Trevor Huddleston: A Life

'This intimate story goes to the heart of Huddleston and definitively explains how a shy English monk came to play a pivotal role in a racial hot-house'

Anthony Sampson, *Observer*

'An honest portrait ... the Huddleston we knew and loved emerged clearly ... we encounter the essential Huddleston ... a beautiful book about a beautiful person'

Desmond Tutu, *The Times Higher Education Supplement*

'This book bears faithful witness to his great achievement ... The core of Huddleston's life ... was the life of prayer. Here the biographer ... one of the most brilliant publishers of his generation, is notably well equipped to understand his subject'

Spectator

'Trevor Huddleston was a dedicated monk and a prodigiously successful political activist and Robin Denniston's wise biography tells the story of how these two ingredients were inextricably linked'

Nicholas Mosley, *Tablet*

DR ROBIN DENNISTON was the editor of Trevor Huddleston's *Naught for Your Comfort*, published by Collins in 1956. He had a distinguished career as a publisher, holding senior positions at Collins, Thomas Nelson, Hodder & Stoughton, Weidenfeld & Nicolson and Oxford University Press. Now retired, he is an Anglican minister looking after a rural parish in north Oxford-shire and a member of the Fraternity of the Resurrection.

Trevor Huddleston, Stepney 1971.

Robin Denniston

TREVOR HUDDLESTON

A LIFE

PAN BOOKS

First published 1999 by Macmillan

This edition published 2000 by Pan Books
an imprint of Macmillan Publishers Ltd
25 Eccleston Place, London SW1W 9NF
Basingstoke and Oxford
Associated companies throughout the world
www.macmillan.co.uk

ISBN 0 330 39311 1

Copyright © Robin Denniston and
the Community of the Resurrection 1999

The right of Robin Denniston to be identified as the
author of this work has been asserted by him in accordance
with the Copyright, Designs and Patents Act 1988.

1 3 5 7 9 8 6 4 2

A CIP catalogue record for this book is available from
the British Library.

Typeset by SetSystems Ltd, Saffron Walden, Essex
Printed and bound in Great Britain by
Mackays of Chatham plc, Chatham, Kent

Naught for Your Comfort was dedicated to Norman Montjane, 'and the Africa he represents . . . with deep gratitude and love in Christ'. Forty-three years later I met Dr Montjane and discussed the book and its author. Huddleston and he had been friends since 1943. Huddleston had told him about his early life, his hopes and his fears for the Rosettenville school at St Peter's (where Montjane was a pupil), and for the future of black urban Africans under the new draconian apartheid laws. They shared everything, despite the difference in age and background. The dedication reflects the primacy of personal friendship in Trevor Huddleston's life. Dr Montjane, working until lately in the students' support unit at Witwatersrand University, is quite clear in his memories of their times together, their talks, what each meant to the other.

I dedicate this life to him, to Michael Rantho, who also shared his reflections of the Sophiatown years, and to the memories of Father Mark Tweedy CR (1912–1989) and Oliver Tambo (1915–1993).

amicus amicis

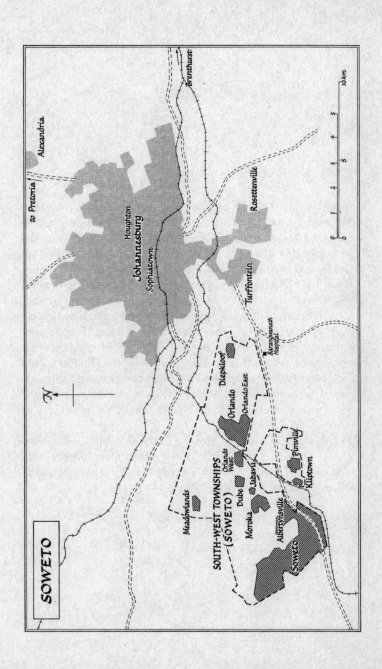

Contents

List of Illustrations

Frontispiece: Trevor Huddleston, Stepney 1971. (*Huddleston Archive, Rhodes House Library, Oxford*)

Foreword to the paperback edition

Certain factual corrections have been made in the light of the very helpful comments of Archbishop Desmond Tutu reviewing the first edition in *The Times Higher Education Supplement*, and from Nicholas Mosley, Fr Aelred CR, Kenneth Leech, Jill Thompson, Michael Terry and Alan Wilkinson. Archbishop Tutu's review included the following account of Trevor Huddleson's 'final triumphant return to South Africa [in July 1998], when his ashes were carried home after the memorial service in Westminster Abbey by the late Alfred Nzo, then South Africa's Minister of Foreign Affairs, to be received at Johannesburg airport with a red-carpet welcome by the then-deputy President Thabo Mbeki and a military guard of honour. He was then taken by motorcade with police motorcycle escort to Sophiatown's Christ the King church for a memorial service. His ashes were interred in South Africa and he was acknowledged as a true hero of the struggle.'

Fr Crispin Harrison CR, Superior has supplied the following details of Trevor Huddleston's memorial:

'In his last years Trevor several times expressed a strong desire that his ashes should be taken to Sophiatown. They were eventually interred in July 1999 at the east end of the church of Christ the King, Sophiatown. On 30 January 2000 the memorial, designed by Henry Paine, was dedicated by the Rt Revd Duncan Buchanan, Bishop of Johannesburg. I preached and Mrs Adelaide Tambo and Mr Abdul Minty paid tribute to Archbishop Trevor. Several hundred people were present including two choirs. After the service the bishop dedicated a plaque commemorating heroes from the diocese who had resisted apartheid, and the parish priest, the Ven Thabo Makgoba, planted a rose bush to honour those heroes who are still alive.

'The memorial to Archbishop Trevor is a garden planted with olive trees surrounding the huge, rough, flat stone over the place where the ashes have been deposited. On three sides long stone cubes provide seats, one of which bears the simple inscription: Father Trevor Huddleston CR, 1913–1998. Three other megaliths stand alongside, between the memorial garden and the road. The rocks, which are heavily scored with drill marks, came from a stone quarry in Naboomspruit.'

ROBIN DENNISTON

February 2000

Preface

One warm winter day in May 1994 two elderly men were sipping tea in Orlando West near Johannesburg. Three others were present. One reminded the other that fifty years earlier they had drunk tea together, looking across towards the great church of Christ the King. Simultaneously and spontaneously the two ancient revolutionaries raised their cups: 'Mission accomplished' they said, and laughed. The two men were Walter Sisulu and Trevor Huddleston.

Trevor Huddleston was perhaps the last great missionary to Africa, whose self-discovery in Sophiatown, the largest of Johannesburg's black suburbs, saw him emerge as one of the post-colonial heroes in the evolution of African nationalism. The story of those years between 1943 and 1956, told in his memoir *Naught for Your Comfort*[1] found readers across the world who recognized in Huddleston an icon at once inspiring and inspired. He was a priest, prophet, pastor they could admire, a human being they could love, whose convictions they could share, whose example some followed, whose attitudes to racial and economic repression bridged a gulf between post-war Western social democracy and the darker, infinitely more exciting, world that evolved during the War in the shanty towns round Johannesburg. Huddleston's reactions to Sophiatown and Sophiatown's reactions to him, when he took the opportunity his monastic order, the Community of the Resurrection (CR), enabled him to straddle that great divide and bring the firm but gentle beliefs and practices of High Anglican Christianity to the noisy backyards and shebeens of Sophiatown, made him the chief white champion

of the non-white oppressed who were his parishioners, neighbours and friends. The years of his prime are covered in *Naught
for Your Comfort*, and the influence of this book extended to his
later years, as readers wrote to him, became his friends, and
worked for him in Masasi, Stepney and the Indian Ocean; by
their love, these people gave Huddleston what he needed – a full
personal and private life in the years of his exile.

Admiration for what he did and what he stood for was never
uncritical or blandly dismissive of his freely acknowledged weak-
nesses and faults. Writing his life story has involved reading the
testimony and memoirs of his friends, all aware of his imperfec-
tions. But Huddleston's shortcomings were so obvious – to
himself more than anyone else – that they help to define his
personality, they are part of his life story and identity, where his
potential fuses with his achievement. They included prickliness, a
susceptibility to self-pity, love of publicity, pride, vainglory, self-
absorption and an intolerance of criticism. This litany was a
regular part of his confessional life, but though there are signs of
such faults in the years of his prime, they did not become a
problem to his friends and his Community until his declining
years. His active work was made possible by his vows of chastity,
poverty and obedience together with a daily life of worship,
prayer and intercession, maintained in the most extreme circumstances. The contrast between his inner and outer lives is far from
being paradoxical; his spiritual life made possible the demanding
changes and routines of his campaign for racial equality and
human dignity under God. This identitification of inner with
outer, between the qualities inherent in him and their expression
in his life and work, pared by his austere lifestyle and set off by
his gift for friendship – he made people think they were better
than they thought they were – is the *leit motiv* of his story.[2]

His consistent and passionate conviction that basic human
rights for all lie at the heart of the Christian Gospel, dominated
his life and work. His Sophiatown years should be seen in the
context of the emerging socio-economic tragedy of generations
of sophisticated coloured and black African people deprived of
human rights. Huddleston had watched 'separate development'

grow from the Smuts government's uneasy non-policy towards an unplanned-for future, into a full-scale programme entrenching indefinite white supremacy, backed by law and the white electorate, which was to last forty-five years. His agenda was to see it off: he made a vital contribution to its eventual dismantling and thereby brought European Christian missionary work in Africa into the history books. In 1996 Professor Adrian Hastings published his definitive account of five hundred years of the Christian Churches in Africa – ranging back to fifteenth-century Ethiopian monastic and royal politics. Against such a time-scale, the history of the Community of the Resurrection in Africa in the first half of the twentieth century might seem insignificant. Yet of South Africa in the 1950s he writes: 'No other decade in missionary history could lay claim to such intelligent vitality.' The five-hundred-year corridor through which he perceives Huddleston's achievement from 1948 until 1993 is Huddleston's prehistory.

Huddleston's contribution to the history of Africa in the twentieth century is therefore a central theme. The four-fold goals of commerce, conquest, Christianity and control that directed the imperialist ambitions of six European nations between 1850 and 1950 may be glimpsed in the life of the last great African European missionary. He came to serve the people through the church. He saw how he could best do that and put the whole of himself into the job. Archbishop Desmond Tutu acknowledged the source of that achievement in 1993, when he associated it with Huddleston's spirituality and dedicated prayer life: 'It was all a consequence of his daily, moment-to-moment encounter with the transcendent and all-holy Trinity in the regular offices of his community, in meditation and in the Eucharist. He took the incarnation and the doctrine of creation seriously; that each person was precious, with an infinite worth because [they were] created in the image of God; that each person was a tabernacle of the spirit of God who sanctifies them as [they are] redeemed by the precious blood of Jesus Christ.'[3] Archbishop Tutu could of course be labelled *parti pris*, as he owed much, as well as contributed much, to their friendship. But he spoke from a Christian involvement in Southern African affairs with a long and

significant history, to which both archbishops became heirs.
Religion had been a dominant force in the country for many
generations. It is close to the heart of Africa. Among Huddleston's
own spiritual forebears, missionaries had been coming and going
to and from Africa and India for a century. By the end of the
nineteenth century, Christian missionary zeal had become a formidable force throughout the continent, bringing to many parts
of Africa education, modern medicine and other more question-
able adjuncts of the Western way of life. And the differences of
dogma and practice within Christanity might well have confused
a less religious continent in which Islam was already dominant.
Within Christianity, Catholics and Protestants distrusted each
other, practised different rites, and made different demands
on their converts. Yet between the Scylla of unreformed Rome
and the Charybdis of unreconstructed evangelicalism, the still
small voice of Huddleston's Community's Anglicanism sounded
throughout Southern Africa, bringing sound education, moral
and pastoral care, and love for the individual.

This tradition brought Huddleston by sea to Cape Town, to a
country whose disenfranchised majority sought equality of opportunity with their white counterparts and whose mission-churches
underpinned native education. By 1943, thanks largely to Huddleston's predecessor Fr Raymond Raynes, the Community of the
Resurrection had assumed an important role in matters of native
South African educational matters –particularly in the new townships growing round Johannesburg – and was already making its
presence felt on issues such as black housing, employment, living
and working conditions, pay – and black rights. Huddleston
seized the baton Raynes passed to him, and for twelve years
thereafter worked with all who shared his concerns; so that by
1954 – through his writings as well as his political activism – he
had become the main white spokesman against apartheid and for
the rights of all Africans, regardless of race, sex, colour or creed,
wealth, ability or age. His political activism was to be cut short
in 1955 by the very man who had appointed him. His subsequent
career might have been no more than a prolonged coda to his
ministry in Sophiatown and Rosettenville, but for the path he

took in retirement, starting in the 1980s. A mutual friend wrote in 1998 that the twenty-seven years of his exile from South Africa might not have happened as far as Huddleston's own assessment was concerned. His new work as leader of the Anti-Apartheid Movement (AAM) and chairman of the trustees of the International Defence and Aid Fund (IDAF) gave purpose to the years of his diminishment. IDAF transferred raised funds to the lawyers and families of those caught up in the armed struggle of the banned African National Congress (ANC) against Pretoria. His leadership of these two key institutions was crucial in mobilising opinion at the UN for sanctions, in the release from jail of President Mandela, and in raising the international pressure on Pretoria to move to relaxations and, by slow stages, eventually to the dismantling of apartheid. His skilful handling of Western politicians, bankers and journalists (learned during his years in Sophiatown) played an important, though unquantifiable, part in the world movement that paved the way for the first democratic general election in South Africa on 27 April 1994. Huddleston's own claims were modest: apartheid's removal was the result of the ANC's armed struggle, and the heroism, suffering and martyrdom of apartheid's victims.

Towards the end of the struggle, in the 1990s, the ANC had its own agenda and some of Huddleston's closest friends from the 1950s felt he had been let down when he attempted to settle in South Africa in July 1995. A place was found for him in a whites-only old people's home; his two months' sojourn there brought out all the worst in him, and he blamed the ANC in general, and Walter Sisulu in particular, for failing him at the last. It was totally unfair, and Sisulu was deeply grieved by this perceived failure of his after they had worked and striven so hard together for a common end. It was Walter Sisulu who had met him at Johannesburg airport and worked hard to make his first return visit in 1991 the time of joy for which they had both long wished. But Huddleston's bursts of irrational anger – often at his greatest friends – had got the better of him, and his quick forgiveness and apology was no longer always forthcoming. However, seven years later and only two days after his death, the

ANC and the South African government, through an unopposed Motion in Parliament, gave eloquent expression to their understanding of Huddleston and his place in history:

Dated 23 April 1998 THAT THE HOUSE:

1. notes with great sadness the passing away of Archbishop Trevor Huddleston on 20 April 1998
2. recognizes:
   a) the enormous contribution that the late Archbishop made to the liberation struggle, and in particular his founding of, and involvement in, the Anti-Apartheid Movement in the UK; and
   b) that his personal relationship with the oppressed majority was such that he will always be known by the black people of our country as *Father* Huddleston
3. believes that, during the worst chapter of South African history, he had the strength, courage and the conviction to stand up against the apartheid oppressor and to mobilise the world to help end the suffering of the people of South Africa; and
4. pays tribute to one of the greatest champions of freedom and equality the world has ever seen, an internationalist who helped to deepen the relationship of friendship and solidarity between our country and the peoples of the world.

S.G. Mfenyan, Secretary to Parliament

This life of Huddleston would not have been started, let alone finished, without the help of four people.

Anthony Sampson inspired Huddleston to write *Naught for Your Comfort* and enabled me to publish it at Collins in 1956. It was he who said in 1997 that this biography should be a celebration of Huddleston's life and work, and I have tried to keep to that advice. Sampson's own account of the new urban African elite in the Johannesburg townships in his book *Drum: An African Adventure and Afterwards* (1956 and 1983) contains brilliantly remembered characters, conversations and contretemps of the early 1950s, as well as a chapter on Huddleston that brings him vividly to life.

Abdul Minty's friendship and support for Huddleston induced the flowering of his later political career and without his advice this portrait of Huddleston could have no claim to fairness. He gave me invaluable information about their great anti-apartheid crusade in its grimmest moments. As chairman of the Human Rights Violations Commission – an offshoot of the Truth and Reconciliation Commission – he also indicated the extent of the apartheid regime's biological warfare manufacture and implementation policy both within and outside the Republic.

Michael Terry, former Executive Secretary of the Anti-Apartheid Movement, who accompanied Huddleston on some of his major journeys, cherished his leadership of the Movement and gave himself unstintingly to the struggle and to Huddleston, has been a great source of help. Finally, Jill Thompson, Huddleston's dedicated secretary and friend in Masasi, Stepney, Piccadilly and Mirfield, sorted his papers so that any biographer working from documents would find much of the hard labour had already been done.

Two other people are here gratefully acknowledged. They are Canon Eric James, who worked for ten years on a biography of Huddleston and travelled to Southern Africa, Tanzania and the Indian Ocean on research trips in the early 1990s, reporting back in a series of journals published by Christian Action. He passed me his Huddleston papers in early 1997 when he decided not to continue. And Joe Rogaly, who was commissioned by Collins to write Huddleston's biography in the early 1960s, and whose typescripts of conversations with his subject have usefully supplemented other sources.

In setting out to celebrate Huddleston's life it has been necessary to research the early history, not only of the African National Congress, but of two more recent and less-documented organizations – the International Defence and Aid Fund and the Anti-Apartheid Movement. Extensive files on both were held for Trevor Huddleston by Mrs Thompson and I have used these, together with some material from the AAM archive now housed

at Rhodes House Library, Oxford. But my accounts of both these
important organizations is necessarily rather cursory, and their
proper historians will in due course publish the full story. I draw
attention in particular to IDAF's work distributing funds to
relatives of political prisoners and victims of apartheid in South
Africa. IDAF's archive contains precious source material for any
future historian of the apartheid years in South Africa. I also
include the testimony of Horst Kleinschmidt, a remarkable anti-
apartheid fighter, whose careful management of IDAF's secret
affairs for ten crucial years materially aided the freedom struggle.

Fr Nicolas Stebbing CR was Trevor Huddleston's infirmarian,
nurse, companion and friend in his last years and grateful thanks
are due to him from all who knew and visited them both at the
House of the Resurrection. In 1998 Nicolas wrote that Trevor
was a 'one agenda' person. He then changed his mind because he
noticed how he was also able, sometimes with effort, to follow
other agendas connected with his personal friends and their
problems and concerns. But I think he was right first time: Trevor
was a one-agenda man and on that agenda was one item, and
that was the destruction of apartheid. This may go some way to
explain why this life has little, too little some may feel, about
individual friends, about those he adopted, whose school fees and
expenses he paid, whose reports he studied, whose legal or
unofficial guardian he became. But another explanation is that
there is little about these people in the records and files. There is
much oral evidence, much hearsay, all amounting to grounds for
the thesis that these personal relationships comprised a second
agenda as important as anti-apartheid. But here I remember
Anthony Sampson's advice, and conclude that, though Huddleston was so important to so many, and so many were perhaps of
equal importance to him, a roll call of speculative theories should
find no place here. Instead I acknowledge gratefully the memoirs
of several of his friends, some of which are incorporated in the
narrative; particularly those of Judge Fikile Bam, Kort Boy, Lady
Molly Baring (later Howick), Hilda Bernstein, Rt Rev Peter
Carnley, Bevis and Anne Cubey, Harry Greenway, Rica Hodson,
Horst Kleinschmidt, Jenny Leggatt, Joe Louw, Columbus Malebo,

Peter Mandelson MP, Don Mattera, Abdul Minty, Norman Montjane, Sally Motlana, Obed Musi, Michael Rantho, Mischa Scorer, Lord Sheppard, Ellis Slack, Alan Talbot, the late Oliver Tambo, Mary Whitnall, Dr Alan Wilkinson, Deane Yates and, above all Fr Nicolas Stebbing CR whose account of the last months concludes the story.

For further assistance I am grateful to the following: Fr Aelred Stubbs CR, Atalanta de Bendern, Anne Cameron, John Allen, Dr Rosa Beddington, Luli Callinocos, Fr David Campbell SSJE, Richard Charkin, Georgina Cope, Sarah Crowe, Liz Davis, Lisa Key, Professor Tom Lodge, Andrew Maxwell-Hyslop, John and Rachael Mitchinson, Nicholas Mosley, Thulani Moyo, Rebecca Porteous, Joan Rampton, Fr Sylvanus CR, Catherine Whitaker, the Superior CR, Joan Wicken and Anne Yates.

ROBIN DENNISTON

Great Tew, January 1999

CHAPTER ONE

HIDDEN TIMES

1913–1943

Some might argue that Trevor Huddleston has already written a memoir of his most important years in *Naught for Your Comfort*, which requires little updating and little further comment forty-two years later. He has also memorialized at length to Joe Rogaly in Masasi towards the end of 1966 and to Eric James twenty-five years later. Both sources, gratefully acknowledged, are incorporated in what follows. Finally, Huddleston's *Return to South Africa: The Agony and the Ecstasy* is a remarkably open and revealing memoir. Huddleston himself thought there was nothing of interest for his biographer prior to 1943, and discouraged those who believed that incidents in his early childhood could be usefully disinterred to explain what happened later. This might seem unhelpful, particularly to the most recent generation of biographers, but the research undertaken indicates that Huddleston might have been right.

He counted among his forebears Father John Huddleston (1630–98), a Benedictine monk and Restoration priest, who helped King Charles II in his escape after the battle of Worcester and, on his deathbed, received the king into the Roman Catholic Church. Trevor Huddleston's father, Captain Sir Ernest Whiteside Huddleston, CIE, CBE, was the son of an Indian army officer who died early, leaving his widow to bring up twelve children. Ernest, born at Murree in the Punjab, was sent to school at Bedford where most of his family lived, but left at fourteen to join the Merchant Navy. Resourceful and intelligent, he transferred to the Royal Indian Marine, attended the Royal Naval College Officers' course at Greenwich, and returned to India where he rose to command the Royal Indian Navy. He was later to serve in the Indian Civil Service, becoming at one period ADC to the Viceroy, Rufus Isaacs (Lord Reading). In 1897 he received the Royal Humane Society's silver medal, for gallantry at sea off the coast of Reunion Island. On 4 August 1904 he married: his wife was Elsie Barlow-Smith, from a prominent Anglo-Argentinian family. They met as school children. Lieutenant Huddleston took his young wife back to India, serving at the naval bases of Bombay, Madras and Calcutta. Their firstborn was a daughter, Barbara. Trevor was born in Bedford four years later, on 15 June 1913. Soon afterwards the family moved to the North London suburb of Golders Green.

Despite the complications of working in India with his family in London, Ernest Huddleston was a devoted father. However, his only son was nearly seven years old before he met his father for the first time, as the War prevented Lieutenant Huddleston from coming home on leave until 1920. Huddleston's mother was deeply committed to High Anglicanism, and by the age of four, the young Trevor served as 'boatboy' – the boy who carried the boat of incense for the thurifer – at St Michael's, Golders Green. Since their mother spent a good deal of her time in India with her husband, Barbara and Trevor were largely in the care of their aunt, Elsie's eldest sister, Mrs Charlotte Dawson Robinson, known as 'Potsa'. Friends from India would call at their home, No. 53 Hampstead Way, and India became part of Trevor's imaginative life.

When he was five, Trevor went to a 'dame' school in Hampstead Garden Suburb but the Church was the main focus of his life – as it was for his mother and aunt. St Michael's was attached to an extreme branch of the Anglo–Catholic Movement, considerably further (though not all the way) down the road to Rome than the Tractarian Oxford Movement in which Huddleston later found his exemplars. Ernest Huddleston did not share his wife and sister-in-law's High Church views but went along with them, apparently without complaint.

At seven, Huddleston went to Tenterden Hall preparatory school in nearby Hendon as a boarder. It was housed in a late-

Georgian House and run by a tiny, furious, former Cambridge hockey blue. At a very early age, while still in Bedford, Huddleston had become friends with Hubert (later Professor) Lamb – a distinguished climatologist. At school, a friendship blossomed with the music teacher, Mabel Druce, and Huddleston played tennis and ping-pong with Phyllis Tyndale and Yvonne Brown, and went to the cinema, the ice-rink and on long 'walks and talks' with them. His school work was variable, but he enjoyed history. He also attended the Robert Mayer Children's Concerts at Central Hall, Westminster, conducted with great *brio* by Malcolm Sargent, and enjoyed Bertram Mills's circus and Madame Tussaud's. He was confirmed at the age of twelve, the year of his father's retirement to London. In an address to an audience of Oxford undergraduates nearly thirty years later, Huddleston spoke of his confirmation as a turning point. The confirmation service was led by the Bishop of Willesden at St Michael's, and it was there that he made his first confession, to Fr St Alphonse, the curate, on Christmas Day 1925. Later he wrote:

> My confirmation was the beginning of what I can only describe as my *real* life. And it came to me through the church ... The starting point for my experience of the Christian life was fundamentally and inextricably set in the context of that visible organism ... I will not weary you with the 'story of my life' – a very uneventful one by any standards – at school and then here at Oxford. I can only say that, as far as my Christianity went it still depended utterly, increasingly, upon the life of the Church wherever I was. I learned to worship, and to pray. I learned to know myself and be penitent, I learned, horribly slowly, a little more of the demands of Christian love and Christian compassion – all *within* that institutional, organic structure, the Church. I could not have conceived the Christian life then as being possible 'outside' that community. I cannot conceive it now. Christ to me was, and is 'present, knowable, real there'.[1]

His father would have liked him to have gone to his old school in Bedford but accepted the wishes of Elsie that their son should go to the leading High Anglican public school, Lancing College, whose buildings – especially the magnificent neo-gothic chapel – were famously described by Evelyn Waugh.[2] He failed to get a scholarship, his coach writing that he was 'not a scholar, just an average, charming, friendly prep-school boy', but the decision was clearly a crucial one.

Lancing's influence on Huddleston continued the process that would culminate in his arrival at Mirfield. Lancing was an all-male enclosed community. Here he started to keep a rule of daily and weekly worship. Here, too, he first felt the call to help the poor, the sick, the lonely. Huddleston's mentor at Lancing was E.B. Gordon ('Gordo'). Another master, Christopher Chamberlin, taught him history and remembered him not for being brainy but for his character. 'He was never one of its leaders, but observed the school closely and quietly; and his friends, men of quality, respected him.' Chamberlin was also in charge of sports, and in 1931 Lancing had a chance of winning the Public Schools Championship in athletics. Chamberlin encouraged Huddleston to compete in the mile run; he came fifth in a large field in which Lancing were runners-up. He was appointed a prefect when only in his fourth year, an unusual distinction. He made friends not easily but deeply, among both boys and masters. They included William Howitt, John Gough, Patrick Cotter, Peter Hadley, Peter Burra, Hubert Dingwall. He struck some as withdrawn, a 'loner', difficult to get to. A colleague thought him 'a sincere and interesting person with a good sense of humour. His tolerance and natural charm made him popular in his house and in the school.' The master of the sixth form rated him 'a good citizen: no flyer'. He played the bugle in the Officers' Training Corps and tossed the mace high into the air ahead of the parade; he also played the trumpet in the school orchestra. He was secretary to the College branch of Toc H, a movement for ex-servicemen established by 'Tubby' Clayton with four principles – fellowship, service, fair-mindedness and the Kingdom of God. Huddleston also edited the College magazine in 1931, and contributed poems to the *Lancing Miscellany*. Since he lived in London, he visited the College Mission in Camberwell during his holidays. It was the height of the depression, and this marked his first introduction to social deprivation and the beginnings of his Christian Socialism. At Lancing he began, consciously, to 'pour iron into his soul'.[3] His faith deepened and strengthened; he began to realise that you cannot love God unless you love and work for your neighbour: 'The real presence of Christ in his sacraments is impossible without the real presence of Christ in man.' Sacramentalism without philanthropy was not enough.[4]

In his last year at Lancing Huddleston's mother died. Three years earlier he had had to endure a lonely grief at the death of his Aunt Potsa. Now, faced with a more public opportunity to mourn his equally beloved mother, he was so little upset by his father's decision to remarry within a year that he was best man at the wedding. In the same year Barbara married, and the family life he had known since a baby was gone for ever. In the summer of 1931 he obtained a place at Christ Church, Oxford, where he read history, not theology.

Early 1930s Oxford was slowly recovering from the war. Ramsay Macdonald's National Government was formed to balance the budget. Gandhi was in London for the India Round Table Conference. Unemployment was out of control over most of Europe, and while in Germany the Nazis won a majority in the Reichstag election, Oswald Mosley was forming the British Union of Fascists in England. Hunger marchers from Jarrow and South Wales passed through Oxford en route to Westminster. In January 1933 Hitler was appointed Chancellor of the German Reich and in South Africa Field Marshal Smuts joined Herzog's cabinet, marking the moment when the South African Party merged with Herzog's Nationalists to form the United Party government. This took South Africa off the gold standard and initiated an era of independence. The world was recovering from one global conflict and heading fast into a second.

Huddleston had three distinguished tutors at Oxford – Keith Feiling, J.C. Masterman and Patrick Gordon Walker. At Christ Church, he was remembered as a good-looking, friendly, devout and austere undergraduate, who went to Pusey House and the ultra-spiky St Barnabas, Jericho, to worship. He joined a holy club (male only) and also the 'Mermaid Club' (white dinner jackets and fancy waistcoats). Later he bought a car, fell in love with a girl 'tall and dark, with an attractive way of not quite pronouncing her r's', then 'spooned' with another girl, dancing till dawn. A keen ballroom dancer, he liked light dance music. But his Christ Church life was not that of Evelyn Waugh. Introduced by Fr Miles Sargent, Huddleston became a Christian Socialist, and worked in gypsy camps during hop-picking in Kent, learning rather incongruously, like many other well-meaning undergraduates, a little of how the other half lived. Like most of his contemporaries at Oxford he was comparatively unaffected by the darkening clouds emanating from Germany, and was not attracted to Stalinist Communism in the Soviet Union. Indeed he remained an anti-Communist all his life, though a fellow traveller on specific social issues in the South African context.

While he seems to have been uninvolved politically at Oxford, his faith developed into a strong devotional life and an equally strong, though less focused, determination to minister to the disadvantaged. It was here that he first began to realise something that became central to his faith and life hereafter: that you cannot love the invisible God unless you find him in 'the brother whom you have seen'. With a friend he went on a mission in Bourne-mouth conducted by Canon Bryan Green and made a retreat at Mirfield. For the hunger marchers, 'thousands of them [who] walked in their pit clothes from the coal-mines of South Wales and the coke yards of the North, to Westminster, life *was* hunger and pain and idleness; without dignity, almost without meaning.'[5] He stayed in College from October 1931 till May 1933 when he took digs in the Iffley Road with John Gough and revised for Finals. He got a decent Second in history. One of the chief college 'scouts', Cyril Little, remembered him as 'a bit of a loner, given to walking a lot, a non participator in sport or the social side . . . a very pleasant courteous man whose subsequent career was to me clearly defined as an undergraduate.' Sir William Deakin wrote of his 'marked integrity and kindness. He mixed easily and simply with his contemporaries. He was not only a dedicated Christian but also quietly self-contained and, in the best sense, sure of himself. He never held forth, and was always good company.' Feiling and Masterman were both revered by Huddleston who found the one-to-one tutorial system to be of great benefit to the novice historian.[6]

Having decided on the priesthood against his father's advice, Huddleston went abroad – Ceylon, India, Burma: then the Holy Land and Florence. In Colombo the sight of Singhalese, Tamils, Portuguese, Dutch half-castes and English all worshipping together may have inspired his later conception of the cosmic brotherhood of the Church and of the world – 'one world'. On his return he went straight to theological college. His High-Church leanings would have made St Stephen's House, Oxford, the obvious choice; instead he settled for a thoroughly middle-of-the-road theological training at Wells. By choosing Wells, Huddleston was joining an important branch of the wider Church, not a small Anglo-Catholic enclave, a twig which might at any time fall off. He wrote about this to Archbishop Fisher twenty years later, since he was labelled extremely 'high' by the establishment but never relished the exclusivity which some of his Anglo-Catholic brethren and colleagues exhibited. His successor at Rosettenville, Fr George Sidebotham, remembered him at Wells as a model student. 'He was up before anyone else and on his knees saying his prayers; after dinner he went straight back to his books.' In his two years there he may have been tempted to become a Roman Catholic, and was gradually drawn to the monastic life.

Wells marked a period of withdrawal. It was Fr Andrew Blair, later Prior of the Community of the Resurrection at Mirfield who directed Huddleston to St Mark's, Swindon, a powerhouse of Anglo-Catholicism and a great training ground for its young parish priests.[7] There he visited, prayed, took a leading part in local church life, daily celebrated mass. The senior curate at the time was John Tickner who wrote: 'He seemed shy and unassuming, except over religion and work. How naturally he went about his Father's business with complete unselfconsciousness and devotion ... Our work was mainly with the railwaymen and their families, centred round the church which the shareholders of the Great Western Railway built for them ... He was one of those naturally good people who base all they do on their realisation of God's love.'[8]

The Community of the Resurrection was founded by Charles Gore in 1892. It was the second men's community in the Church of England to emerge from the Anglo-Catholic Revival of the last years of the nineteenth century. It realized the ideals of the earlier Tractarian, or Oxford, Movement, which sought to rediscover the beliefs and practices of the early church before the supremacy of both Rome and the Reformation obscured them. Its leaders felt the ancestral roots of their faith, overladen by later accretions (both Catholic and Protestant) were to be found in the eucharistic life of the early centuries of Christianity. Gore and five friends made their profession at Pusey House, Oxford in 1892, and for forty years thereafter he worked for, and with, the slowly growing Community to make a deep sacramental connection between individual sanctity and the needs of the world. Similar emphasis appears in several other Anglican religious communities flourishing in the 1930s: the Society of the Sacred Mission at Kelham, near Nottingham; the Society of St John the Evangelist at Cowley ('the Cowley dads'); the Franciscans at Cerne Abbas, Dorset; and the Anglican Benedictines at Nashdom Abbey, Burnham, Buckinghamshire. Within sixty years, Charles Gore's Community grew into a great worshipping, teaching and missionary organization, politically inclined towards the left.

Huddleston was brought to Mirfield by Fr Andrew Blair in 1939, having become a deacon in 1936 and priest in 1937. He was professed in 1941 as a full member of CR, and took the threefold vows of poverty, chastity and obedience, which were to become his lynchpins for the rest of his life. A few letters from elderly, now deceased, priests and laymen testify to Huddleston's strong faith and excellent conduct as a young High Church curate in a working-class parish. But they could have applied equally to many other promising curates.

The years dominated in Europe by Nazi and Fascist oppression culminated in a war that took Britain from the brink of defeat in 1940 to slow recovery towards the end of 1942. Huddleston spent the early war years in his novitiate at Mirfield, chafing at his enforced absence from the action.

CHAPTER TWO

SOPHIATOWN

1943-1953

In 1943 Fr Raymond Raynes, newly elected Superior of the Community of the Resurrection, after a distinguished decade serving the Anglican Church of South Africa, returned to Mirfield where he met Huddleston on the doorstep and impulsively decided Huddleston should go to Johannesburg to carry on where he himself had left off.

Africa in 1943 was in turmoil. In a dozen African countries from Morocco to Chad, from Somalia and Ethiopia to South West Africa several thousand kilometres distant, African movements of national liberation were stirring. For nearly a century the colonial powers – Portugal, Spain, Belgium, Italy, Germany, France and Britain – had fought for their chosen portions of the continent, exploiting its mineral wealth as well as the resources of its indigenous peoples. Trade had followed the flag and much of this European colonisation for Africa was carried out in the name of Christianity. Trevor Huddleston's own Community of the Resurrection had been active in Southern Africa for many years, its missions and schools bringing the diurnal round of the Anglo-Catholic Movement to the Xhosas and Zulus in their charge. But by 1943, the Second World War had given Africans a new sense that European dominance was not an inescapable fact of life. However disparate the countries and tribes of which it was composed, Africa was ultimately for Africans. One African caught this new spirit in a vivid phrase, 'We owe our independence to Adolph Hitler.'[1] But Churchill's Atlantic Charter, including its confirmation of the right of all peoples to choose their own form of government, was a bigger inspiration to the African

National Congress (ANC) than Hitler. Lord Lugard, High Commissioner in West Africa, had written: 'For two or three generations we can show the Negro what we are: then we shall be asked to go away. Then we shall leave the land to those it belongs to.'[2] Lugard's vision was not realised as bloodlessly as he would have hoped, and in Southern Africa it did not apply at all.

Race relations in twentieth-century South Africa began to deteriorate five years after the Anglo-Boer War: the Boers reasserted themselves in the Transvaal, and in 1907 Transvaal joined the Cape, Natal and the Orange River Colony to plan a constitution for a new, single South African dominion. The new constitution was not only a retrograde step for liberal opinion in England and the Cape, but became the basis upon which South Africa moved in world affairs from 1910 onwards. By the time of Huddleston's arrival, a whole generation had grown up knowing nothing of life without the colour bar. As Nelson Mandela said from the dock in 1964, 'Fifty years of non-violence has brought the African people nothing but more and more repressive legislation.'

Elsewhere in Africa the former colonial powers had been more radical and less creative in their dealings with the continent. By 1912 France had swallowed most of Morocco and handed much of Rwanda–Burundi to Germany to keep the Germans sweet. Italy grabbed the former Ottoman lands that became Libya. Only two African powers remained independent – Ethiopia and Liberia. The Peace Conference of 1919 confirmed Britain as Europe's leading residual imperial power. Britain acquired Tanganyika from the defeated Germany and divided Togo and Cameroon with France. Belgium took Rwanda–Burundi. The League of Nations invented the 'mandates' for small African nations judged 'not yet able to stand alone in the modern world'.[3]

However, the mandates were largely a sham. Until 1948 Britain, France, Belgium and South Africa ruled them as arbitrarily as they did their other colonies while, despite the League of Nations, Italy was allowed to invade Ethiopia. But the War brought a change in European attitudes to Africa and Africans, many of whom fought with distinction for the Allies. Imperialism was presenting more problems than opportunities in the poverty-stricken parts of the continent and 'both the men of God and the men of business had begun to see that formal empire was counterproductive.'[4]

Meanwhile the British connection was growing thin, frayed and taut. As one of the leading dominions of the Commonwealth, South Africa's soldiers, sailors and airmen – white and non-white – served alongside French, Polish, American and British forces in North Africa. Its Prime Minister, Field-Marshal Smuts, hated by most Afrikaners, was one of Winston Churchill's most valued colleagues and a member of the British War Cabinet. Its strategic position guarding the shipping routes to the Far East was vital to the Allied war effort. South African public opinion, however, was not wholly behind Smuts's pro-Allied policies. The anti-British legacy of the Boer War still hung heavily over Afrikaner politicians, while to non-whites of every shade, the opportunity to train, travel, and serve alongside the armed forces of the Allied countries brought a new awareness of basic human rights. On the ground substantial support for the Nazis was everywhere apparent. Many leading Afrikaner politicians, some to achieve high office in successive Nationalist administrations, had Nazi connections and sympathies. Dr Malan, Johannes Strijdom, Hendrik Verwoerd, John Vorster were all Nazi sympathisers who regretted Allied victory and General Smuts' association with it. The leading Nazi was the father of Horst Kleinschmidt, who later converted to the ANC.

The process by which Europe scrambled out of Africa since 1945 has been well described by Thomas Pakenham.[5] A distinguished South African writer regards the middle years of the twentieth century in Africa as having had 'the greatest effect on the shape of the world and the nature of human relationships.' There was 'a revolution in racial attitudes . . . which caused the great powers of the West to withdraw their hegemony over billions of coloured people round the globe, allowing nearly a hundred new nations to come into existence in the space of a single generation.'[6] Three years before Huddleston's arrival, 400-million British subjects had been liberated pending the post-war partition of the Indian sub-continent in 1947; many more millions followed them in Burma. After 1947, France and Holland hurriedly adopted similar policies towards their Asian and African colonies. Libya became independent in 1951. By 1956 France had let Morocco and Tunisia go, and had fought a vicious war in Algeria; by March 1957 many African nations were independent. Over the next ten years, European powers tried, increasingly frenetically, to extricate themselves from Africa. France, Belgium and Britain perceived that they should get out before they were kicked out. Compared to the Algerian conflict, the Mau Mau revolt in Kenya in 1950–8 was a mild affair, and in 1960 Harold Macmillan delivered his famous 'winds of change' speech in Cape Town indicating that the age of imperialism had run its course. Uganda and Tanganyika subsequently went their own way, and a Conservative government in Britain, masterminded by Huddleston's friend, Sir Evelyn Baring – the Governor-General of Kenya and adviser to successive British governments on African affairs – brought Jomo Kenyatta out of prison to lead Kenya to freedom in 1963. Southern Rhodesia, dominated, like Kenya, by white settlers, might have gone in the same direction, but a Federation including Nyasaland and Northern Rhodesia was put forward instead. Belgium pulled out of Rwanda–Burundi in 1960 and soon Portugal remained the only residual colonial power. After its dictator, Dr Salazar, died in 1970, Portugal quit the continent under international pressure and led by an electorate which saw its domestic economy drained by the needs of its African empire. Guerrilla wars and genocide followed in its wake. On 18 April 1980 Lord Soames watched the Union Jack hauled down in Rhodesia, and the independent nation of Zimbabwe came into being.

Much of this happened during Huddleston's African years, and was completed after he arrived in Mauritius in 1978. He found himself in an ironic situation as heir to a missionary inheritance in which serving Africans meant looking after their well-being on European lines, with the help of district officers from the Colonial Office, while, in country after country, nationalist movements were showing that people wanted his like to go

away and let indigenous Africans look after themselves. That he
was aware of the inherent contradiction of his position and the
instability of his power base – which he longed to see erode into
a post-imperial future – and yet achieved a balance between these
forces, is a measure of his self-knowledge and of the size of his
achievement.

The South African response to the European departure from
Africa was slower than elsewhere, and Huddleston's part in it
was crucial. In the north, east, west and centre of Africa, increasingly unstable regimes were shored up with European money
waiting for the revolution which, when it came, proved costly in
human terms. But in Southern Africa an apparently more stable
situation had developed. A comparatively prosperous white
minority, English and Afrikaners, ruled over a beautiful, rich and
temperate land. Meanwhile, the problems created for the disenfranchised black and coloured populations whose labour underpinned that prosperity, were steadily worsening. If the British
Liberal establishment had always envisaged a qualified franchise
for non-whites and progress via education and the civilising
influences of Christian missionaries and pragmatic business people, towards some sort of eventual qualified equality, the reality
was very different. Educational opportunities, particularly for the
new and growing class of urban blacks drawn to the towns by
the prospect of work, were provided not by the government but
by overseas missions. Only the worst-paid jobs, with the worst
conditions, were made available to them, while poor whites
earned more for carrying out the same duties. Huddleston was to
be particularly incensed by the stark contrast between the living
conditions of Europeans of all classes and non-whites. The War
had brought many thousands of Africans from their tribal
reserves to meet industry's need for workers in the mines and
factories of the Reef – the urban and industrial belt on the
Witwatersrand where gold was discovered. Before squatter camps
were established, few had anywhere to live between shifts. But
the camps themselves, lacking even the most basic infrastructure
such as sanitation, soon generated serious problems of their own.
Unofficial community leaders, who had learned the arts of under-

world management in the armed forces, took command of them, creating the perfect breeding-ground for systematic crime and violence. The white forces of law and order were strengthened to crack down on all protest movements, and new laws quickly introduced to punish those publicly opposed to the system. Needless to say, there was no social security available for non-whites.[7]

So Cape Town was Huddleston's port of entry into a continent already seething with a determination – at whatever cost in human and economic terms – to be free. But these were the years of 'separate development' following the regressive policy – caught in the phrase 'white supremacy, now and always' – which was introduced in stages after the Nationalists came to power in 1948, voted in by the overwhelming determination of the white electorate. Smuts had taken his time to address the 'native problem'. But the increasing prosperity of the South African economy, stemming not least from the fruits of black men's labour in the mines and factories of the Reef, had accentuated the problem of maintaining the strength of the labour force in areas close to the workplace while also fulfiling the contradictory requirement of separate development. The United Party had taken some steps towards improving conditions for urban non-whites by adopting some of the main findings of the Fagan Commission on Native Laws in 1947. This report, sharply criticised by the white electorate, was a belated attempt to construct a positive native policy, and presupposed the impossibility of total segregation. But a year after the Report was made public, the Nationalists were in power, and were instituting a legislative programme to erode what was left of the rights of natives, while continuing to exploit the black labour force. Although too little and too late, the Fagan proposals for a viable native policy might have maintained stability for a while, had the mood of the white electorate not already hardened.

There were many causes for this hardening of white attitude, but the one most relevant to Huddleston's ministry to the urban non-whites of Johannesburg was the growth of the South Western townships round the city centre like 'hessian tents stitched to a pinstriped suit'.[8] Johannesburg's domestic and industrial workforce (and a growing number of office menials too) had to commute daily (often two or three hours each way) in order to live with their families. Rudimentary housing estates, constructed at Orlando (originally a model township), Newclare, Rosettenville, Pimville, Meadowlands and Alexandra Township, littered the veldt to the south and west of the city. Exceptionally, in one such settlement – Sophiatown – blacks could own their own houses. This anomaly was unacceptable to the white electorate.

By the time Huddleston left England for Cape Town in July 1943 the tide of the World War had turned; the Cape route was comparatively safe for Allied shipping. Russian victories in the Ukraine, and the Western Allies' successes in North Africa were still partly offset by the continuing success of the U-Boat campaign against convoys sailing the Atlantic. Many CR brethren had become padres in the British armed forces: to his chagrin Huddleston was not chosen for this work. Father Raymond Raynes, later to become head of all the Community's activities in Southern Africa, had been in Africa for nine years when he was elected Superior CR in January 1943, and returned to Mirfield in April as a troopship chaplain. CR's commitment to Southern Africa was crucial both to the Community and the people it served. The Community had been invited to undertake work in South Africa as far back as 1903, just after the Boer War. CR was established by 1943 as a major force in native education, religion and social improvement, providing almost all the manpower and resources to improve the lot of the hundreds of thousands of urban Africans round Johannesburg. By 1938, six years into Raynes's posting as Provincial, the mission had built three churches, seven schools and three nursery schools catering for over 6,000 children.

Raynes hated leaving and his send-off was an emotional one. 'Do not be sad,' he told the people, 'I will send a new father to you.'[9] He found him in Huddleston who was the priest who opened the door for him the day he returned to Mirfield, and looked after him through the illness he had contracted on the voyage home. Mutual respect was established immediately and it deepened throughout Raynes's remaining years. Huddleston greatly admired Raynes for what he had achieved locally for African advancement during his years there, and for his rock-like spiritual strength and self-discipline. Raynes had the ability to *feel* what it was like to be an African.[10] It took little time for Huddleston to feel the same, but he felt inadequate to the task laid upon him. Raynes told Huddleston: 'There is much you will learn only by experience about Africa and about Sophiatown in particular. I know that in time you will probably want to change things and do new things ... that is what you are going for ... be unendingly patient with the people – and you will be rewarded by their love and their confidence; and try to be meticulously just – for that is what they look for in the Church and in her priests. They get little of it in the world.'[11] And Raynes, despite later aborting Huddleston's career as an 'agitator', never criticised his brother's politics or conduct, and eventually made him his confessor. Physically similar, both men were tall, with cropped grey hair, strong profiles, decisive movements, expressive hands, ready smiles and a sense of humour. The controlling force for both of their lives was the daily and hourly seven-fold Benedictine Office, daily mass, regular confession and absolute obedience to the Lordship of Christ. But there the similarity ended. What released Huddleston's charismatic qualities of leadership was the increasing freedom with which he was able to respond to the affection and respect of his African flock. Neither Raynes nor any other Christian minister displayed so openly the love Huddleston felt for those to whom he ministered. Archbishop Tutu singled out this as his most unusual and powerful quality: 'He was so un-English in many ways, being very fond of hugging people, embracing them, and in the way in which he laughed. He did not laugh like many white people, only with their teeth, he laughed with his whole body, his whole being, and that endeared him very much to black people. And if he wore a white cassock it did not remain clean for long, as he trudged the dusty streets of Sophiatown with the little urchins with grubby fingers always wanting to touch him and calling our "Fader" with obvious affection in their little voices. He loved us – tremendous. He was fond of letting you sit on his lap . . . His office in Sophiatown would have very many street urchins playing marbles on the floor and the next moment when he had shooed them out he would be meeting ambassadors and high-placed officials and leading businessmen.'[12] Much later this delight in close physical contact with young boys was to bring him, in a vastly different society, to the brink of collapse and beyond. But in Africa it was the key that turned his love for urban Africans into a potent energy to assert their human rights.[13]

Huddleston had a big operation to manage; several hundreds of people who looked to him for guidance and leadership on many aspects of life; the pastoral care of thousands more; as well as the education of the young and their subsequent employment and general well being. Some have criticised the decision to give such a large job to a relatively young and inexperienced priest: Raynes had not, except formally, and ex-post facto, consulted the Community: he saw his successor and took the decision entirely on his own. His style was abbatial, Benedictine, not consensual. But Huddleston would have known how important South Africa was to the Community's worldwide activities, and anticipated the demands that were to be laid on him, from returning brethren, from common-room discussion, and from knowledge of the Community's commitment to its Southern African responsibilities. Raynes had identified in Huddleston the one man in CR capable of taking on what he had so successfully developed. It was an inspired choice.

Huddleston had sailed from Liverpool on 29 July 1943. The ships went in convoy and his was bombed off Spain. It was a ghastly journey. They were anchored off Freetown for ten days, and no-one was allowed to leave the ship because of wartime regulations. The convoy eventually arrived at Cape Town in the first week of September. Huddleston was met in Johannesburg by Fr Goodall CR, and taken to mass in Sophiatown: 'The doors opened and I was engulfed with this flood of kids and I thought I'd never tell one from the other . . . of course I spent the next years doing just that.'[14] Shortly afterwards he met Dorothy Maud who had done so much with Raynes for the Community in support of its interracial work. He was worried about his responsibilities, for all the Africans of Johannesburg – except those in the city centre staying in the backs of white people's gardens as live-in servants, and except Alexandra township – were to be his parishioners.

For the first few weeks Huddleston stayed at the priory in Rosettenville but was anxious to settle in Sophiatown. He, three other fathers and the women church workers of Ekutuleni (or 'place of peace', next to the Priory) were the only Europeans in the township, except for a Roman Catholic mission with one priest. All the other white clergy of all denominations came and went by car.

On 4 October he was inducted into his new parochial responsibilities by the then Bishop of Johannesburg, Geoffrey Clayton, who quoted St Paul's words to Timothy as his text: 'Let no man despise thy youth.' Clayton was his boss so far as the life of the parish was concerned. Sophiatown was to be the microcosm of his vocation, with Rosettenville, Johannesburg, and eventually the whole of Southern Africa forming concentric circles around his womb-like true home.

In February 1944, Huddleston moved into No. 73, Meyer Street, Sophiatown, with four other CR brethren. He was almost the only person with white skin in the sleazy but partly beautiful township of some 70,000 souls. Bloke Modisane was only one of many writers to praise Sophiatown, but he was born and grew up there. He described it as being 'like our nice-time parties or the sound of a penny whistle, or mounting compulsion to joyousness, but always with a hint of pain. Sophiatown was also like our weekends, it was the reason, or rather the excuse we used to stop the progress of time, to celebrate a kind of wish fulfilment; we cherished Sophiatown because it brought together such a great concentration of people; we did not live in it, we were Sophiatown.'[15]

But if Sophiatown provided the fuel to drive CR forward as missionary parish priests, the provincial headquarters of the community's work in South Africa was some miles distant, at

Rosettenville, from where several parishes, a mission outstation in Penhalonga, Southern Rhodesia, and many schools, hospitals and mission stations were administered. By 1944 the Rosettenville centre at St Peter's Priory included St Peter's school – a boys' secondary boarding school; and also St Peter's theological college which the future ANC leader Oliver Tambo applied to join in the early 1950s. This was an important establishment in which 'a very large proportion of the native ordinands of the Province of South Africa receive their training.'[16] At St Peter's, Tambo, then teaching physics, and Huddleston, the school's superintendent, became lifelong friends. Huddleston's predecessor had moved his headquarters from Rosettenville to Sophiatown; their church there, of Christ the King, was the pride and joy of CR. Huddleston always preferred, even loved, the friendly but dangerous life of the Sophiatown streets and backyards. On his very first day, he went to a school mass in church and saw 'nothing but row upon row of black, curly heads. It seemed quite impossible to imagine that there could be so many children' but these were only half the children in one school. 'Within a few weeks I was beginning not only to know them, but to compare them mentally with other children I had known.'[17] Huddleston could relate one-to-one with an astonishing number and variety of people, but his deepest love started with the children of Sophiatown. 'The Sophiatown child is the most friendly creature upon earth and the most trusting . . . You will be walking over a playground and suddenly feel a tug at your sleeve or a pressure against your knee: and then there will be a sticky hand in yours. 'Hallo, Farther, hallo, Seester, how are you? Hallo, hallo, hallo. . . .' You are *home*. Your children are all around you . . . you belong to them and they will never let you forget it.'[18] Later that first day Huddleston sat with Fr Leo Rakale on the window seat of the Priory house and they went through the mass in Xhosa and Tswana, because Huddleston wanted to learn and use these languages as fast as possible to build on the Anglo-Catholic religious practices already introduced by Raynes. Away from the children and parochial concerns, the brethren said the Office (not sung, as at Rosettenville) in the tiny chapel. 'You can really say the Divine Office seven times a day and still lead a very active life,' Huddleston was later to remark.[19]

His day began at 5.15 a.m., in church by 5.30 a.m. This, including mass, went on for two hours, and breakfast was taken in silence. Then there was Terce, and Huddleston was in his office by 8.30 a.m. for office work or visiting. His mornings would be spent interviewing people with particular problems – a subtenant not paying the rent, an Indian landlord cutting off the water supply – but he might also visit a school, perhaps to teach scripture, or take communion to the sick, in home or in hospital. He joined or started committees to focus white support for African causes, giving much time each month to shriving the nuns, always followed by crowds of small children. He started a little guild of servers at the altar – 'I wanted them to get some social life. Once a week after supper they met, a younger and an older group. There were a hundred or more of these kids; they grew up with me, and I got the feel of the whole of their way of living.'[20] Lunch was at 12.30 p.m., after endless problems, domestic, social, economic, moral, religious. In the afternoon there would be meetings with officials or work focusing on specific social problems, and he would get back from such meetings at 6.30 p.m. for evensong, then supper, followed by a servers' meeting or choir practice or some church guild; Compline was at 9.30 p.m. Thereafter the Greater Silence would regularly be broken by the noise of a large town enjoying itself.

When winter set in the first year . . . 'when the wind was blowing dust across the veld and the frail little shanties were almost torn from their moorings,' the Johannesburg City Council set up soup kitchens. But the people boycotted them – they needed homes, not soup, and guessed that Huddleston might be another well-connected do-gooder: he was nearly set upon by squatters and 'was pulled from behind and shoved very hard into one of the shacks'. In January 1946 the same thing happened again, but by this time, the Anglican priest Michael Scott, one of the few white voices challenging the status quo at that time, had come to live and minister to those in 'the Shelters'. Scott had returned to South Africa shortly before Huddleston's arrival in

1943. When he arrived in Johannesburg Scott was appointed assistant priest to the coloured community and chaplain to an orphanage. He lived in a rondavel (one-roomed hut) on the outskirts of neighbouring Sophiatown. Speedily, Scott set about discovering what successive government committees of enquiry had recommended be done to alleviate distress among the growing thousands of squatters, only to find that, while recommendations for improvement already existed; all serious commitment to implement them was lacking. So he formed the Campaign for Right and Justice, which itself generated a scheme for regional planning and its implementation. This won considerable support from local Europeans. The Campaign collapsed without government support, but it made Scott famous, and he then lent his support to the campaign for passive resistance in Durban in 1946, for which he was imprisoned after witnessing violence and cruelty inflicted on Indian women as well as men.[21] After a spell in jail, Scott was declared a prohibited immigrant in 1950, but continued to campaign for the rights of expropriated African tribes and communities from abroad. Huddleston candidly and penitently admitted that he failed to understand and support Scott's principled stand and the suffering it entailed for Scott. 'To my shame,' he later said, 'I did very little to help him.'[22] His moving tribute at Scott's funeral is also a confession.[23] On the text 'What does the law require of thee – to do justly, to love mercy and to walk humbly before thy God,' Huddleston recalled his listeners to: 'those blue remembered hills of our young days of commitment to the struggle for human rights and human dignity in South Africa ... the no longer shared friendships of action. I have not got, and I never had, his prophetic vision. We had arrived together in 1943 – Michael to work in the Coloured Mission in Johannesburg which covered much of the same territory as the African parishes of Sophiatown, Orlando and Pimville to which I had just been appointed priest-in-charge. To me those first months [in Sophiatown] were wonderfully exciting but I was far too immature to read its meaning in terms of either present suffering or future tragedy ... It took me the best part of four years to understand it wasn't the symptoms but the disease itself that had to be fought. It took Michael about four weeks.'

For in that winter of 1946, Huddleston refused Scott permission to celebrate Holy Communion with his people in the Shelters known as 'Tobruk' on somewhat specious grounds. Archbishop Clayton (the former bishop of Johannesburg) told Scott that Huddleston, 'believes that it is undesirable . . . I have complete confidence in his judgement.' Scott and Huddleston corresponded inconclusively and Scott later accused Huddleston of being misled by the opinion of others and ceased to be his penitent. Huddleston replied that Scott found in every issue some fresh occasion of persecution. But there is evidence that, despite his otherworldliness, Huddleston threw himself effectively into the grim life of the shanty towns almost from the start. And it was the Squatter Movement that deepened his opposition to the regime.

By 1945 the huge communities outside Johannesburg housed 250,000 people in conditions of squalor unbelievable to those who had not seen them. Brother Roger Castle CR on a visit to Africa in 1947 wrote of one of the townships: 'Acres and acres of sacking hovels and no sanitation, no amenities of any kind.'[24] The urban blacks of the reef had but dimly been recognized as a sociological development of significance to the future of the country when Anthony Sampson went to edit the picture magazine *Drum* in 1951, and his subsequent book about his experiences is the first revelation of the significance of this development.[25] Urban Africans were very different from rural Africans with their subsistence farming, tribal orientation, Muslim or animistic faiths and practices, and political innocence. Many of those, including some from St Peter's, who worked and joked their way to maturity in *Drum*'s newsroom, were, by contrast streetwise, alienated, cynical and unpredictable.

CR's involvement with this new breed of parishioner had not developed strongly until Huddleston's arrival, but Raynes had spent endless hours leading deputations to protest at the lack of social amenities, calling in the press, addressing meetings of the multi-racial Joint Council established by Johannesburg City

Council and above all succouring individuals and families in particular distress. Later Fr Claude Lunniss CR continued the work, visiting (for instance) every house in Orlando (numbered 1 to 6,000 in their redbrick rows.) Both men encouraged white groups to attend their churches and visit the locations. 'Fifteen years later', Nicholas Mosley wrote, 'when all white missionaries were thrown out of Orlando, their work had had its effect.'[26]

But Huddleston's 'effect' was different. He was not a visitor, rather a neighbour, a fellow townsman. He was looked upon as a saviour, and not only by Anglicans; many of the young black men (stigmatized as 'tsotsi' or thugs) – who didn't attend church – met Huddleston and became close friends. There were many others: Oliver Tambo; Don Mattera; Michael Rantho; Hugh Masekela; Ezekiel (Eskia) Mphahlele; Arthur Maimane; Nimrod Tubane; Maurice Manana; Walter Sisulu; Stephen and Norman Montjane; Walter Makhulu; Nelson Mandela; Simeon Nkoane; Peter Abrahams; Kort Boy; Chinkie Modiga; Columbus Malebo; Fikile Bam; Desmond Tutu; David Nkwe. George Mbalweni saw Huddleston at his home because, like many of 'Huddleston's boys', he had been in serious trouble: 'people respected him a lot. So did I – he was very clever. You couldn't move. He watched everything quicker than you.'[27] These are but a few of the names which recur in his diaries right through to the 1990s.

He soon became friends with the ANC President, Dr Xuma and his American wife, and Harry Madibane, headmaster of the local high school. New friendships were made, too, at the monthly parish council meeting. After a week he forgot about colour for ever. Raynes had warned him about Sophiatown living conditions, about knifings, about illicit beer, about tsotsis. 'I had to deal with their problems and listen to their confessions. Most of them lived one family to a room. It was difficult to get any privacy.'[28] Despite the squalid living conditions and the lack of satisfactory alternative accommodation, the Municipal Council was already planning the destruction of Sophiatown, because the white suburbs nearby were also growing and encroaching on it, producing an unacceptable juxtaposition of black and white. As early as October 1944 Huddleston moved in the Diocesan Synod that 'this House deplores the recent proposal in the City Council to expropriate the African people of Sophiatown in that it is contrary to the principles of Christian justice, and that copies of this resolution be sent to the Administrator of the Transvaal and the Johannesburg Municipal Council.' Exactly a year later, he preached at St Mary's Cathedral, Johannesburg, on the text, 'Is it well with the child?' (2 Kings 12, 5–6.) on parental responsibility in the crowded urban life he now knew well. He started by asking: 'What is the greatest responsibility of the African people today? Should it be to build an African nation free of want, fear, oppression? Important, but without a good home life, impossible.'[29]

Huddleston knew from Raynes's briefing what to expect in the attitude of the authorities over education. There were many battles at the municipal level from the very start: 'There was filthy housing, a dangerous situation at Orlando with the squatter movement, and running battles over the Pass laws.'[30] He began to associate with known Communists and, anxious to achieve a measure of equality and justice for all, to find a new world beyond the Church. He joined the Institute of Race Relations where he attended meetings of the Joint Council, convened monthly to deal with every kind of abuse – housing, rent rackets, water supply problems – and had Africans and Europeans for members. Huddleston later said: 'I learnt my basic sociology on the Joint Council.'[31] Raynes had served on it, and the distinguished liberal statesman J.H. Hofmeyr (Minister of Finance and Education in the Smuts government) encouraged it as a meeting point between the races.

Early on in his African ministry Huddleston understood that any good parish priest had to combine local politics with his pastoral care. CR had become partially politicized in South Africa years before Huddleston arrived, but its important position in the middle of Sophiatown only enhanced this process of politicization, and Huddleston responded to the extraordinary atmosphere in Sophiatown even more enthusiastically than had Raynes. In 1988 he told a television interviewer, 'I learnt everything from

Sophiatown. It was one of the most vital places on earth. I think the main characteristic of the African people is this extraordinary zest for life at all kinds of level. I loved every minute of my life there.'[32] In a letter to the Johannesburg *Star* he pointed out that the root cause of crime among natives lay in the evil social and economic environment in which urban Africans struggled to lead decent lives. What was needed was a direct and honest policy in housing, labour, education and recreation facilities for the townships. He was to return to this theme again and again, and often condemned many of his activities as 'ambulance work only' when what was needed was irreversible social change, racial equality, a new view of how people of all colours could live together in harmony.

In 1945, Huddleston discovered that white schoolchildren were entitled to a free midday meal whereas black children, whether in school or not, had no right to anything. The sheer unfairness of this provoked him as much as the all too evident malnutrition of black children, and within months he had started the African Children's Feeding Scheme. That year, he also inaugurated a church newspaper in the vernacular and opened a new mission station at St Benedict's. By 1947 what Huddleston called his 'philanthropic period' was in full swing. On 18 May he told readers of the Johannesburg evening paper, the *Star*, that Orlando, 'the largest non-European suburb in the Union,' had no resident doctor, no regular milk supply, no swimming pool or bioscope.[33] Violent crime in the city was on the increase and he sought a subsidy for one of the squatter schools at Jabavu stating that more could be done, and for less expense, by educating young would-be thugs than by doubling the police force. On 23 July he wrote that Sophiatown and Newclare residents had asked to be transferred to Moroka squatters' camp; 'better a shack of your own on a 20 ft by 20ft plot than as subtenants sharing with others.' On 7 August he opened a new school for natives at Orlando, and, two months later, registered his support for the Africans' desire to relaunch the 'African Citizens' Guard' following the murder of Elias Mokoetsi, the principal of the Anglican mission school in Sophiatown by a young tsotsi.[34] The police were unwilling to back the move. On 4 December, the *Star*, encouraged by the journalist Olga Price, commented on Huddleston's activities on behalf of the underdog in the Sophiatown, Orlando and Pimville mission districts, and the crime wave became local headline news. Six weeks before, Huddleston had formed a multi-racial body to work for better native housing, education, and 'a sane labour policy', but this initiative, called the Active Citizens' League, did not prosper. By 3 January 1948 the menace of the city's native criminal underworld was growing, while the law-abiding black parents of young children had to go out to work (5 a.m. till 7 p.m.) to pay the bills. 'The church is attempting the colossal task in the townships and locations of Johannesburg by making the care of such children one of its prime responsibilities ... For their neglect, for their sufferings, we shall one day have to answer before God,' wrote Huddleston.[35] Later that month he observed that the government would not pay for native education for the 4,000 to 5,000 now adrift in Sophiatown and Orlando. On 25 February, speaking in Pretoria about native housing conditions, he commented: 'The public has shown no sign of wanting to know what conditions were like – one tap to fifty families in Jabavu/Moroka – a population of 224,000 to the square mile.'[36] By March the urban Africans proposed to build their own schools with their own labour but this move was said to be unfair to the blue-collar unions and disallowed. In June Huddleston appealed for funds for nursery schools and re-launched the ailing Active Citizens' League.

But by now the General Election had been won by the Nationalists and the time was rapidly approaching for a more confrontational position. By the end of 1948 the press had reported Huddleston's first public protest, when he spoke from the back of the Johannesburg magistrate's court in November against the eviction and destruction of the homes of some of the 40,000 families within his parish. It happened during the hearing of one of fifteen cases where native Sophiatown landlords were being prosecuted for failing to comply with municipal orders that wood and iron buildings should not be used as dwellings. George Ndhlovu had refused to throw one family onto the streets and was about to be fined. Huddleston stood up and insisted on standing till he had been heard: 'simply that it is unjust to penalise a man for an offence that is not his fault but the fault of society.'[37] Evidence was supplied that some of the shacks were only 6 to 8 ft high and were in an insanitary condition; up to eight families lived in one shack and eviction would force people to live in even worse conditions. The magistrate refused to hear him. Huddleston refused to sit down. The magistrate adjourned the court and left. He commented acidly on the feebleness of his action in *Naught for Your Comfort*, observing that 'making a nuisance of oneself in a magistrate's court' was rather pathetic. 'I thought so that night, and I think so today.' But he did notice marginal improvements following his outburst.[38]

At the end of 1948 Huddleston had written to Evelyn Baring: 'Life is very interesting politically at the moment, and it looks as if we may have a first class crisis on our hands early next year. In the meantime things aren't any easier. Yet somehow or other the very fact that they may be so difficult makes one glad to be out here with the Bantu.'[39] On Christmas Eve he wrote a Christmas sermon for the *Star* on the subject of philanthropy. 'Like patriotism,' wrote Huddleston, 'philanthropy is not enough . . . It is clear that a Communist witch hunt is about to begin, and that "Communist" covers the acts, words and speeches of those who voice the grievances and frustrations of the native people. To meet the rising tide of native nationalism, there is the policy of oppression: the trampling underfoot of the right to freedom of speech and freedom of the press; the pursuit of totalitarian methods in all their naked horror.' He added, 'I write as a Christian priest not a politician.'[40] By 10 January 1949 he was preaching in the cathedral that 'we are allowing the State to treat the largest number of its subjects in a way that is an affront to the dignity of man – and so an affront to Almighty God, who became Man . . . The time has come for the churches to try and meet to frame a constructive Christian policy.'[41] Despite his words, his association with the now-banned Communist party members, together with his appearance at the magistrate's court, showed that he had developed; he had become tougher and better able to cope with the demands of hs political activism without compromising his Benedictine lifestyle. A friend of his, then under his spiritual direction remembered the early days:

> When I arrived in Sophiatown at the end of 1943 Trevor Huddleston had been there only a few months, though he appeared to be already settled and established. I had seen him at Mirfield, but did not really know him. The impression he made on me was of a very shy, unworldly, spiritually minded man. He seemed to be awkward in his movements and gestures, with the typical motion of his huge hands which he still has. One felt that the job of following Raymond Raynes was taking everything out of him and that he was constantly stretched and very tired. Yet at the centre this was a very special person. I loved him from the start and both wanted to obey him and at the same time to protect him. He became much tougher and more able to cope with the constant demands made on him. He became more worldly and less overtly shy. He began to smoke a great deal and to enjoy being the leader and centre of a large group of workers. This did not in any way affect his devotion to Our Lord. He needed to be tempered and toughened if he was to survive what was to follow. His prayer life and daily mass and monastic offices were never crowded out by pressure of other work. They were the centre and strength from which he moved to the circumference of action.[42]

One of Huddleston's most fruitful friendships of this period was with Olga Price (later Horowitz) of the *Star*. He had already appeared in this evening paper as a man to watch, but the publicity generated by this friendship was to prove of particular importance when he was elected Provincial CR and removed to Rosettenville towards the end of 1949. 'She was a great buddy. She would get me the headlines to get a cause moving.'[43] Other close friends were Evelyn and Molly Baring, who came to visit, and Huddleston in turn was able to use the High Commissioner's residence in Johannesburg for rest and recuperation. Another was Sybil Pollock (the sister of Sir Ernest Oppenheimer's first wife).[44]

She came slumming and soon became a friend, introducing him to the Oppenheimers at Brenthurst. Among the Communist activists were Hilda [Watts] Bernstein, with whom he worked on a number of social protests, and Ruth First.

While Huddleston's move to Rosettenville as the newly elected Provincial CR extended his range and influence, leaving Sophiatown after six formative years was a terrible wrench. In retrospect he thought of it as the happiest time of his life; and he remained a legend there, nicknamed 'Die Jerry' because of his close-cropped hair, his tall cassocked figure striding through the township, surrounded by African parishioners. Photographs of Huddleston adorned backyard walls. Anthony Sampson recalls the first time he met Huddleston in Sophiatown when Huddleston asked the then young editor of *Drum* picture magazine if he would take on a bright St Peter's alumnus, Arthur Maimane. 'Huddleston came in, a tall dignified figure, wearing his long black cassock, with a worn leather belt round his waist, and a cross dangling from the side. He had a long face with a deep chin, greying, close-cropped hair and direct eyes. He spoke with a simple directness, as if Arthur and *Drum* were all that he had ever thought about.'[45]

Sampson saw Huddleston frequently in the next three years, 'at African functions and Congress gatherings, at European cocktail parties and fund-raising meetings. All roads seemed to lead to Huddleston. I went to the funeral of Oubaas, to find him conducting the burial service. When one of our staff who was unhappy in *Drum* found other work, I found that it had been arranged by Huddleston. Many of the best members of our staff were sent to us by him; two of them he sent after they had been expelled from St Peter's.'[46]

Huddleston himself singled out three key friends of this period, pointing to their stories as illustrations of the apartheid regime's increasing erosion of the liberty of individuals. One was Stephen Ramasodi, who was refused a passport to take up a place Huddleston had secured for him at a leading Episcopalian school in the United States because it was said that the boy would be unsettled by exposure to the liberalising conditions under which blacks were then living on the East Coast. The second was Helen Navid, an agnostic and communist, whose anti-apartheid work had led to her receiving a banning order, preventing her from leaving the country. A public protest meeting was called, which Huddleston was the only European to address. For he had earlier been in long discussion with her, 'struggling to see some light, to make the right decision, knowing that it would alter the whole course of her life.'[47] The third was Oliver Tambo, future President of the African National Congress who, but for his health, would almost certainly have preceded Nelson Mandela as South Africa's first head of state when apartheid came to an end. Huddleston liked to remember Tambo sitting on his *stoep* sometime in 1955 and telling of his childhood in a large, non-religious family with illiterate parents, his mission-school education, and his arrival as a pupil at St Peter's Rosettenville at the age of sixteen.[48] For Tambo, Huddleston was the living evidence that the Church sided with the African people in their struggle. Their friendship withstood the test of time, and was always subservient to the cause they both served so unremittingly. When Huddleston left Britain for Masasi in 1960, Tambo was the only person at the station to wish him godspeed. When Huddleston arrived in Kenya on church business, or later in the United States, the exiled Tambo, successfully promoting the ANC cause abroad, would slip into the back of the church where Huddleston was celebrating evening communion, and sit there silently. In 1991 it was Tambo who saw Huddleston off from Johannesburg airport after his return visit. 'It is his friendship of nearly fifty years which is my greatest strength and consolation and the ground of my hope for the future of the African National Congress and so of South Africa.'[49] His death removed a vital prop in Huddleston's understanding of the past and hope for the future. It is fitting that on 27 January 1998 the busts of the two men were unveiled together in the stately hall of South Africa House, Trafalgar Square, both lonely warriors and wanderers, celebrated belatedly for their parts in the long battle to destroy apartheid. Huddleston's speech in honour of Tambo was short, pithy and extremely moving, delivered from a wheelchair three months before his own death.

By comparison, Huddleston's encounters with the man who claimed to be his boss, Archbishop Geoffrey Clayton, were frosty. Huddleston had his first row with Clayton some years earlier. 'The war was still on, so it was probably 1944–5. There were a lot of women missionaries who were jolly tired and had been out the whole of the War. The army was getting its men home, chartering ships for the purpose.'[50] Huddleston, who was trying to get the missionaries home, put up a motion in the Synod on Clayton's advice, only to find it opposed by Clayton from the chair. 'I don't believe in pulling strings,' Clayton snapped to the Synod, 'and I hope you don't either.' Clayton 'simply wiped the floor' with Huddleston, who, nothing daunted, accosted him at the door, saying 'I think you behaved extremely badly.'[51] It was not a good start to what proved to be a stormy and unreconciled relationship. Both were forceful characters; neither liked being crossed or put down in public. In correspondence after Huddleston's enforced departure from South Africa, Clayton made it clear he did not want Huddleston back; an unlikely possibility after which Huddleston hankered spasmodically throughout 1958.

In 1950, the year after Huddleston's move to Rosettenville, government legislation replaced the Pass System with the Population Registration Act, and the Group Areas Bill. The Pass Laws compelled non-whites to carry identification papers at all times while the Group Areas Bill made possible the enforced removal of whole communities. Together with the Suppression of Communism Act and the Bantu Education Act in 1953, these bills were to become the cornerstones of Nationalist native policy. Their implementation unequivocally forced apartheid upon Johannesburg's non-whites, and to oppose them became Huddleston's overriding concern. Writing in the *Star* on 13 May he compared 'our apathy to their hunger and hopelessness: our presumptuous superiority abusing their patience and courtesy; our blind acceptance of their labour as a right which is ours for the taking: in a word, our refusal to accept them as persons – all this will in the end bring upon us the judgement of God.' He was writing because 'for the third time in some ten years a decision has been taken to expropriate the native peoples living in Sophia-town and its adjacent areas.' He knew that the expropriation was taking place not 'because the City Council really wants the Native to be better off [but] to meet the demands of those European ratepayers who . . . have encroached on an existing native area and now object to its proximity . . . I have known and loved these people for six years,' he continued. 'I have been in and out of their homes day after day. I have seen their sorrows and shared them to the best of my ability . . . The average European cannot hold a candle to most of these men, women and children of Sophiatown.'[52] His public statements became more frequent, making him enemies among the white electorate; a fresh wave of native crime perturbed the Johannesburg citizenry: the tsotsis were blamed. Again Huddleston pointed to the horrendous living conditions as a cause of inevitable crime. As recently as February 1950, he had written to the press about the conditions he had shared with the 60,000 other citizens of Sophiatown; 'where a shack is home', he wrote, 'we just get on with it.'

Part of his parochial responsibility, the nearby township of Newclare, was in particular crisis. 'Something was stirring beneath that strange mixture of slum and open space, in those crowded backyards. Indian shops were set on fire and looted,' perhaps to stir up racial strife between African and Indian, recounts Huddleston in *Naught for Your Comfort*.[53] 'Gradually the true picture emerged and was clarified,' he continues. 'A [black] Basuto gang, calling themselves "the Russians" (but having nothing whatever to do with the Communist party anywhere) had entrenched itself at Newclare.' So the locals formed a civil guard. 'Men, armed with heavy sticks and moving only in groups of a dozen or so, patrolled the streets after sundown . . . Meanwhile, the weekend clashes in Newclare continued and became more bloody . . . But still, for some strange reason which has remained unexplained to this day, the police did not disarm "the Russians".' Two months later this civil guard was declared illegal and conditions in Newclare became impossible: 'people began to move out of their homes and to erect shacks and shelters in the open . . . Within a week 200 families – 1,500 people – were living there, with a public lavatory in one corner and an iron fence all round it.'

It was a little under two years after the violence had first erupted that the authorities decide to respond. On 2 July 1952 the City Council and the police got together and decided to evict the squatters. 'I was asked to see what I could do to persuade the squatters to go back to their homes and face "the Russians". I went as swiftly as I could to the camp, taking the field-officer of the Institute of Race Relations. It was a very tough proposition, to persuade people who had been terrorised out of their homes that they must either walk back into terror, or be exiled. As we drove out to Newclare [the officer] was almost in tears: "It is impossible, Father: impossible! What have these poor people done? It isn't their fault. It's these Russians. We know the Basuto government has files full of evidence against the gang's leaders." '
After Huddleston had made a fruitless trip to the High Commissioner's office in Pretoria, the City Council applied for an eviction order against the inhabitants of Newclare. Huddleston returned to Newclare itself to discuss the emergency with the squatters' leader, Dhlamini. The priest contacted the squatters' lawyer, Lowenberg, and then dashed to the Magistrates' Court, where a hearing for the eviction order application was already in progress. Told he had no standing and could not speak, Huddleston endured two adjournments, during which the ANC collected evidence from those driven out of Newclare by the 'Russians'. In the ensuing stand-off, Huddleston decided to use a small nursery school the Mission had built to save the squatters' children from the worst of the winter cold. He collected 'a miserable £300 for blankets and basic comfort'. Meanwhile a tornado had hit nearby Albertynsville and within three days thousands of pounds worth of clothing and food were contributed. 'I have always felt that this was an interesting comment on the conscience of White Johannesburg. Stirred to immediate and most generous action by a tornado, it could remain utterly impervious to what was happening day after day to hundreds of its own African citizens in its midst.'

The legal battles dragged on.

I spent a good deal of time trying to organise what comfort and shelter I could at the nursery school ... I used to spend my evenings bathing the small ones and wrapping them up in their warm blankets. It was a wonderful experience – the gradual unfolding of confidence and trust which it produced: the sense of being expected each evening at bedtime: the grubby hands thrust into mine, the noisy chatter and laughter. I shall never forget the nights at Newclare ... I was there on the morning the lorries arrived ... a vast new temporary camp was set up where 60,000 others, from the previous squatter movements at Orlando, had for four or five years already been living ... I have told the story not only because I know every smallest detail of it but because I think it illustrates better than most events the kind of thing I have tried to fight against over the years.

Pondering his motives, he asked: 'Is it because I saw so much courage and gaiety in the midst of so much degradation? Or is it, perhaps, because a little African boy leapt from his blankets and kissed my hand?'[54]

Many readers of his book, and this, will see this defining episode in Huddleston's life not as the moment of his becoming political, but the moment when he accepted fatherhood, responding with love to the love of African children.

On 22 March 1950 Huddleston told the press there were 57,000 homeless in Johannesburg, and a week later that implementing the Western Areas Removal Scheme (the expropriation of all non-whites from Sophiatown, Martindale and Newclare) would cost the Council £1,600,000. Later in the year Huddleston was criticized for being the tsotsis's supporter, but his friend and pupil, Ezekiel Mphahlele pointed out to *Star* readers on 27 July that 'Father Huddleston lives among the tsotsis and their parents.' If his concerns still centred on those in his immediate patch whom he could help, this must have been because the full horror of apartheid did not emerge until 1953. But if his assimilation process was a slow one, the native situation in South Africa under the Nationalist government was changing rapidly, producing a radically new concept of how apartheid could work in practice.

1951 saw the introduction of the Bantu Authorities Act
and the Separate Representation of Voters Bill which further
entrenched the separate development and administration of white
and non-white communities. Huddleston at this time consorted
with known Communists but denied that he was anything other
than a Christian Socialist. He spent three months on leave in
England, where he saw the film of Alan Paton's *Cry, the Beloved
Country*, deplored the falseness of the Festival of Britain and
continued 'to take his share in framing and speaking to resolutions of Synod which condemned apartheid'.[55]

The African National Congress, founded on Gandhian principles of non-violence, was the oldest political party in South
Africa and had always worked to integrate all races into a
democratic system rather than advance the interests of any particular group. Since its founding in 1912 its achievement had
been modest and its membership restricted mostly to African
gradualists. After four decades of seeking change through peti-
tions, deputations and public meetings, in 1949 the Youth League
(which included Walter Sisulu, Oliver Tambo and Nelson Mandela) fostered a new militancy. They drew up a Programme of
Action calling for civil disobedience, strikes and boycotts focused
on 26 June, which they christened Freedom Day. By 1952 this
movement had gathered sufficient momentum for the ANC to
make direct calls for apartheid legislation to be withdrawn. This
was the start of the Defiance Campaign and drew a swift and
violent response from the government: within seven months 8,500
protestors were arrested and imprisoned and new laws passed –
the Public Safety Act and the Criminal Law Amendment Act –
which made any acts of protest, or even newspaper reports of
such protests, illegal. With increasing frequency and thoroughness, the special political branch of the police conducted raids in
an effort to uncover evidence of subversion resulting in a total of
fifty-two ANC leaders and many members of the Communist
Party of South Africa (SACP) being banned from attending any
public political gathering. In the general election of 15 April 1953
the Nationalists increased their majority from 73 to 94, thanks in
part to its exploitation of white fears aroused by the campaign.[56]

By February 1953 Huddleston had identified himself entirely with the struggle of the African and Indian Congress.[57] Despite the suppression of the Defiance Campaign, public meetings continued and on 15 February Huddleston spoke in front of nearly 1,000 Congress delegates in the Trades Hall, Johannesburg. The *Rand Daily Mail* was there to report his speech: 'It has been the teaching of the church throughout the centuries that when government degenerates into tyranny . . . laws cease to be binding on its subjects . . . The future of South Africa is in *your* hands, that is certain . . . I pray God that he will give you strength . . . I identify myself entirely with your struggle.'[58] After the meeting he told Sampson, 'I've been trying to pluck up courage to say that for months. I'm glad I've taken the plunge.'[59] This was a watershed, because what he now publicly allied himself with was sedition.

Four months later, on 28 June 1953, another protest meeting took place at the Odin cinema in Sophiatown: 'It was a lively exuberant meeting attended by more than 1,200 people, none of whom seemed intimidated by the presence of dozens of heavily armed policemen.'[60] It had been called to decide what action could be taken to oppose the government's intention to remove blacks from the area. Huddleston recorded the meeting. 'When, after mass, I arrived at the vestibule, there was already a small group of Europeans, two or three men, arguing with some of the African and Indian delegates and claiming that as they were the CID [Criminal Investigation Department of the South African Police] they were entitled to come to the meeting. This I thought to be quite untrue, but, to make quite sure, I went into a neighbouring shop and rang a lawyer friend of mine who confirmed my opinion.'[61] Yusuf Cachalia, a prominent Indian Congress leader was arrested, 'in an atmosphere of tension, [which] seemed to me quite criminal,' and then forcibly assaulted. 'The people rose to their feet in the dark hall, 1,200 of them, and made their anger known as the police hurried towards the exit . . . I protested to the officer in charge and was threatened with arrest myself.'[62] Huddleston also discovered that the police were waiting outside the doors of the cinema, ready and armed in great numbers. Had the people inside the cinema reacted, the result could have been a massacre.[63]

Another witness was Nelson Mandela, only recently unbanned from attending meetings of any sort:

> Shortly before the meeting was due to begin, a police officer saw Walter and me outside the cinema talking with Father Huddleston [who] shouted to the policemen coming towards us, 'No, you must arrest me instead, my dears.' The officer ordered Father Huddleston to stand aside, but he refused and the police moved him out of the way. Inside the hall, I saw Major Prinsloo come swaggering in through the stage door, accompanied by a number of armed officers . . . He walked over to the podium, where Yusuf Cachalia had already begun to speak, and ordered the other officers to arrest him, whereupon they took him by the arms and started to drag him off. Outside, the police had already arrested Robert Resha and Ahmed Kathrada. The crowd began yelling and booing, and I saw that matters could turn extremely ugly if the crowd did not control itself. I jumped on the podium and started singing a well-known protest song, and as soon as I pronounced the first few words, the crowd joined in. I feared that the police might have opened fire if the crowd had become too unruly.[64]

Don Mattera, a self-confessed gangster tried and acquitted for murder, has written of Huddleston's spiritual and physical charisma and his abhorrence of violence, in a powerful memoir entitled *Memory is the Weapon*.[65] Don Mattera remembers the Odin Cinema meeting in which he felt the force of Huddleston's persona:

> As the people gave way for him to pass I remember moving towards him and I stood almost in his path. His long, bony fingers rubbed my hair and he smiled deeply and seriously. He had made a reputation for himself as an outspoken foe of the policy of apartheid, as well as of crime and violence especially among black people . . . There was a hush when Father Huddleston stood up to speak. Like many others, I

had only heard him give sermons, and read about him in newspapers . . . While he spoke [agreeing with the last speaker but calling nonetheless for non-violence] uniformed police-men, all armed entered the hall and approached the Indian speaker [Yusuf Cachalia]. Father Huddleston pushed madly through the crowd, his big wooden rosary firm in the thick belt around his waist. 'Wait,' he shouted, 'we must not have violence here.' . . . I watched the lanky priest with the bony fingers and aquiline features move through the crowd. He appeared to be tired and I felt a strange love and pity for the man. What force was there in him, that made others succumb? Even the police whom I had challenged and fought in the streets had heeded and feared him . . . Admiration pounded in my heart and I followed him from a distance, my knife tucked secretly under my shirt. And from nowhere the greet-ings began, until a huge crowd of children was following the priest as if he were a religious Pied Piper. Some of them touched his heavy black robe and the rosary that swung from his belt . . . I watched the priest smile; his grave, deep-set eyes change before the innocence of childish abandon and joy. In that moment I made myself believe that he was happy; or that happiness could flow out of a man who had earlier that day averted bloodshed.

Father Huddleston was an integral and important figure in the life and history of Sophiatown and the country as a whole, Mattera comments. His most powerful image of the man comes in a description of his own return from the Catholic convent school in Durban, when he attended an Anglican mass at which Huddleston was officiating. He asked the priest about doctrinal differences between the two churches; 'Father Huddleston smiled and shook his head very gently . . . He then rubbed my head tenderly, and pressed the long, bony forefinger of his right hand into my ribs, where my heart was beating fast. "There, my son, there, in your heart beats the true church of God." '

Huddleston's behaviour at the critical Odin Cinema meeting marked him out as a future leader. From this point on he had the unwavering support of the ANC's leading activists, Nelson

Mandela and Walter Sisulu. But Huddleston needed enemies as well as friends, anger as well as love, to propel him into political protest. By 1953 he had found the cause to which he could give his heart and soul – not just wrongs to be righted, people to be helped and championed, protests to be made, policies to be changed – but the energising force of an enemy that had been identified, and now had to be fought and destroyed. This negative aspect of Huddleston's achievement is worth emphasizing. Anthony Storr, an authority on spiritual leaders, has argued convincingly that a key moment in the making of a great spiritual figure has often come when he or she identifies an enemy, and makes a rallying call against that enemy.[66] Some of the power of Huddleston's austere, well-argued and well-founded attacks on the cruelty and injustice with which he was daily confronted in Sophiatown and Rossettenville derived from a growing mutual antipathy between this 'effortlessly superior' leader of the non-enfranchised majority in the townships, and the white electorate who saw in the policies of the apartheid regime a quick route to the good life. Huddleston himself wrote: 'It is not apartheid which has provided the Nationalist Government with its immense and growing dominance over all other European groups and parties in this country. It is not the thirst for such a negative state of affairs as 'separation' *in itself* that has so stirred enthusiasm and multiplied votes. It is something much deeper and much more appealing. In a word it is *white supremacy, now and always*.'[67] Certainly the personal venom directed at Huddleston grew strongly at this point. When Nicholas Mosley went to Johannesburg in 1960 to research his life of Raynes he observed that Huddleston 'was still an anathema to most whites'.[68]

Letters from Huddleston to Alan Paton, author of *Cry, the Beloved Country*, suggest that the recurrent depression to which Huddleston was later subject started during this period.[69] However, little of the depression is discernible in Huddleston's recollection of his Sophiatown years. In an interview with Cyril Dunn of the *Observer* in 1955, he said: 'The impression [Sophiatown] made on me was one of immense vitality and gaiety, in spite of everything. I felt completely au fait with the people, shrewd and quick-witted like the people of Camberwell [South London, where he had been on a mission]. It is a community, not an abstraction like Orlando, in spite of its backyard shacks. There was something tremendously alive and real about the whole show there . . . I was there to run a parish, with three others, but it did seem to me that one couldn't do the job at all without getting involved in these social problems. Father Raynes had set the pace . . . We are the only Europeans who ever lived in Sophiatown, the only white people.' Speaking of Michael Scott in 1945–6, he commented: 'I was a pretty cautious political racketeer. I had nothing like the guts of Michael S. I went to visit him when he got imprisoned in Durban. He went out to live in the squatters' camps . . . Hofmeyr was still alive and if you wanted to press things you could go to him and know that something would be done . . . He got native schools to be eligible for school feeding. One felt that one was making a little progress, though nothing like enough.' Huddleston told Dunn he turned political over housing, in particular over the Newclare squatters. He fought government policy for six months in 1952, but 'all they did was to dump the squatters out on the veld at Moroka.' But it was in 1953, as a consequence of the implementation of the Bantu Education Act and the suppression of the Defiance Campaign, that Huddleston burnt his boats by joining the ANC. His new persona remained rooted in his love for Sophiatown and the urban Africans he served. He said that this period had taught him 'the meaning of love in such a way that no other time or place could ever supplant it.'[70]

It is this love he celebrates in chapter seven of *Naught for Your Comfort* in a memorable piece of sociology, which is both a vivid yet simple memoir and a rare *apologia pro vita sua*:

The overcrowded rooms . . . wherein whole families must sleep and must perform all their human functions as best they may. . . . Again and again, hearing confession, I have asked myself how I can advise these children, how warn them, how comfort them when they have fallen . . . I can shut my eyes and see old, blind Margaret, tapping her way along the street into the darkness which has been hers for many long years. Or there will be old Tryphena Mtembu. She has spent all her years ... mending sacks and inhaling cement dust into her old lungs so that she is never free from a fierce cough. She lives in a single dark room and 'does' for herself ... Or Piet, crippled with arthritis, infirm and with no pension after thirty years' work in a furniture shop ... It would be easy to list a score of others, who have lived in Sophiatown for the better part of their lives ... folk who live ordinary lives in extra-ordinary conditions ... The only thing that is meeting the need for a sense of 'community', of 'belonging' in the broken and shattered tribalism of the town-dwelling African is the Church.[71]

Thirty-six years later, he was to make this link between his love for the people of Sophiatown and his growing political engagement even more explicit:

I was working in those days in a slum area of the city, which now no longer exists ... But in my day Sophiatown, one of the oldest African areas in the city, was very much alive. And my whole experience of poverty – my whole experience of what is meant by the word urbanisation in the African context, my experience of that other word you see so often, 'detribalisation', and its effects, one's understanding of racial conflict actually in the heart of where it hit hardest – all this I learned within the context of this slum parish in Sophiatown. This was, of course, a very wonderful experience and one which I suppose more than anything else shaped all my views and my thinking, not merely about sociological problems, but about religion itself – changed my views certainly, and gave me a completely new approach to life. There is always a honeymoon period in life, when you fall in love, not only with somebody else but with something else, with the job that is really worth your life. Nothing can take the place of that period ... In a place like Sophiatown you want to improve living conditions, to give more space and more room for people to live, instead of having them live in single rooms, with one tap in the yard, and one lavatory in the yard, serving

about a dozen families. You obviously want to do things
about this. But immediately you are up against the problem
that if you do try to do this in the wrong way you may uproot
a complete community, and create all kinds of new problems
which are just as hard, just as difficult to tackle as the old
ones.

Huddleston was the father, a real father of many in the servers'
guild. Each evening groups of children would gather in the Priory
while Huddleston studied. He was there to answer questions and
help with difficult words, like any other parent. It was a quiet
place to read. Forty-two years later, he 'met many others of my
children and knew the ecstasy . . . the love that does not fade or
decay or disappear with the years.'[72] Sally Motlana was one of
these children: 'CR was home to us as we were nine children of
parents both of whom worked as domestic servants . . . Father
Huddleston was a man of prayer and very few words. He loved
praying. Each morning at 11.45 a.m. he left the Priory for the
church and all the children would follow him and he would try
to speak to each. We were not English-speaking, we didn't
understand what he said: we just loved being with him, walking
down the aisles, rehearsing the nativity plays. He was a fearless
man, no man was as courageous as Father. When the removals
came, Father walked round the people, comforting and blessing
them.'[73]

'However much Africans grumbled about whites,' writes
Anthony Sampson, 'most of all whites who were trying to do
good, there was always one strange exception, whose existence
was of incalculable importance – Father Trevor Huddleston.'[74]
Sampson admired Huddleston's political life ('so practical and
comprehensible, so much what others would wish to have done
if they had the courage and strength'), and spotted that this
activity was powered by his monastic life. His name was a legend.
'He wandered into the cinema, listened to meetings, joined a
bread queue in the early morning. He started a cocoa club for
young tsotsis, and enrolled them as servers in the church. He had
walked between two tsotsis in a knife fight. Everyone knew his

name in Sophiatown.'[75] As he was a close friend of Oliver Tambo, Evelyn Baring, Yusuf Cachalia, Secretary of the Indian Congress, 'most distinguished visitors to South Africa seemed to find their way, somehow or other, to Huddleston's cell.'[76]

CHAPTER THREE

AFTER SOPHIATOWN:
CRISIS YEARS

1954–1956

In the previous chapter I have tried to put together a picture of Trevor Huddleston's early years in South Africa. The picture includes changes in the racial policies and politics of the government; the effect of wartime conditions on the newly urbanized Africans; Huddleston's encounters with the harshening apartheid regime; his personality change – from tentative and unsure to confident and outgoing; from spiritual and interior to politically aware and astute. Throughout all this he maintained his prayer life and habits of meditation and withdrawal, while developing a new-found facility for making friends wherever there was a commonality of interest and convergence of commitment.

By 1954 Huddleston had found an appreciative audience abroad, and learned that he got more media attention at home if he dealt direct with newspaper correspondents in North America and Europe. He liked journalists and they liked him: he gave them good stories, good photo-calls. On 8 February 1955 he opened a photographic exhibition of the Western areas with a speech claiming that South African pressmen were afraid they would get into trouble if they spoke out; that the facts were not presented to the public: 'It is much better these days to hand press statements out to the Press representatives of overseas newspapers and let them publish what is going on here. Then these reports can be sent back to South Africa for the public to read.'[1]

He spoke as a supporter of the African National Congress

and ANC's fortunes between 1953 and 1955 relate to Huddleston's own change of views. New government legislation was
successfully driving the ANC leadership apart. It was not that
it had become more militant since 1953, nor did its leaders at
this point believe in the inevitability of the armed struggle; but
the Malan government interpreted the demand for equality as
an implicit call for violent revolution, along Soviet lines, and
hardened its condemnation of Communism and Communists,
many of them high in the ANC as well as the SACP. In fact
African political activity was subdued in the second half of
1953, the new legislation carrying a draconian message for any
would-be revolutionary. Chief Albert Luthuli had been elected
ANC President-General but he, like Walter Sisulu (re-elected as
Secretary-General) and Nelson Mandela (First Deputy President),
was prohibited from attending meetings and confined to Johannesburg. Protest against the new legislation continued and gained
some support from the United Party (Liberal) opposition but the
annual Freedom Day strike of 26 June was a modest affair.[2] Two
days later the meeting to protest the Western Areas Removal
Scheme took place at the Odin Cinema. On 21 September Dr Z.
K. Matthews (though an anti-Communist), and Nelson Mandela,
put forward measures to strengthen the ANC by means of a
multi-racial Congress of the People, on Communist lines, and
Mandela urged the implementation of the 'M-Plan' to establish a
network of underground cells for mass organization. Soon afterwards the report of the Tomlinson Commission for the Socio-
Economic Deployment of the Bantu Areas was published, having
been commissioned by the Nationalists who had simply ignored
the 1948 Fagan Report's main finding: that total segregation was
impracticable. Tomlinson legitimized apartheid on anthropologi-
cal grounds and the government speedily accepted its recommendations, striking a direct blow to the multi-racial and democratic
aspirations of the ANC leadership. This hastened the formation
of a number of splinter groups among the younger, more radical
ANC activists, who were becoming impatient for change. The
most significant of these was to formally break from the ANC in
1959 to form the Pan Africanist Congress. But apartheid had not

gone unnoticed at the United Nations where the ANC conference of December 1953 was regarded as a watershed. Sisulu, travelling without a passport, was able to visit Britain, Holland, Israel, Romania, Poland, Czechoslovakia and spend five weeks in China to report on the Defiance Campaign at first hand. The conference, on his return, called for an economic boycott against selected business and governmental organizations.

The two actions of the government that brought this phase of the anti-apartheid struggle to its crisis were the Bantu Education Act of 1955 and the Western Areas Removal Scheme already mentioned. Huddleston was uniquely placed to observe the immediate and deadly effects of the workings of the Bantu Education Act, whereby all non-white education had to be handed over to the Department of Native Affairs. As Superintendent of St Peter's, Rosettenville, he had daily experience of the frustration of young Africans with promise and ability condemned to a minimal curriculum. Writing later he knew that 'the whole burden of educating the African fell upon the shoulders of the Church for nearly seventy years.' Until 1940 *every* school in South Africa owed its origin, its buildings and its supervision to the Christian Missionary. By 1955, 90 percent of the schools were church schools, though dependent on government grants. The Community of the Resurrection ran the largest primary school in South Africa, with 2,000 pupils, yet only one in three children could find a school place. The Mission schools were hopelessly overstretched and there was a pressing need for change. African teachers were only too aware of the difference between 'the African Missionary School in its poverty and the European Government School in its wealth'. The government, through the Eiselen Commission (on which no missionary or African served) responded to the situation by creating the Bantu Education Act, 'one limb to subserve a vaster creature called the Bantu Development Plan.'[3] On 25 March 1955, Huddleston's comment on the Bantu Education Act, or 'education for servitude' at Education Week, organized by student bodies at Witwatersrand University, was given prominence in the *Star*. The Act 'emptied of meaning all that was understood by the word 'education' . . . Mission

schools had to be eliminated because Dr Verwoerd had said
the schools were unsympathetic to government policy. The whole
purpose of this 'new thing' called Bantu education was to condition native children to acceptance of the apartheid world, of
the unalterable fact of White supremacy, so that, when they grew
up, they would be neither bewildered nor surprised nor even
unduly depressed.'

Opposing the Act by closing the schools rather than handing
them over to the government was Huddleston's final and most
lasting contribution to his personal anti-apartheid campaign.
Bloke Modisane was 'visibly moved' by Huddleston's decision to
close his beloved St Peter's, rather than see it become a school
for servitude under the new legislation But many schools were
handed over. Opinion on what was best for African children
was sharply divided – particularly within the Anglican Church,
and all Catholic schools remained open – for which Mandela
thanked the Pope personally in June 1995. The ANC's reaction
to the Bantu Education Act was flawed, uncertain, fissiparous –
reflecting a wide divergence of non-white opinion throughout the
nation. Luthuli was sick and marginalized by continuous government surveillance and Dr Z.K. Matthews still clung to hopes
of involving the United Party in opposing Pretoria. Opposition
to government policy would have eventually grown effective
without Huddleston's personal input but there would have been
insufficient support for the more radical ANC reaction of young
activists like Mandela, Tambo, Sisulu and Joe Matthews without
the formidable and disinterested commitment of Huddleston to
the struggle.

Aware of growing opposition to Huddleston's high-profile
political stand and association with known Communists, Fr
Raynes came to Johannesburg in June 1954. The contrast
between the two men was now more striking. While Raynes had
been active in championing racial justice at the municipal level,
Huddleston agitated against each of the acts of government that
entrenched apartheid – the Group Areas Act, the Population
Registration Act, the Suppression of Communism Act, the Criminal Law Amendment Act – at a national level. He was now a

national figure, whose opinion was sought on many different topics. Because he had a talent for writing and public speaking and because of his personal popularity with reporters – clear about his own convictions and well-informed about his opponents' – he had become the ideal spokesman against the policies which the church thought evil. He was also brave, simple, with genuine empathy. As time went on, the leadership of the African and Liberal forces became more and more focused upon him personally, as did the anger of his opponents.

The greatest single cause of Huddleston's anger and despair was the implementation of the Western Areas Removal Scheme. As Chairman of the Western Areas Protest Committee, he fought with all the weapons he had to alert public opinion, without any lasting success. The day of the removal of the residents of Sophiatown (those with freehold rights unilaterally expropriated) began as he stood 'once again where I have stood so many times before, at the low altar step in St Mary Magdalene's chapel in the Church of Christ the King . . . "I will go unto the altar of God, even the God of my joy and gladness." It is still dark outside, there are about twenty communicants. Normally I would know exactly the appearance of the street outside, the familiar sounds of dawn in Sophiatown; the first steps of men walking down the hill to the bus stop; the clop-clop of the horses as they draw old Makadu's cart out of his yard for another day's coal hawking; a baby crying, a cock crowing, distant voices as people greet each other in the half-light . . . it is the beginning of the end of Sophiatown: because from now nothing will ever be the same again in this little corner of South Africa: because today the great removal is beginning, and all the people I know and the houses they live in will soon be scattered, and Sophiatown itself will crumble into dust.'[4]

Many journalists had got up early at Huddleston's tip-off. Rain was falling slowly. 'Suddenly . . . there comes a sound I have never heard in Sophiatown before. It is the sound of men marching . . . A detachment of African police under European command marches raggedly but purposefully past us, down the hill.' He talked to the journalists and walked past the bus queues in the rain, where some gave the forbidden Congress sign and greeted him, some shook his hand. 'A whole fleet of army lorries was drawn up. Lining the street were thousands of police, whites with rifles and revolvers, blacks with assegais. The Commissioner of Police was himself in a VIP car, in hourly contact with the central government in Cape Town . . . In the yard opposite the bus station military lorries were drawn up: 'already they were piled high with the pathetic possessions which had come from the row of rooms in the background . . . I deliberately put my arm round Robert Resha's shoulders and looked up at the camera. "Move away there . . . you've no right here . . . get out I'm telling you." '⁵

Again and again Huddleston was moved on by the police, who were acting on the orders of the Minister of Justice. Afterwards he held press conferences, wrote newspaper articles, and appealed to prominent people everywhere. 'When the removal took place, with the precision of a military operation, on 10 February 1955, foreign journalists from all over the world reported on it, and the words many of them quoted, and the face many of them photographed, were the words and the face of Trevor Huddleston.'⁶

Alan Paton told CR's historian Alan Wilkinson that the government destroyed Sophiatown because '[white people] could not stand living in close proximity to so many black people. . . . They would have been delighted, too, by the fact that they would also be doing some harm to the work of CR in Sophiatown . . . 'The intense dislike the government had for Huddleston further increased antipathy between Calvinism and Anglicanism when Anglicans [like CR] insisted they were part of the true church.⁷ By now Huddleston was identified by the government and wide swathes of the white electorate as the leading champion of non-white protest: their dislike and distrust hardened into anger and hatred. But to non-white South Africans he was a hero: more than a hero, a saviour.

On 25 June 1955, a little over four months after the first of the Sophiatown removals, the ANC and other anti-government bodies convened a new 'Congress of the People' at Kliptown and there acknowledged Huddleston's achievement, unique amongst whites. This was part of a continuing political process orchestrated by leading white Communists who had written a Freedom Charter without much consultation with Congress leaders Chief Albert Luthuli and Dr Z.K. Matthews. For this reason the political police were there and made a detailed record of what was said and done.[8] After singing Nkosi Sikelel' iAfrika (later to become the South African National Anthem) and welcoming delegates, the Chairman, Dr Conco announced 'a new feature in the liberation struggle of the people of South Africa. It is Isitwalandwe. There will be here presentations made to individuals who have distinguished themselves in the struggle of the people of South Africa.' The individuals were Chief Albert Luthuli, Dr Y.M. Dadoo, head of the South African Indian Congress, and Trevor Huddleston. Explaining that Isitwalandwe was a high honour given for outstanding national or war service, the Chairman went on, according to the police note-taker, 'every man who was given this honour got the highest distinction in African society.' The speaker hailed Huddleston 'in recognition of his many years of honourable service in the cause of the nation, and as a man of experience and affection in which he is held by both men and women, African, Indian, Coloured and Whites, who seek to build a better life for our country on the basis of equality.' The title of Isitwalandwe was then presented to Huddleston 'because he has given us without fear, his courage and services. He has refused to compromise whether in the field of education or freedom of speech.'[9] Huddleston replied:

Mr Chairman and friends, I find it very difficult to express my gratitude for the honour which I was awarded this afternoon. It is a great pleasure to receive the title of Isitwalandwe on an occasion like this. I cannot help feeling sad that of the three people to whom this honour is given, I am the only one who is present to receive it, and I don't know whether it is to be blamed on the part of our friends, the police, or not, but the fact is that I am here. [There must have been the noise of trains in the hall] I would like to give you one personal message, but I will wait for the South African Railways to

finish their work first. I have never known the South African
Railways to be so efficient as they are this afternoon, and I
am quite sure it is a demonstration to this Congress by the
Minister of Transport. The Minister of Justice is very well
represented here in the background and I hope they have a
happy afternoon to see if they can spot some of their friends
in this large gathering . . . Here in Kliptown this afternoon we
have only one answer to the government in this country. The
government in this country wants to deprive people of their
rights, the government in this country uses unconstitutional
methods, methods which are used to deprive the majorities of
their rights. Here this afternoon . . . we meet openly. We want
to discuss freedom. We meet to plan a charter which will be
the basis of action for the coming years. Those are the
principles we hold so dear, of justice and of peace in our time,
and so I thank you from my heart and I wish this Congress of
the People every blessing in the years to come. Thank you
very much.

It was Oliver Tambo, one of Huddleston's closest associates,
who as Acting Secretary-General of the ANC prepared and signed
the Report of the National Executive Committee which formed
part of the police dossier. In it 'Isitwalandwe Huddleston' was
commended for remaining at Sophiatown throughout the day of
the removal, 'amongst the people and participating in the "resistance".'[10] The presentation to Huddleston at the Congress of the
People marked his graduation to active militancy.

Non-white housing problems were now going from bad to
worse as the squatter camps were levelled, Sophiatown itself
destroyed and its inhabitants driven away to Meadowlands. In
these circumstances of squalor and degradation crime inevitably
increased and for the white population this was a threat to
security, rather than the symptom of a cause they should seek out
and rectify. White people had regularly and systematically ill-
treated their black workers, not just with terrible quarters and
food but with regular physical punishment, often for imaginary
offences. To keep the native in his place was simply to 'know the
native' and that included the self-fulfilling conviction that natives

could not feel pain and should not benefit from the recent arrivals of creature comforts from North America and Europe. Any whites who challenged this *weltanschauung* brought upon themselves automatic and almost universal derision: they had betrayed their own people. They tended to include a minority of Johannesburg residents, many Jewish, and some members of the Communist Party of South Africa, which had become respectable in 1943 because the Soviet armed forces had beaten Hitler and saved the Allied cause at Stalingrad in October 1942. Under his strong leadership and practical approach to problem solving, this small band became Huddleston's allies. Helen Navid and Olga Horowitz have already been mentioned, but Hilda Bernstein, Helen Joseph, Ruth First, Mary Benson and Jasmine Rose-Innes were other women who came under his spell. Ruth First, wife of Joe Slovo, was murdered by a letter bomb in 1986 and Helen Joseph and Jasmine Rose-Innes died in 1995 and 1998 respectively, and to each Huddleston remained a family friend, a colleague who changed and gave meaning to their lives and inspired them to continue to give themselves to the anti-apartheid cause. The strength of these relationships harboured dangers of which his CR brethren were all too well aware.

In September 1955 Huddleston spent his annual holiday with Alan Paton. Paton and Huddleston had met in 1944, when Paton was superintendent of the Diepkloof Reformatory which played games against St Peter's Rosettenville. For all their differences, a friendship developed between them that endured for many years. During the holiday, Huddleston wrote most of *Naught for Your Comfort*, working through the day with few breaks, and never re-writing. While there he received Raynes's letter re-calling him from South Africa. These two unconnected events were to propel him to international celebrity status. It is extraordinary that he managed, in the midst of this major personal crisis, to finish the book. Many preachers find it easy to write publishable journalism, and there are similarities between preparing a sermon and writing press articles. Huddleston had been trained in the preacher's craft, his style was elegant and sometimes eloquent, even passionate. He could sum up an argument, draw a picture, needle his opponents, inspire young readers, all by writing, in his neat hand, what was in his mind. Rarely did his work need editing. When the typescript of *Naught for Your Comfort* arrived at Collins it had already had the benefit of Anthony Sampson's advice that he should forgo objective prose and write up his own personal experiences in his own way – excellent advice as Huddleston later acknowledged. His editor at Collins had only to lift what became chapter one out of its position near the end. Its particular compelling power, a rhetoric approaching poetry, expressing his anguish, as well as the inevitability of his obedience, at his recall was irresistible. In a brief preface, he apologized to CR for publishing a book at all.

By this stage, some of his white supporters, including church leaders, were beginning to express the opinion that Huddleston was getting too fond of personal publicity and acclaim, too keen to see his picture in the papers. Even Paton, recalls his biographer, felt that Huddleston, at the time, 'had a conviction of the rightness of his own views . . . which led him to pursue what he saw as the right, but to condemn and accuse those he saw as being in the wrong . . . He also had an egotism and a love of publicity which Paton found uncomfortable.'[11] Within the Church, many – including Archbishop Clayton of Cape Town – advocated appeasement. Huddleston, living closer to the action, saw that this could not work. Despite the seriousness with which he observed his threefold vows of poverty, chastity and obedience, he believed it was right and necessary to defy unjust laws and oppose the arbitrary, racialist use of authority. His hatred of gradualism, a response to apartheid favoured by British government ministers as recently as the late 1980s, was expressed with equal vehemence, since it arose from his conviction that apartheid was irredeemably evil.

By the end of 1954 Archbishop Geoffrey Clayton, who agreed with Huddleston's opposition to the Bantu Education Act, decided nonetheless that he could not continue as Visitor of CR in South Africa. Though he had no personal quarrel with Huddleston he disagreed with him 'rather fundamentally'.[12] Huddleston – still an unregenerate High Churchman in ecumenical affairs – was already in episcopal black books for joining a hundred other South African Anglican clerics in a letter to the *Church Times* that deplored the action of the Provinces of Canterbury and York in offering full recognition to the newly reconstituted Church of South India. So profound were the doubts of the signatories about the Church of South India's doctrinal purity that they threatened to withdraw the South African Church from full Communion with the Provinces in protest against what they saw as a dilution of Anglican Catholic faith – a challenging if not provocative action which drew down on Huddleston the wrath not only of Clayton but of Geoffrey Fisher, Archbishop of Canterbury, who had led the South India démarche. Clayton declared that Huddleston no longer had respect and confidence in him.[13] This came as a terrible shock to Huddleston. However, four days later Huddleston informed Raynes that he had contacted the Archbishop at Johannesburg airport and persuaded him to change his mind. '*He could not have been nicer.*' Blaming himself for provoking Clayton, Huddleston told 'my dearest Superior' that 'it was my fault was in writing too strongly: I have been pretty wore-out [*sic*] by this endless crisis and said too much.'[14] Raynes was careful not to apologize to Clayton about Huddleston who, he said, had the highest regard for him.[15] The Church, Huddleston believed, was now caught up in a tragic situation which needed immediate and desperate measures . . . 'The state has already become a tyranny, and . . . Christians with a conscience should be prepared to resist its laws and take the consequences.' Thus Huddleston's public stance on apartheid was complicated by the growing mistrust the hierarchy had about his very successes as an agitator for racial and political freedom and his views on ecclesiastical matters. In February 1955 Raynes, who had visited Huddleston in June of the preceding year, sent Fr Jonathan Graham to Africa to report on all CR activities there, in particular the pros and cons of allowing Huddleston to continue down the road he had set himself and, by implication, his brethren.

Raynes's choice of Graham was significant, for he was to be the next Superior. Graham was no particular friend of

Huddleston's and found the flamboyant style of his increasingly uncontrollable colleague distasteful. But he was impressed when he saw Huddleston at work. He praised him and acknowledged the process whereby 'Huddleston's prayer and pastoral love had led him to make a stand and to seek worldwide publicity'.[16] 'In Sophiatown he lived and learnt in the heart of an African township and with immense thoroughness set himself to know, love and serve the underprivileged and the sinners. Not just to love and serve, but to *know* deeply and in detail the life of the African. Though one may first be struck by his affection for Africans and go on to marvel at his unsparing work of service to them, it is not long before one meets evidence of a profound and detailed, if lightly worn, knowledge which lies behind them both . . . He is heart-whole and single-minded and uncomplicated to a degree which is the envy of lesser men. There are no reservations, no pettiness, no querulousness; everything about him is fresh and wholesome and in perspective and integrated; the whole man is there at everyone's disposal, whether the claimant for his attention is a dirty schoolboy or an Archbishop, an eccentric or a bore . . . Gifts of leadership are there in plenty but they are never displayed, just naturally incorporated into the whole character.' Graham observed that Huddleston was 'news' and his opinion sought on every conceivable subject, but he only spoke on matters where 'he feels it right to speak'. But it was as a pastor that he excelled. Under accumulated weight of the years of injustice and oppressive legislation against which he fought, he was still able to give undivided attention and care to all – his own brethren and the nuns he shrived – who needed him.[17]

By the spring of 1955 the pressure was becoming acute, and the strain was showing. Police followed him everywhere. There was constant harassment and the threat of arrest, imprisonment or deportation, provoked surely by his intensifying use of the press through his friendship with foreign correspondent Cyril Dunn and with Olga Horowitz of the *Star*. He was a frequent visitor to her office, where she was able to turn his letter of protest into a feature article for overseas syndication straight on the typewriter, both of them smoking away furiously. In the largest nationwide police raid ever undertaken in South Africa, the police raided the St Peter's Priory and took away most of his papers, though typescript drafts of his book were secretly conveyed to the nuns next door who ensured they eventually reached London. By the end of September 1955 the authorities were thought to be waging a personal war against him and some said that the destruction of Sophiatown had been accelerated just to spite him.

It was also about this time that he was diagnosed as diabetic and treated with daily injections of insulin that continued from then until his death forty-three years later. Huddleston's physical as well as inner strength was tested many times over the years to come. Raynes knew little of this, though he feared he would not get proper treatment in prison. Dorothy Yates, a good friend and wife of a local headmaster, believed Raynes thought Trevor would die in prison, and it was a risk he was not prepared to take. But even at this late stage he doubted, talking to many who feared for Huddleston's safety. 'I am his Father in God,' Raynes said.[18]

On 24 October 1955 it was announced that Huddleston was to be re-called to Mirfield to take on the important position of Novice Guardian. On that day the *Star* published a leader headed 'Father Huddleston':

> There must have been many occasions when goaded by [his] outspoken and often unconventional opposition to their policies, the Government have murmured 'who will rid us of this pestilent [sic] priest?' ... From the South African point of view it is to be regretted, for it is desirable not only that there should be fearless critics here but also that they should be men whose lot is cast with the South African people ... In his dozen years here he has had the advantage, which many of his critics have lacked, of intimate contact with the Native peoples whom he had made it his business to champion. In consequence he has enjoyed a unique esteem and authority among them.

A few days later what was described as 'the whole truth of Huddleston's recall' was featured in the same paper.[19]

There was no question of his not accepting Raynes's decision but Huddleston left no one in any doubt of the depth of his private desolation. The 'whole truth' was a reference to an airmail statement from Fr Raynes at Mirfield, emphasizing that it was 'no easy thing to decide to re-call him and no easy thing for him to accept, but obedience requires both ... I wish it to be clear that this statement is the whole truth about the matter.' The whole truth or not, Huddleston continued to give grave offence on two public occasions which followed in quick succession; one a broadcast on radio, and the other a sermon which was broadcast uncut on the SABC. On 1 November the sermon was the subject of a news story in the *Rand Daily Mail*, while a leading article in *Die Transvaler* also reported 'his final shot at the supporters of apartheid before his departure to Britain.'[20]

Huddleston issued a statement to the Press about his 30 October sermon, claiming it was based entirely on Holy Scripture. 'Can a single section of it be described as unscriptural? ... Christians were once called men who turned the world upside down, i.e., revolutionaries, and the Christian Gospel is and always will be revolutionary.'[21] On 3 November the *Rand Daily Mail* reported the presence of a group of plainclothes police clustered round the door of the Trades Hall in Central Johannesburg where 500 people listened while Huddleston, the first speaker, told them South Africa would never be a free and happy country until people dropped expediency, and stopped conniving with the activities of government 'because they don't hurt me personally'. The meeting had been summoned to protest the implication of recent police raids. In the context of Raynes's decision this may be seen as Huddleston's final act of protest.

Reactions to the re-call announcement came swiftly. Oliver Tambo wept when he heard the news.[22] The Federation of South African Women called on citizens to sign a petition to CR asking that Huddleston should be allowed to stay, their argument strengthened by a letter Fr Raynes published in the London *Observer* pointing out that the brethren broadly shared Huddleston's views and approved his actions. The Federation's statement said: 'Father Huddleston is more widely loved, respected and

followed than any other man in the land today.'[23] By way of
contrast an infuriated member of the press section of the State
Information Department claimed that 'God, in his infinite wisdom
has contrived that Huddleston "should go from there gorged with
pharisaical fulfilment and unctuous content".'[24]

The same letter also mentioned Huddleston's forthcoming
book, 'a potential bestseller'. The first chapter of *Naught for
Your Comfort* is in essence a threnody for his years in Sophiatown and Rosettenville, brought to an untimely halt by a deeply
undemocratic process whose force he had no thought of combating, though he did ask many friends and supporters to see
if the Superior would change his mind: Alan Paton was one.
There were those who questioned Raynes's motives in snuffing
out such a promising activist career. Was he really only worried
about Huddleston's health, given the likelihood of regular and
perhaps prolonged imprisonment? Was the new job as Novice
Guardian, really so important and really so suited to Huddleston,
that such desperate courses were necessary? Did Huddleston's
charismatic leadership of a national movement challenge thwarted
ambitions in Raynes himself, who had in his time done great
work for Sophiatown? Speculation even now, over forty years
later, continues.

Raynes visited Deane and Dorothy Yates in December 1955.
'He was in a state of tension, smoked incessantly and drank
strong black tea – not good for his ulcer ... I am still quite
certain Raymond was gravely concerned about Trevor's diabetes.'
Since 1948 the politicians had been making apartheid laws and
now, for the first time, they were taking action (forced removals)
in accordance with what those laws prescribed. Mrs Yates
believed that 'the Nationalists were obviously on the brink of
direct action' to silence Huddleston, and that 'he did not have the
support of his Community or the Church hierarchy'. She added
that the real achievement of Huddleston in South Africa was that
he overcame his own desire to conform. 'Trevor fell in love with
South Africa,' she concluded. 'If you are open to love there is
nothing in the world more appealing than the joyful warmth of
South African blacks, especially children. This love was his glory

and his tragedy. Perhaps if he had been able to love all of us his voice might have been heard by more of us. He seemed to see all whites as involved in a system inexplicable except in terms of evil to be opposed and eradicated.'[25] She referred to the case of Stephen Ramasodi. The story bore eloquent testimony to the regime's hatred of Huddleston, who had secretly organized a place for Stephen at a top Episcopalian school in Connecticut. At that time 'the Nat coppers in Sophiatown were arresting young Africans and giving them the usual treatment simply on the ground that they were "Huddleston's boys".' Hence the need for secrecy. When his application for a passport to travel to America was refused, Stephen was distraught, and his parents were furious with Huddleston, Mrs Yates having met them 'combing the streets of Johannesburg one night looking for the boy, who had disappeared.' Mrs Yates concluded that by now Huddleston was doing more harm than good, as his efforts to help individual Africans immediately attracted savage reprisals aimed at breaking him.

So, was Raynes right? At the time few outside the Community thought so. To the African community, CR had taken away their leader and champion just when he was most needed, because it was afraid of the Nationalist government. To white activists and commentators, who would shortly be themselves in danger of summary arrest and imprisonment, Huddleston's relentless non-violent opposition to apartheid seemed crucial. A correspondent to the *Star* said: 'Talk to any Bantu and see how his face lights up when the Father's name is mentioned.'[26] It was not just the problem of understanding what lay behind such an arbitrary decision, but the loss of an opportunity to change the course of South African history, through Huddleston's success in arousing world condemnation of apartheid. Raynes delivered to Dr Malan an unexpected and certainly undeserved reprieve by withdrawing Huddleston, despite sharing his nominee's views on the evils of apartheid, and widely praising his achievement in South Africa.

Meanwhile the seventeen service committees of African women who worked voluntarily and for many years ran the African Children's Feeding Scheme – which became known as the

African Self-Help Organization – knitted a huge travelling rug which was presented to Huddleston in the Pimville Communal Hall on 13 December.[27] That very day Huddleston published a fine article in *Forum* assessing his twelve years in South Africa; 'It was at Sophiatown that I realised that whatever one might try to do in the field of social welfare ... it would still always be ambulance work only ... What is needed, quite simply, is social justice.' On 20 December, Cassandra of the London *Daily Mirror* made Huddleston his 'Man of the Year': 'For 12 long years [he] has fought an untiring, desperate, lonely battle against hatred and intolerance in the worst slums in the world. For twelve long years he has endured the malevolent ill-will of the South African government ... To watch him, as I have done, working in the squalor of the shanty towns and to see children race up to meet him is to know he is a great and good man.'

This was Huddleston's finest hour, and remembered as such by two of his closest associates: Desmond Tutu and Oliver Tambo. Tutu wrote in 1988, 'we just want to thank God very much for the wonderful, wonderful person who made us blacks realise that not all whites were the same.'[28] Two years after this, on 25 September 1990, Oliver Tambo, the Secretary-General of the post-apartheid ANC, back from thirty years in exile, faxed Huddleston a handwritten testimony to what his friend had meant to Tambo's generation in the struggle to achieve liberation, prompted by the publication of *Father Huddleston's Picture Book*:[29]

I remember as if it were yesterday, your arrival in racist South Africa, my motherland, where even those who abhored [*sic*] racism chose to be silent. The Church had to tread carefully and many people felt that their lives were threatened.

You arrived – armed with truth as your sword and integrity as your breastplate and ready to follow the master to the cross if necessary. I remember Sally telephoning me at St Peter's and saying 'Brat', this new priest who has just arrived at St Cyprian's should prove to be just what our people need – a man who is prepared to work with the people – this might

prove to be a worthy find.' I once said to Chief Luthuli that
the road to freedom would be long and hard and many will
drop out along the way, but I believed that Father Huddleston
would be with us to the end.

I remember above all the morning when you and Robert
Resha faced the bulldozers that entered Sophia Town [sic] to
forcibly remove the people to Meadowlands. My mind reels
back to numerous fights – the Bantu Education Act, which
resulted in the close of St Peter's Secondary School and the
alternate arrangements to open a replacement school ... the
Sophia Town square meetings, the Congress of the People at
which you received your 'Isitwalandwe' our highest award –
given to giants of our struggle and a giant you were – even
then. I get back to the people of Sophiatown and Newclare
who never failed to notice and register your love for the
children and the youth and your tireless efforts to advance
progress in their chosen disciplines. A few examples are Hugh
Masekela, Jonas Gwangwa, Archbishop Desmond Tutu,
Archbishop Walter Makhulu, Rev David Nape, Dr Nthato
Motlana.

One of the songs that was sung at your farewell concert
sung by schoolchildren says:

> When my education is threatened
> When gloom and hunger strikes
> When police bully us and demolish our homes
> And word of reason falls on deaf ears
> There is always *one* white man who
> Stands and fights with us unwaveringly
> – Father Huddleston

When you left South Africa there was a series of farewell
concerts in your honour throughout the country ... We the
people of South Africa will never forget that. You have been
an invaluable friend to us. Even away from South African soil
... you kept close to the Anti-Apartheid struggle even when
health was not giving you an easy time. Your contribution to
the struggles of our people and nation is outstanding and
History shall not forget that. *Father Huddleston's Picture*

Book gives us pride in the pictures of your work in South Africa but I know that there are a lot more pictures both produced and indelibly printed in the minds of our people that ought to have been included. I hope very soon someone will put the record of your life in its true perspective. I wish I were in a better state of health to do this. However, I hail you and squeeze your hand very tightly. 'If God be for us who can be against us?' O.R. TAMBO.

1955 was the crisis year for Huddleston. It had begun with the destruction of the only place he would ever call home, it was to end with the closing of St Peter's and his imminent and enforced departure from the land he loved. '*Partir, c'est mourir un peu,*' and I am in the process of dying: in the process every hour,' he wrote.[30] His future was bleak but surprising, for by mid-1956 he had become a famous author – his face the most photographed of any Christian except the Pope, his stand on racial equality admired by millions. But something in him had died. Raynes had killed it.

Had Huddleston been allowed to stay on he would undoubtedly have been included among the 156 Treason Trialists, and after acquittal five years later, re-arrested, harassed, imprisoned for as long as his political will survived. And since he had nothing to lose – no family, no children to bring up, no income, no hostages to fortune – that would have been a very long time. He did not court imprisonment and was never himself imprisoned – as Arthur Blaxall and Michael Scott, fellow Anglican priests were – but he was familiar enough with the double standards of the South African prison system to know that any sufferings of his in prison would never match those of his non-European colleagues. So would he have been able to bring forward the collapse of apartheid earlier, had he been allowed to stay and follow his chosen career to whatever destiny awaited him? Opinions vary. Those who believe so also believe Raynes had a great deal to answer for not only in removing such a charismatic protest leader but for undermining Huddleston's *raison d'être* almost terminally.

'I am totally in the dark', Huddleston wrote to Lady Molly Baring from Rosettenville.[31] He declared he would be 'thankful when all these farewells are finished; it really is too much of a strain. Indeed I beg your prayer.' Later in the year he wrote to her from Mirfield: 'I can only take this exile as a sort of penance, which indeed I have earned, and pray it may be not too hard to bear. I know it is hard for you to understand but England is so utterly empty and meaningless to me.'[32]

I met Huddleston first after it was all over. The impression he made on me was formidable – but it was of a grief-stricken man who had undergone some major surgery, endured some serious debilitating and irreversible illness, lost some vital part of himself. He was interested, friendly and involved as our common interest in the success of his book developed into a deep family friendship; but it was impossible not to feel the aura of one who was really elsewhere. The present was a poor substitute for Sophiatown, and he could not conceal it.

Raynes had claimed that CR needed a new Novice Guardian and needed Huddleston in Mirfield to do the job. That never seemed the whole truth and very soon seemed a weak link in the chain or argument that brought Raynes to Johannesburg in late 1955 to implement his decision, and bring both of them back to London in 1956. How, one wonders now, could anyone as intuitive and intelligent as Raynes have thought for a moment that to implement his decision was in Huddleston's best interests? Or that of the Community? The alternatives were no doubt riskier but to adopt one of them would have been to acknowledge the overriding importance of Huddleston's work among the urban Africans who had grown up alongside CR, which had become Mirfield's great contribution to twentieth-century history.

The Community remained positive that Raynes had made the right decision on both counts. However it must have been as unclear then as now whether re-calling Huddleston was indeed in the long-term interests of the Community. The debate over the balance between the Benedictine 'life' and 'work' was perennial in CR. In April 1955 Huddleston reminded Graham (then in Johannesburg) that the strong, apostolic missionary life he was then leading was incompatible with the closed 'claustral' life of the Benedictines on whose Rules CR modelled its own. He went on to defend his years as Provincial:

> We have been led to play quite a part in the present crisis. And that, not only by *sharing* in the passion of our people, but to some extent by leadership . . . many Europeans as well as African Christians . . . look to us to stand firm on principles realising that we are in the strongest possible position to do so, having nothing to lose . . . Our witness is essential. Not popular but still essential. Closing St Peter's still left a large and important parish, St Benedict's House – expanding rather than contracting; the only African Provincial Theological College; two large and well-run hospitals; the care of ten women's religious houses. Finally South Africa offers a very special and precious opportunity to brethren . . . to be a bit venturesome: a bit strong in initiative: a bit of a nuisance maybe.

Huddleston's advocacy in his own cause is powerfully apparent but Graham was unimpressed, opposing all points in the argument.[33]

Anthony Sampson talked to Raynes for over three hours on the evening of 23 January 1956: 'Trevor had shot his bolt, and was in danger of putting others in trouble. Africans had petitioned him, Tambo had changed his mind. Now he felt that Huddleston, despite his great sorrow at leaving, was inwardly relieved at his re-call, after the great strain and frustration.'[34] It was Raynes's conviction that Huddleston would have become a national protest leader, despite his monastic vows and personal unwillingness to accept such a destiny, that made him determined to stop Huddleston's new career as an agitator before it got out of hand. Raynes told another priest as much during a 'holy party' at South Park, Bletchingley some time later when his own death was imminent. He had found some peace in his last years as spiritual director of a group of friends who organized a series of high church religious retreats over several years. His presence and participation dominated the proceedings, and he left an indelible impression on many, including Nicholas Mosley. One evening in 1959 after a long day of talk and prayer Raynes and one of the priests on the retreat, Peter Wyld, drank whisky into the small hours of the morning. Emboldened by drink, Wyld asked Raynes what had been the real reason for his decision to withdraw Huddleston from South Africa. 'They would have taken him away and made him king,' he said.[35] The question remains: why, knowing this, did Raynes prevent it?

CHAPTER FOUR

HOME AND AWAY

1956–1960

Huddleston wrote his own goodbye to Sophiatown:

> The grey smoke from a thousand braziers hangs over the streets, makes the square tower of the church appear ancient as if upon some Umbrian hill, wraps the whole place in a soft and golden evening shadow. And in those rooms and yards and playing or talking in those streets are the children whose names I know and whose characters I know too. And coming home from work are John and Elias and Michael, who first greeted me twelve years ago and who are part of my family in Christ. Tomorrow I shall take the Blessed Sacrament to old Piet, crippled and bedridden with arthritis, and afterwards we will talk about his family problems. And later in the day I shall have a cup of tea with old Ma Malunga and see if I can coax her into that deep and fascinating chuckle that I love to hear. And probably in the evening Harry will drop in to tell me how things are going in his school and what sort of Matric. results he is likely to have ... And my mail will certainly include at least one letter from some friend of mine beginning: 'Dearest Father ...' and ending '... your loving child.'[1]

Sally Motlana was one of hundreds of African children at the airport. 'There were many soldiers ... Father smiled and said: "Have courage. The Lord is always with us." '[2]

The other goodbyes were over. Huddleston was packing under the CBS TV arclights; Fred Friendly, legendary television reporter, led the team to cover his departure. He was flying, not to Britain

but to New York. Providentially he had been invited, at Alan
Paton's prompting, to address a commemorative dinner of Kent
School, Connecticut, then celebrating its 50th anniversary year.
The prospect of a glamorous trip to America on the way home
made the partings easier.[3] The invitation was made before news
of his re-call had become public. He landed at Idlewild at midnight in early March 1956. There he was asked by the FBI if he
was or had ever been a Communist, and learnt that he and Paton
had both been reported by Pretoria as Communists to the US
authorities. Fortunately the US Consulate in Johannesburg had
ensured VIP treatment for him: it was high season for Communist
witch-hunting in North America.

His visit to New York and Connecticut was a celebrity affair.
Doubleday organized a publicity programme: he addressed the
dinner guests with a detailed and well-informed account of Christian education in South Africa. Then his publishers gave a press
lunch at which the *Life* representative commissioned Huddleston
to write about the Huddleston jazz band. *Presbyterian Life* subsi-
dised a trip to the Deep South, where he met Martin Luther King
Jr in Montgomery, Alabama. He was given an office in the basement of King's Little Rock Congregationalist Church. King told
Huddleston: 'they call this the cradle of the Confederation and it
sure is rocking.'[4] They exchanged their experiences of their respec-
tive bus boycotts. From there Huddleston went on to Tuscaloosa,
Tuskegee and Jackson, Mississippi where he met the Secretary for
the National Association for the Advancement of Coloured People
and learnt of some of the atrocities being inflicted on blacks –
lynchings, murders. But he was an onlooker, not a participant, and
never exploited his 1956 American experiences to become a public
figure. He took a 100-mile taxi ride to meet Louis 'Satchmo'
Armstrong and to tell him about his young trumpet-playing protégé
Hugh Masekela. Armstrong handed over his own instrument which
Huddleston had sent back to Masekela in Johannesburg. The story
of how Huddleston bought the now internationally renowned
musician his very first trumpet, incidently launching what was to
become the Huddleston Jazz Band, is one of the most touching
moments in *Naught for Your Comfort*.[5] Most appropriately, it

was this very instrument that Masekela played at Huddleston's memorial service in Westminster Abbey on 29 July 1998.

Back in New York he resumed the fame circuit, lunching with Eleanor Roosevelt, interviewed by Ed Murrow, photographed by Karsh of Ottawa. *Naught for Your Comfort* had just been released in Britain and the reviews were reported 'very flattering and long'.[6] Huddleston enjoyed all this publicity and VIP treatment, feeling for a time that there might be life after South Africa. In mid-April he flew in to Heathrow. At my office in St James's Place I was told that he and Raynes would hold a press conference, and I volunteered to drive them to what was described as a secret destination, revealed in due course as CR's Retreat House at Hemingford Grey, near Cambridge. In the wake of the successful launch of the book I had been awarded a company car, barely big enough to accommodate the legs of these two tall monks. Conversation was sticky, and consisted mostly of anecdotes of their travels round America, statistics of meetings addressed, interviews given, celebrity statuses compared. Perhaps my presence inhibited anything closer to their needs. Neither of them was good at directions and, in pouring rain, I inadvertently drove the car into a field of corn. Neither seemed at all alarmed or surprised, and the welcome at the Retreat House was warm, the food and drink excellent.[7]

Back in London Christian Action and the Africa Bureau had arranged meetings for him all over the UK. Collins threw a party for him at their St James's Place office where his elderly father appeared from his Devon home and enjoyed the *réclame* of his only son. Canon John Collins and Michael Scott quarrelled about sharing a platform with Huddleston and about who should speak besides him. Though both men (according to the Collins files) were equally concerned to give Huddleston fullest possible scope, and to recognize him as the most outstanding and courageous Christian exponent 'of the cause we all serve', Collins insisted and won.

The effect of the fortuitously timed publication of his book, on himself, and on his work for South Africa, cannot be underestimated. Early demand was difficult to satisfy and the book was enthusiastically, respectfully and widely reviewed. In South Africa, local publication meant that his book could not be banned, but it was difficult to get hold of, and publicity came more from local re-use of American and British news stories and reviews than what was written on the spot. A local publisher commissioned Alexander Steward to write a half-hearted rebuttal, published as *You Are Wrong, Father Huddleston*.[8] Another surge of publicity and further sales followed his return to England from his American tour. Huddleston spoke to packed houses at the Central Hall, Westminster, the Albert Hall, St Paul's Cathedral, Oxford and Cambridge (where an overflow meeting had to be set up) and to a huge public meeting in Manchester's Trade Hall. Subscription sales were bolstered by the news of his re-call to Mirfield. He had become a major public figure, somewhere between a hero and a martyr. His story and personality inspired many with a new conviction that if the Anglican Church could produce even one man like him, there must be more to it than they realized. It was this factor that marked him out from other white people, equally brave, equally committed, who also fought apartheid. *Naught for Your Comfort* heightened the awareness of a whole generation, not only to the evils of apartheid, but also to the surprising fact that here, arising from the apparent somnolence and equivocation of the Church of England, was a passionate and heroic priest whose actions and convictions derived somehow from the same source. Readers of *Naught for Your Comfort* learnt that religious, social and political commitment could still lead to greatness, could call forth dormant qualities of self-sacrifice in unlikely places, could change lives. Alan Paton's *Cry, the Beloved Country* and Anthony Sampson's *Drum: A Venture into the New Africa*, in their different ways, also introduced to the British reading public a new, stark, exciting, cruel and sometimes crazily hilarious community of the repressed and the irrepressible – and for those white South African readers who managed to find copies of these books in their local bookshops – the revelation that all this existed not far from their own doorsteps.

The world to which he was reluctantly returning presented few challenges, and inadequate opportunities for the loving service he now knew he could give. His responsibilities were to be limited to the guardianship of some twenty novices and a growing number of postulants. Living at Mirfield he was, at least technically, required to ask permission to post a letter or go for a walk. Invitations to speak were screened with Raynes and only a limited proportion agreed by him. As early as 11 February 1956 he was asking Lady Molly how was he 'ever going to adapt to the West Riding? I just cannot begin to think . . . As things are at present I see nothing but darkness . . . I do want to be good about it, but I find it just fearfully hard going. And I cannot see the point.'[9] Later he reflected that if he'd refused to leave Johannesburg – hundreds of people urging him to do so for conscience's sake – he would not have made the contacts in England which eventually led him to Masasi. 'At every point there is the touch of God . . . Of course none of this means you have got to like obeying and removing yourself from a loved place or job. There is no sin in not liking it, but you must obey.'[10] There may be an element of disingenuousness here, that he was feeding a biographer with words he felt he ought to say.

It was quickly apparent that, far from being an ideal Novice Guardian, he was hampered from sufficiently carrying out his duties by the incessant invitations to speak which came by every post. He could not turn down these many opportunities to challenge the young, who saw in Huddleston living proof that the Christian gospel could be lived out in the contemporary world; that social activism was not just for eccentric deans; that where he had gone others could follow with a new confidence in the Christian calling to serve. Under Raynes's guidance Huddleston had found a new interest: 'I spoke at every public school in England, I should think, and a great many others, including girls' schools and comprehensive schools.' He went to the schools for weekends, meeting and talking with children and teachers. He always had to start by talking about his experiences in South Africa but soon grew weary of recycling old memories and moved on to the Gospels 'which is where I wanted to be . . . They came

in great numbers. I wasn't talking about anything except God.'
He also led the mission to Leeds University with a big team. At
that time 'missions' to universities or individual parishes were run
by teams of clergy and laity and led by some powerful preacher,
priest or personality. Meetings, services, visits, addresses were all
part of the mission to bring, or in some cases bring back, living
Christianity to the targeted groups. His presence in English public
schools is remembered with awe by many now in their fifties and
sixties. But his frequent absences from Mirfield undermined the
need to oversee on a weekly or even daily basis the spiritual lives
of his postulants. His celebrity status and Franciscan belief that
all who feel they are called should test their vocations ensured
that numbers would grow dramatically, adding to a workload
already under strain through his intermittent availability to them.
Perhaps he may have expected too much from some of them.
Huddleston agreed with his colleague Brother Zachary that he
was a lousy Novice Guardian. 'I was given novices from a post-
war generation of varied backgrounds – the West Indies, a
Yorkshire mill town, Oxford – and I hadn't had time to get the
feel of their ideas; I was never sure that I had the right judgement
of their vocations ... I should have weeded out half of them
before they started.'[11] Summing up, he said, 'it was the least
satisfactory period in my life. I was very close to Fr Raynes and
it was not an easy time for him, or for me, or for the community.
It was the end of an era.'[12]

Raynes, already seriously ill, found it impossible to retire
voluntarily as Superior. He learned, while on a mission in North
America, that Jonathan Graham was to be the new Superior.[13] It
was Graham who quickly saw that Huddleston could not combine his work as preacher with being Novice Guardian, so
appointed him Prior of the London House in Notting Hill where
he lived from 1958 till 1960. Huddleston continued to address
public meetings, mostly on racial matters, and new friendships
became of growing importance. He was always at his best with
nuns, and in Mother Clare, the Superior of the Deaconesses at St
Andrew's House, in the slums near Portobello Road, he found
a close companion and confidante. Her successor as Mother

Trevor Huddleston, aged ten.

Lancing College, 1931.

Southwold, 1933. Huddleston, on holiday from Oxford, with friends (from left to right) Mary Mackay, Yvonne Brown and Gerald Brown.

The team at St Mark's, Swindon 1937.

Opposite, top: Sophiatown, 1948. High Church Anglicanism in Southern Africa.

Opposite, bottom: Sophiatown, 1952. Pastoral work.

Above: Huddleston and Alan Paton look on as the Huddleston Jazz Band rehearse. Hugh Masakela (left) plays the trumpet Huddleston bought for him. The trombonist is Jonas Gwangwa.

Above: Orlando, 1955. The opening of the Olympic-size Huddleston swimming pool.

Opposite, top: Odin Cinema, June 1953. Huddleston attempts to intervene as the police arrest Yusuf Cachalia, leader of the South African Indian Congress.

Opposite, bottom: The Freedom Charter, adopted at the Congress of the People, Kliptown, 25 June 1955.

Above: Huddleston addresses the Congress of the People, Kliptown, 1955.

Left: Huddleston receives his Isitwalandwe medal at the Congress of the People.

Superior was Mother Joanna, who memorably recorded the influence Huddleston made through example:

> *The primacy of his prayer life*: however early the novice got down to prepare for the eucharist in chapel, [Huddleston] was always there first, a still, silent figure. However late he came in at night, and most nights he was very late and *very* tired, he went into chapel to pray before going to bed. When he talked about prayer it was so much part of him and so dynamic that an agnostic could hardly doubt its value.
>
> *His humility*: he never thought he was any good or could do anything well and was very nervous before he spoke at a meeting. He really made one feel he thought he was quite as inadequate as one was oneself, which made what he said in the way of advice or help much more real and telling, and one would take anything from him and not get hurt.
>
> *His gift for being right in the situation of the moment*: although he loved Africa and the Africans and obviously must have felt very impatient with the superficial worries and problems of people in this country and their concern with material things and grasping after luxuries, he could still put himself completely into a person's or a group's situation and produce constructive criticism and advice.
>
> *Personal relationships*: he had a greater depth of relationship with people than anyone else I have known. He was always charming and courteous and one loved being with him. He had the gift of making one feel one was the only person that mattered to him at that moment however tired or worried he was ... He seemed completely to understand all about one and established an on-the-level relationship through which one could trust him completely and say anything one liked and be certain of just the right reaction and answer. This applied at all levels – social, intellectual and spiritual, though in fact the three were integrated and not separated in him.
>
> *A man of God*: one felt this really was so. That God worked through him, he was transparent to God ... He himself

always emphasizes that anything he has done has only been because God has used him. One felt this was so, his considerable abilities were developed and used to the full by God. He is a prophet, having that closeness to God that makes him see things as they really are, and the authority to proclaim them – not only the world situations but the ordinary day to day personal situations.

Africa was his love and it must have nearly killed him to come back . . . but he never breathed this . . . Only from little things like the way his face lit up when he spoke about Africans . . . did one have any inkling that he might have other thoughts than those concerned with what he was doing at the moment.[14]

But he told the CR novitiate in the middle of Lent 1957: 'I am more and more uneasy at the idea of delivering pious addresses when there is nothing immediately to emphasize in our common life: the divorce of piety, devotion or whatever you care to call it, from the common life as a whole: the substitution of ideas of my own for the true working of the Holy Spirit, as he leads you . . . I am horribly aware at present of a certain barrenness, perhaps the result of a fairly strenuous year, which makes it difficult to give you anything refreshing or new.' In March and May 1956 Sampson talked to Huddleston and recorded that 'he would become an African bishop if asked. He wants above all to go back to Africa.'[15]

But this time of self-doubt was also one where he vastly expanded his range of friends. Enthusiastic readers wrote him letters; to most of these he replied, and in some cases meetings followed and friendships developed based on nothing more than mutual attraction shading into mutual love and care. This is an area into which a biographer must tread warily. His relationship was different with every friend. Of the many friendships formed over the years it seems reasonable to select two. The first is Jenny Leggatt, who met him in the aftermath of *Naught for Your Comfort*, and fell in love with him. He knew it and he loved her deeply. He looked after her spiritual welfare for many years, seeing her through several crises, making himself available whenever she needed him, sharing suffering and joy, well beyond the requirements of any spiritual director or confessor. It is not unusual for penitents, male or female, to fall in love with their confessors: what was unique was Huddleston's response.

The other was Mischa Scorer, a Westminster schoolboy, also an enthusiastic reader of Huddleston's book. Scorer invited him to talk to Westminster's God Soc. They met many times, usually on the steps of Church House, Westminster, in Dean's Yard. Huddleston arranged for Scorer to see David Astor of the *Observer* newspaper about becoming a journalist. In August 1957 Huddleston was writing to Mischa that 'love is not love apart from truth ... I am so nervous now of "wanting" for selfish reasons, that I am wholly prepared to stand aside too. (At least I think and hope I am!)'[16] And the next month 'I love to know you as you are – even the bad bits – because I think, in fact I know, that I do care greatly for you: and anything I *can* do to help and guide, I most gladly will.' By September 1957 Huddleston was writing to 'Dearest Mischa' about constitutional delimitation in South Africa, as the cause of the swing to the Nationalists there.

Returning from an exhausting but successful tour of Ireland late in 1957 (a country where he was always particularly welcome) with nine full-length sermons, two public addresses and meetings with Lord Mayors and archbishops, Huddleston wondered whether he would ever see the end of 'this strange whirl of activity'. He continued to help Scorer's journalistic ambitions, talking to Sir Christopher Chancellor ('a really great friend') and Victor Gollancz as well as Pierre Collins. He told Scorer of his meetings at Oxford in November with the Joint Action Committee Against Racial Intolerance. They both went to a party at Anthony Sampson's in early December. On 26 December Huddleston wrote: 'You give back immeasureably more by your love and friendship than in any other possible way ... Of course I love you.' They had become father and son – something each lacked previously. Later: 'I do pray for you at every mass each day, and always after Compline. But more often than that, really, for you are much in my thoughts, dear Mischa ... *much* love as always.' And revealingly on 6 February 1958 that he shared 'a fearful inability to cope with the demands of really secondary interests. I think it *is* awfully hard to learn priorities and especially so when you've rather let yourself go in the past . . . I truly *do* know your love and trust in me and am immensely grateful. After all, dear Mischa, I have no right to any of it, and I'm only thankful that you feel you can write to me as you do . . . I love you, and that's that . . . I really shan't change, I'm sure! Because I love you for yourself, not for your virtues!!! Longing to see you.' Another vivid memory from this time was that of an old Communist friend, Jack Linscott, who used to take Huddleston to the theatre and send him anti-capitalist press cuttings. 'Through him I knew I especially loved old people,' he later remarked.[17]

Huddleston's perceptive comment to Mischa Scorer about his sharing an inability to cope with secondary interests shows his own awareness of his need to prioritize. From 1943 to 1998 his priority was the liberation of South African blacks, but back in the West he grew sick of repeating old speeches about South Africa without being there, and neither his preaching, nor being Prior in Notting Hill could provide the springboard his energies and commitment, his new-found abilities as a manager and leader, required. There was a dawning realization that this sort of life could not be lived for more than a few months. His African friends – those able to travel – found him changed: Hugh Masekela wrote to him: 'our relationship was not the same as it was in South Africa where I would sit on your knee almost every day and pour out my heart to you . . . It was impossible to establish the same old wonderful atmosphere.'

CR's new Superior, Fr Jonathan Graham, was aware of the problem. Raynes's action in removing Huddleston as Provincial in Southern Africa had created an impossible situation. It had not benefited the Community, it had weakened CR's influence over events in South Africa, it had all but destroyed both Raynes and Huddleston.

In recent years CR had been torn between following the Tractarian practices of Gore and Frere, and Raynes's enthusiasm, shared by many members, for more extreme catholic practices such as prostration, frequent confessions, self-punishment and having many altars for individual daily masses. On 12 June 1959, after spending his last months at Mirfield, miserable and in pain, Fr Raynes died. Huddleston wrote to Molly Baring on 17 June 1958: 'I saw him twice in hospital, desperately tired. Never has the veil seemed so thin. I just cannot feel him other than as marvellously near.' The two men were bound by a symbiotic relationship paradoxically strengthened by the ties that were strangling them both. Obedience conquered all. Their lives were changed by Raynes's decision to take Huddleston from South Africa: if Raynes, while making his confession to Huddleston, ever spoke of it we shall never know. The evidence suggests not. But Huddleston's new predicament – no job, no call, no enthusiasm – was widely known within the Community and particularly to Graham.

By October 1959 the new Superior wrote to Huddleston's longtime friend, Sir Evelyn Baring, now the government's chief administrator in African affairs, saying that he was 'much exercised in his mind about [Huddleston's] future'. Huddleston had been home for three years and he had too many outside distractions: everyone was asking him to speak and preach; 'hordes of people had become his disciples and his correspondence was staggering.'[18] This would have been no secret to Baring, whose wife kept her letters from Huddleston. In late 1958 he had written to her: 'I am confused to know what one is really meant to be at. I honestly seem to be so little use and yet so much in demand . . . It's this endless pull between public and hidden life, with Africa in the background, which is so tricky.' The only job left to Huddleston was Graham's own and 'that would be too small a sphere for him,' said Graham. 'What about an African bishopric, if one should ever become vacant?'[19]

Baring heartily agreed: one month later Masasi did fall vacant.[20]

The circumstances under which this vacancy occurred and how the ultimately benign influence of Archbishop Geoffrey Fisher of Lambeth affected the outcome are particularly interesting, and reveal unexpected qualities in both men – sentimental in Fisher, almost slavish in Huddleston. Baring wrote to Fisher who, after some hesitation, agreed on the desirability of Huddleston's return to Africa, but away from South African politics. Masasi was not only thousands of kilometres from Cape Town but racially and politically very different. Independence from colonial rule was only two years off; the work of Christian missionaries of all denominations had to be unobtrusively wound down and, particularly in the fields of education and medicine, integrated into the local scene at local and national levels. South Eastern Tanganyika, with its centre at Masasi, would remain poor economically because of its geography and lack of mineral and other resources: no political, still less religious, change was going to alter African life in the area. Ecclesiastical leadership needed to be firm but gentle, sensitive to the rising tide of nationalism and the indigenous strength of Islam throughout the continent. Such sensitivity was not part of the spiritual equipment of most missionary clergy. Tanganyika had benefited from the work of Christian missionaries of all persuasions, but in choosing its own non-Western road to a socialist society, as would be defined much later in the celebrated Arusha Declaration of 1967, with its emphasis on self-reliance and communality, it stepped forward into an ideologically confusing and economically impoverished place in the African world – free but fragile. Huddleston knew this, and approved of Julius Nyerere, the prime mover behind the declaration, who was soon to become first head of the state of the independent Tanzania.

Masasi was a small town a hundred miles inland from the coast of Southern Tanganyika, half way up the coast of East Africa. The diocese was 200 miles from east to west and north to south. It had links with Zanzibar and controlled by the same Catholically-inclined missionary society. But shortly before Huddleston's arrival both dioceses were to become part of the new Province of East Africa, headed by a redoubtable Anglican priest, Archbishop Leonard Beecher. The retiring Bishop of Masasi, Trevor Lucas, was a staunch Anglo-Catholic of the old persuasion, and his departure gave Fisher a further opportunity to withdraw Central and East Africa from the direct control of Canterbury. Fisher wrote: 'the new Province was about to be born with its splendid alliance of CMS [Church Missionary Society – low] and UMCA [Universities' Mission to Central Africa – high] bishops.' It could be observed that this factional and confusing missionary picture may have been one of the reasons why, despite valiant and intelligent efforts, numbers of converts were not large when Huddleston arrived – and do not seem to have grown disproportionately as the result of his ministry there.

Fisher's earlier problems with Huddleston are recounted with some freedom by Huddleston in *Naught for Your Comfort*.[21] They had met at the Community mission station at Penhalonga in 1955 and after supper found themselves disagreeing strongly about the use of political weapons to achieve social and racial justice for Christians. He asked Fisher what these political weapons might be and found that 'he seemed to object to my use of "force" as being contrary to the teaching of Christ . . . When I suggested to the archbishop that there was at least one occasion in the Gospel when Christ Himself used force – to drive the moneychangers out of the Temple – he replied that this was "symbolic".' Fisher was offended when their after-dinner argument was made public, and later claimed that he was only making a debating point, but that Huddleston had anyway been dangerously indiscreet even to mention the matter. This was thought to have been the cause of Fisher's initial reluctance to send Huddleston to East Africa, and his eager acceptance of the happy opportunity created by the formation of the new Province, no longer under his jurisdiction, which would enable it to elect its own bishop, freeing him from his dilemma. 'The new Bishop would have to live in, learn from, and give himself to, the new Province. Obviously it was far better that the new Province should have the responsibility of choosing the new colleague.'[22]

Fisher claimed that by this time he had no hesitation of any kind about Huddleston. 'Trevor would be in the full sense of the word a godsend.' They wrote to each other quite glutinously for a while, but something must still have rankled because the evidence of the Huddleston–Lady Baring correspondence suggests that Fisher remained difficult to shift and delayed the appointment to Masasi for several agonizing months, with Huddleston moaning and groaning in a distinctly non-episcopal way.

In Masasi it was Canon R.G.P. Lamburn who was holding the fort as Vicar-General (VG) during the interregnum.[23] Under existing rules, Fisher had absolute discretion to appoint, but by custom consulted diocesan clergy and a committee of UMCA advisers, to which Huddleston himself may have been appointed. Despite putting these customary arrangements in place, Fisher proceeded off his own bat to invite a former bishop of Masasi, Leslie Stradling, then Bishop of South West Tanganyika, 'to go back to Masasi.' At this point no one had thought of Huddleston for the job. Stradling's re-appointment was approved by the clergy in Masasi. But at Mirfield Fr Andrew Blair was prompted by Graham, who had already been in touch with Baring over the matter, to write to Lamburn suggesting Huddleston might be a candidate.[24] The great advantage of Huddleston joining the team was immediately apparent to Lamburn who wisely took it upon himself to write to Canon Broomfield, head of UMCA, saying that while Stradling's return was unanimously acceptable in the diocese, the possible appointment of Huddleston was the preferred option. All the Masasi clergy agreed when they heard. Broomfield approached Fisher who, although he remembered differently later, refused (according to Broomfield and Lamburn) to consecrate Huddleston unless all the bishops of the (as yet unincorporated) new Province approved. That ensured the delay, but Lamburn and senior clergy agreed to wait another eight months. Fisher duly arrived to hand over the dioceses of Kenya and Tanganyika to Beecher, with whom he visited Masasi: the new Province then unanimously agreed to Huddleston's election.

In England Huddleston, who had been kept informed by the Barings, the Superior CR and Canon Broomfield of UMCA, took a holiday from the press, who had eagerly picked up on his new career move. He had been staying with the Barings at Howick in August when the telegram came from Dar es Salaam announcing his election. According to Lady Howick, 'he was over the moon, the prospect of leaving England again was so wonderful, he was as jubilant as a schoolboy, and delightfully pleased and unselfconscious at all the congratulations, both private and public, of the next few days.'[25]

He then left Howick to prepare for his return to Africa.

CHAPTER FIVE

MASASI

1960–1968

To understand the place of Tanganyika (or Tanzania, as it became after union with Zanzibar in 1964) within the burgeoning African national movements, and of Huddleston's election as Anglican bishop of Masasi, some account needs to be given of the global pressures on East Africa in the late 1950s. Anti-colonial movements, fuelled by traditional tribal rivalries, had brought independence but neither peace nor prosperity to several nations in the sub-Saharan region. In East Africa this was to culminate in Julius Nyerere's emergence as President of Tanganyika's one-party state after independence in 1961.

To the west, the nationalist movement had triumphed but some West African presidents, precipitated suddenly into high office, lacked experience or maturity. To the south, Southern Rhodesia resisted the tide of black nationalism from the north, and, abetted by successive British governments, allowed white supremacy to entrench itself in a vast territory. Huddleston never forgave British politicians of either party, Harold Wilson especially. He met a number of Labour leaders in 1960, but apart from Aneurin Bevan, found them less interested in combating apartheid than in promoting their own careers. As we have seen, French, Belgian and Portuguese electorates were struggling to divest themselves of their former imperial territories, which had become an insurmountable economic burden. The withdrawal from Africa was in full swing but it was to take three more decades and much avoidable slaughter before the deed was done. In Kenya, long a British enclave run on colonial lines from London, with Kikuyu and Maasai tribes fighting each other, the

Kikuyu leader, Jomo Kenyatta, was in prison when the Governor-General, Sir Evelyn Baring, asked Huddleston for advice. The bishop disclaimed any expertise in Kenyan politics.

In the area of East Africa between the prosperous farming regions of Kenya and the broad British acres of Rhodesia, Masasi was a poor network of rural communities, lacking roads, electricity, infrastructure, natural resources or much in the way of radical ambition for change, except for the aspirations of those Africans who had attended the Mission Schools. The diocese of Masasi occupied the south-eastern corner of Tanganyika bordered by the river boundary with Mozambique to the south and the Indian ocean to the east, extending into relatively un-populated areas 200-miles inland and 200-miles northwards through Muslim coastal areas to Kilwa on the Rufiji River. It was indeed a strange backwater for Huddleston, with his recent experience of danger, high-profile political protest and worldwide fame. He appreciated his new situation quickly and adapted appropriately. He described his diocese in these words: 'It is the size of England and lies between two great rivers, the Rufiji and the Ruvuma. For over half the year the rains are falling, there is no direct road to Dar es Salaam; many of the roads into the villages become impassable to cars and lorries; movement is slowed down . . . Yet ours is the most highly literate region in the country.'[1]

The original settlement was a mission for freed slaves at Mkomaindo where the area's main hospital was later located. Served by a succession of able and strongly motivated missionaries, doctors, nurses and teachers, the mission established a high level of literacy which in turn produced a generation with raised expectations and a very limited range of career options. Politics and nationalism were only two strands in the complex twine drawing East Africa into the middle of the twentieth century. Religion was intensely important, too. The area had been pre-dominantly Muslim for centuries: Muslims held most official government and local posts and disliked the activities of Christian missionaries of all denominations – Roman Catholic, High Anglican (UMCA), medium high (Society for the Propagation of the

Gospel – SPG) or low church (CMS).² Christian converts had been maltreated, threatened and even murdered by Islamic activists. However, Huddleston felt the force and appropriateness of Islam and came to admire many Tanzanian officials who were Muslim. Islam aside, there were counter-productive groupings within Christian missionary 'outreach' in East Africa. The Roman Catholics maintained a strong, externally funded German Benedictine centre close to Masasi – staffed by monks living in babylonian comfort with their own large electrical generator – which tolerated Anglican activities in the area because they were the responsibility of the Anglo-Catholic UMCA, and thus similar in their worship and convictions to those of the true Catholic church. UMCA priests and bishops accepted a discipline closer to Rome than to Lambeth, and some older priests practised more ultramontane masses than the post-Vatican II liturgies enjoined on African Roman Catholics, whose altars had been moved to the centre of the church so that mass could be said or sung facing the people. The Roman hierarchy regarded High Anglicanism simply as a step closer to Rome, to which all roads led, eventually. They poached converts from the Anglicans, offering a substantially improved quality of life: Huddleston and his colleagues resented this but could do little about it.

All this church history should not be allowed to obscure the fact that Islam was closer to the people and villages of Tanganyika. Christianity in whatever form came from Europe, whereas Islam belonged to the people of the area. The Christian churches offered modest handouts, baptism to obviate the pains of hell. Huddleston's predecessors, particularly Bishop Lucas, had been attempting, largely without success, to benefit from some of the emotional force of the local rite of circumcision – undergone by all young men at puberty – by associating it with the less painful rite of confirmation. Some missionaries deplored circumcision but others saw in such an association the opportunity to entrench Christianity at a key moment in life.

There were 50,000 Christians in Huddleston's diocese. Confession, regular communion, Bible study were peripheral, but in the key area of education there was missionary money and the manpower resources into which the nascent nationalism of the area could tap. Roman Catholics provided education and collected souls. Anglicans had a wider remit, to deliver universal literacy, the passport to progress in the modern world. And their pastoral work, of a very practical kind, spearheaded by teachers and doctors, had prepared the way for the arrival of more politically conscious religious leaders, of whom Huddleston proved a prime example. His concentration on the educational system within the Masasi diocese was a well-timed response to the needs of the nation, for which its President would award him Tanzania's most important decoration, the Torch of Kilimanjaro, amost thirty-five years later in 1994. It was also a response to the partially accepted need for Christian missionary activities to be scaled down and adapted to the requirements of the new nationalism. While his appointment might have seemed a retrogressive step, in that he was a white European import rather than an indigenous product of the country's fragile Christian tradition, Huddleston was determined that his successor should be an African, and that as soon as that person had been identified, he would go. Meanwhile education had to be extracted from its missionary penumbra and presented in good order to the emergent one-party state. Huddleston's achievement in that area, explored by Professor Terence Ranger in his contribution to the Huddleston *festschrift*, may well prove to be one of his most important achievements.[3]

His other priority was the improvement of primary health care throughout the region, where leprosy was still rife, and in particular at Mkomaindo hospital. Here he recruited a group of four specialists – first David Gill, then (in early 1967) Bevis Cubey (a surgeon – ophthalmologist), followed by Frank Johnson (a gynaecologist) and Brian Wheatley (a surgeon). These four friends, drawn by Huddleston's charisma, were moved to undertake mission hospital work under the auspices of the United Society for the Propagation of the Gospel (USPG), 'a process of recruitment [Huddleston] pursued with typical zeal from remarkably tenuous origins'.[4] They responded to his invitation and their work was aided by regular visits from the remarkable Michael

Wood of the Nairobi flying doctor service, Christopher Wood (a specialist in social medicine) and Harold Wheate (a leprologist). Several Dutch doctors made significant contributions to primary health care in the region, as did Maurice King, who later wrote the core textbook on the subject.[5] The matron at Mkomaindo hospital married another of Huddleston's recruits, Alan Talbot, whom he had first met at Mirfield while Novice Guardian.

Huddleston's first logbook of his Masasi years opens with a description of his arrival at Mombasa: 'The *Warwick Castle* entered the harbour of Mombasa early on Sunday morning, October 1 1960. After three weeks in a crowded and noisy ship it was an immense relief to have arrived in East Africa, and I promised myself that, if possible, I would never travel by passenger-liner again.'[6] Some other passengers may have cold-shouldered this easily recognized and controversial figure, but a family group, the Wyndhams, befriended him. A Wyndham niece travelling in the same ship 'noticed the rather unkind way some of the South Africans on board treated him,' and took him to her family home. This was the beginning of a friendship that was to last until Huddleston's death in 1998. On arrival, he was upset to learn that his consecration had been postponed owing to a meningitis scare in the Masasi area. He went into a rage about having to come so far for nothing and threatened to return home by the next boat: the next day he apologized for his outburst.[7] His consecration took place on St Andrew's Day at St Nicholas's Chuch, Dar es Salaam. Enthronement followed on 7 December and 'we started the happy years of Trevor's episcopate.'[8]

In early February an ANC escapee from Johannesburg, Edward Kumalo, sought sanctuary with him. Other messengers from the world he had left behind became a weekly postal delivery of between forty and 100 letters, many requiring long replies, to those under his spiritual directorship. On 4 March his post held an invitation to head the mission to Oxford University in February 1963, a significant step in his upward ecclesiastical career. On 18 April Cassandra of the *Daily Mirror* sent him an admiring article he had written about him.

Despite these positive endorsements, the logbook quickly begins to reveal loneliness, depression, angry self-criticism and, despite his rigorous observance of the Community's rule, a dryness in his prayer life. By 9 June he complained to himself that he had no one to talk to, and on his 48th birthday he noted that 1961 had been the toughest year of his life: 'The rains came and went, the temperature was in the 90s. There was almost no electricity, no bathroom, and nothing of the comings and goings of community life' to which he had grown accustomed. On 30 September he left for Nairobi and by 8 October was in London visiting old friends, including the new Archbishop of Canterbury, Michael Ramsey.

From London he travelled to the United States, at the invitation of the Revd Richard Young OGS (Oratory of the Good Shepherd) to raise funds and initiate a liaison between UMCA and the American Episcopal Church. UMCA was using Huddleston as a fund-raiser. This was something he did reluctantly, but successfully. He visited Chicago, San Francisco, Boise, Salt Lake City, Denver, Fort Collins, Kansas City, Wichita, Philadelphia, Princeton, Boston, Newhaven, New York, Washington, Sewanee and Milwaukee. Reporting to UMCA, he noted a stream of bishops and others visiting America, including the Archbishop of Capetown and the Bishop of Guildford, all discreetly pressing their cases. He did not enjoy his role as 'spoiler of the Egyptians' and begged to be let off similar journeys in the future. His American contacts were to prove vital, yielding money and volunteer workers: but there were strings attached to both, which did not always make for easy relations or relaxed encounters.

Back in London, 1961 saw the Monday Club created by a powerful group of right-wing Tory MPs opposed to Macmillan's 'winds of change' policy in Africa. At the same time South Africa was preparing to withdraw its application for re-admission to the Commonwealth and become a republic. Opposition to the government had intensified after the massacre at Sharpeville in March of the previous year, in which 69 Africans had been gunned down by police. On 29 March 1961 the Treason Trials had finally ended after four years with the acquittal of all the accused – but their subsequent re-arrest and harassment led eventually to the Rivonia Trial in 1962. In the meantime, Mandela and Sisulu had persuaded the National Executive of the ANC to endorse the armed struggle and on 16 December 1961, MK (Umkhonto we Sizwe or 'spear of the Nation'), the newly founded military wing of the ANC, exploded its first bombs at power stations and government offices. Six months later Mandela was arrested and sentenced to life imprisonment for sabotage, Walter Sisulu was sentenced to six years and went underground and Helen Joseph was placed under house arrest. All were good friends of Huddleston's and one can only imagine that this increased his sense of isolation in remote Masasi.

Back in Tanzania preparations were well in hand for independence, and Huddleston was soon back at what was to be his daily routine for the next eight years: administering the schools, churches and medical centres of his diocese. He spent long hours driving in his battered Renault alone along dirt tracks in order to reach the remotest villages. There he would celebrate the eucharist, hold confirmations, sort out one *shauri* (problem) or another – a school's finances, a quarrel, a shortage of medical supplies – before returning to Masasi for more meetings, interviews, reading and writing. In an interview some years later he was to reflect: 'I used to read more in Masasi than I had since leaving Oxford. We live by the sun there. No one goes out after sunset.' His reading covered the expected theology and biographies but he also read sociology ('anything to do with children') and modern novels, particularly Iris Murdoch, Graham Greene and Margaret Drabble. 'It's very important to keep in touch that way.'[9] In many ways, Huddleston continued to lead a CR life in a non-CR context. One immensely enriching new element was his growing friendship with Julius Nyerere, then still opposition party leader. Since Raynes's death, Huddleston had not had a boss or senior colleague to whom he found it either appropriate or rewarding to defer. He found it now in Nyerere. 'He was a man for whom I would do anything.'[10] After Nyerere there would be no one. The Huddleston–Nyerere relationship – two unreconstructed socialists in a decreasingly idealistic world – like that between him and Oliver Tambo – remained close for many decades. Huddleston always used the respectful 'Mwalimu', meaning 'teacher' when addressing him.

Huddleston began to prepare for the forthcoming Oxford Mission. Dr Eric Mascall, the *eminence grise* of High Anglican theology reassured Huddleston who doubted if he was clever enough for his audience: 'I am sure you are the right person for the Mission . . . you can do the really important thing . . . and that is to show the young men and women the relevance of the Christian faith to the real issues that are convulsing the world today.'[11] Nicholas Mosley and I both offered him advice on the subject and the approach he might take. Friends and helpers also came to visit, including Michael Scott and Donald Chesworth, Huddleston co-opting the latter to develop hospital and agricultural projects. Huddleston was working away at his Swahili and could preach, though haltingly – and he thought badly – in the local language.

On 5 March 1962 he noted: 'The greatest joy in the world is to minister to souls and *at last* I'm beginning to be able to do so again.' Yet at the same time he described himself as 'tired and cross and depressed largely for lack of companionship and simple comfort.' Some of this depression may have stemmed from his diabetes. While out visiting villages in March and April, though active and cheerful, he had two blackouts resulting from failure to balance his insulin and carbohydrate intake. Despite the presence of new friends, in particular Archdeacon Ronnie Cox and Father Alan Talbot, Easter saw him with 'a bitter feeling of loneliness and purposelessness', not helped, it seems, by the success of the German Benedictines nearby who had succeeded in winning over Anglican converts with the promise of better living standards. On 18 June, however, he received £5,000 from Harry Oppenheimer in South Africa, which, followed closely by a visit by Anthony Sampson, cheered him up again. Sampson described his 'miraculous' journey to Masasi ending with 'sharp turn down track with high grass all round, and up a hill to the mission: a long grey stone cathedral across the hill, a steep thatched house above it. A toot on the horn, and out comes Trevor's tall white figure, astonished and welcoming. We drink Bourbon, from a special padded container given him by Americans – and long talk.' Sampson watched Huddleston talking Swahili with the children who 'swarm onto his porch' but was unsettled by what he saw as 'distressing rivalry with Roman Catholics'. He left Masasi in a Piper Apache plane, 'with Trevor surrounded as always by children, in front of the little airport hut.'[12] Other visitors that year included the Wyndhams and Sir Evelyn Baring. The last day of the year began, after the usual 7 a.m. mass, with 'a morning at my desk, interrupted by visits from many children! A visit to the hospital at Mkomaindo; heavy rain ... hot and sticky.' Eleven days later, he wrote: 'Last day in Masasi till May 3. I can find no sort of joy in going ... It has been a very full two years ... I have learnt a great deal. I have made many mistakes. I have failed over and over and over again in charity so that I could almost despair. Yet I *do* believe God has called me, and in spite of two years of *failure* I want to go on.'

After attending the Provincial synod in Nairobi, lunching with Bishop Leslie Stradling and visiting his friend Arthur Maimane from Sophiatown days, now in exile, Huddleston flew to England for more meetings at USPG, visits to friends and a Community Retreat at Mirfield: 'a v. warm welcome exactly 24 years since my first mass as a postulant.' From there, in bitter cold, he went to Oxford, and Christ Church, his old college. The Oxford University Mission week began on 11 Februry 1963 with his main address in the Examination Schools at 8.15 p.m. every night, followed by question sessions, visits to many of the colleges, and, of course, Pusey House. 'On the final Sunday we had a High Mass in the Cathedral (Howell's "Aedes Christi") at which I pontificated ... most beautifully sung and very simply and reverently done ... After the evening "mission" a truly *great* crowd, and the amplifiers broke down for the first time; but no harm done.' One of the Community of St Mary the Virgin sisters rescued him for a rest at Wantage.

Missions, particularly high-profile ones like that at Oxford University, have to be judged by high standards. The University's Vice-Chancellor, the distinguished philosopher Walter Oakeshott, wrote to Huddleston about it afterwards in donnish terms: 'no assignment could be more exacting . . . no one could speak from the experience to which the undergraduates would more readily respond, than yours. Rightly, this is the one thing they mind about, passionately; and some of them mind enough, I think, to do something. You must have a very vivid impression of contrast; and what you said was absolutely fair . . . what you are saying is something we all need desperately; and the men who can say it as you can with authority can be counted on the fingers of one hand.'[13] I think he was trying to say: 'well done and thank you'.

It was while resting in Wantage, on 19 February, that Huddleston learnt of his father's death. After addressing a large post-Mission gathering at Pusey House and recording a TV interview at Elstree studios he left London for Plymouth and the funeral.

Visits in London and Scotland followed. On 5 March he went with Mary Benson to see *King Lear* in which his new friend Irene Worth[14] was playing Goneril: 'a magnificent but most exhausting play.' Desmond Tutu visited him, as did Albie Sachs, and later he dined with Edward Boyle, then Minister for Education. A visit to Cambridge followed, then preachments at Ely, Coventry, Oundle, Bloxam, Birmingham, Marlborough: 'fifty meetings so far!'

Back in Masasi at the beginning of June electricity had come at last to his beloved Mkomaindo hospital. Confirmations and the inevitable *shauris* crowded in on him. 'All these things *depress* and *worry* me so much I can hardly bear to go on. Where are we going? Is there any hope?' On 19 July he celebrated his twentieth anniversary of setting out for South Africa but it was '*not* a happy day this year. I cannot shake off this constant worry and depression, and each day seems to add some new cause for anxiety, and I don't know how much of it is my fault or not. Moreover I am lonelier than I have ever been.' Huddleston cannot have been an easy colleague, for all that he was a considerate boss. He believed that close colleagues did not want his company and there was 'no *joy* anywhere. My prayer-life is as dead as it could be . . . Life is strangely, utterly empty of joy and peace. It must be my fault. But where?' On 27 July after a day of *shauris* he found snags in every department of the training College: 'it needs great wisdom and I feel my own lack of this very much.' Archdeacon Ronnie Cox, the excellent administrator of the diocese was by now on sabbatical and Huddleston missed him sorely. An infuriating talk with the Catholics on the Transfiguration of Our Blessed Lord led to his conclusion that 'the RC line is that we are simply a stage in the conversion of everyone to Catholicism'. He was also deeply concerned about the apparent lack of African leaders ready to take over the running of the Anglican church in nascent Tanzania.

Huddleston's frustrations continued in this vein, with only occasional respite, through the rest of the year. In September he preached his first extempore sermon in Swahili. Visits from Donald Chesworth and Dr Eric Williams, were welcome but time consuming. Children coming to claim the footballs he had organized for them delayed business too. Indeed the second part of the year seems dominated by encounters with children. He had adopted a little blind boy, Robert Isa and spent much time with him. He also loved taking groups of boys to the coast to swim and play games on the sand.[15] The rains came on 10 November, and within nine days he was writing that he was 'desperately tired all the time – no enthusiasm, no hope and no encouragement. I know I am being very hard to live with too, but I am quite unable to shake off this darkness. My prayers are virtually meaningless. I have the feeling that no one in the diocese – NO ONE – really has any use for me except as a source of gifts: money, jobs, rides, footballs.'

Again, there are signs that developments in South Africa and New York were adding to his frustrations. Arthur Blaxall, a white priest–colleague in the anti-apartheid struggle had been sent to jail for possessing ANC literature; while in New York, Michael Scott's one-man crusade on behalf of Namibian freedom from South Africa was bearing fruit. Two former colleagues were carrying the torch for African independence while Huddleston was grappling with local problems at once disheartening and insoluble. His early years in Masasi, outwardly useful, cheerful, efficient and effective, were giving rise to periodic depressions so intense that he longed to escape from what he saw as a cycle of hopelessness. Time and again his logbook returns to the lack of love and sense of failure he felt towards his pastoral work, the management of resources and the transfer of authority and responsibility.

A *coup d'état* in Zanzibar on 13 January 1964, led by the revolutionary forces of Sheikh Karume, established the island as an independent state. This was followed a week later by a copy-cat army mutiny in Dar es Salaam. January 21 was a day of rumour: European officers were being replaced by Africans; Indian shops were closed: a radio broadcast by Nyerere did little to dispel the confusion. In fact, he had been forced to call on the recently departed British forces to return to discipline his own army. By the end of April, the upheavals of the New Year had resolved themselves into the union of Tanganyika with Zanzibar, a not unproblematic alliance, given that Karume was a military dictator and possibly an anti-Asian racialist. Neither of these chimed with Nyerere's passionate socialist and egalitarian beliefs but he made the compromise in the name of African unity. Humiliating as the mutiny and its aftermath may have been, it was the first and last challenge to Nyerere's dominance of the independent Tanzania.[16]

Huddleston was by this stage already feeling restored, perhaps by a sense of achievement over the hospital with Maurice King, which gave him 'a deep sense of joy and purpose'. On 5 May he made the interesting observation in his logbook that Masasi was 'at the beginning of quite a social problem with broken homes and no strong supporting tribal life.' Further generosity by the Hilden Trust: £6,000 for the completion of the UPS (uninter-rupted power supply) kept his spirits up, and a positively ecstatic Huddleston records a day off on 13 June. 'After breakfast with ten children, off to Lindi. All very excited and very happy. Arrived at 11.15. Went shopping. Gave them an enormous meal at "hotel". Then to beach for a swim and football on the sands and home again by 4.30. ALL very well behaved and yet full of joy. A real delight.' Another logbook entry for 22 July shows

fascinating insight into the questions that were occupying him
around this time:

> I did not sleep till after midnight and at 5.30 a voice called
> 'baba' – it was the kid from Maritsa – a Muslim boy – who
> wanted to pee. This he did, without another word, and went
> to bed again. Somehow this single word 'baba' in *That*
> context has set me thinking about a whole range of subjects
> connected with 'Fatherhood' (as against 'paternalism'): a) His
> trust in me, a stranger; b) The word itself was enough – no
> need for explanations; c) I reacted to it immediately, didn't
> have to force myself to get up, as I do so often! d) Africa
> today – not Paternalism but Fatherhood needed; e) These
> children who seem to need affection or security or something?
> f) Linked up with the ordination – Fatherhood in action in
> the church; g) My own possessiveness a denial of this; h)
> African and European relationships in the church – 'Pastor'
> so *apparently* cold compared to 'Baba' etc; i) 'Abba' etc; j)
> Sexuality and fatherhood; k) 'Islam' and Xtianity – almost
> enough material for a book.

What a book that might have been!

August 1964 saw plans develop for a hospital and farm institute
at Mahiwa, funded in part by Denmark. Huddleston also led a
Mission at Makerere University in Uganda, preceded by a half-hour
meeting with Tom Mboya, the Kenyan political leader. He was
impressed by the varied backgrounds of the missioners, especially
the Nigerians, and blamed himself for preaching too intellectually.
He also attended the opening of Dar es Salaam's University college
and noted a very good speech by Julius Nyerere ('though an
attempt to justify preventive detention didn't convince me!') Later
that month he had a half-hour interview with Nyerere who he
found 'far more care-worn, grey and tired, but very friendly.'

The year continued with much action on the building and
education transfer fronts, but on 3 October Huddleston lost his
temper – '*mea culpa*' – over a problem in the Education Officer's
office, a recurrent cause for concern. A week later a flood of
refugees arrived from neighbouring Mozambique, then attaining

independence, and Huddleston came to the rescue with blankets, food, clothing, a doctor. Nyerere made a visit to Masasi where he opened the new Mahiwa school with a superb speech that left Huddleston in high spirits.

After Christmas, and a remarkable year for coping with many difficult matters, flutuating blood sugars brought on serious fatigue, depression and sickness. Huddleston's closest friend in CR, Mark Tweedy, came to stay, but he too was in a state of depression, and the visit seemed to have done neither much good.[17] However, a new resolution to go on safari to every parish in the diocese to discuss fund-raising and self-help was implemented. Three days after Tweedy's departure, towards the end of January 1965, Huddleston flew to Mauritius for a VIP visit, staying with Donald Chesworth. He returned on 3 February, to a crisis over funding teachers' pay and improving their working conditions in the school at Chidya. Many European teachers resigned and on 21 February they were joined by the superintendent himself. The financial crisis had arisen because local Christians would not give more to churches now perceived to be alien imports. Relations with the Roman Catholics improved. Depression loomed but passed away. Good Friday was celebrated with Stations of the Cross at Chidya 'in mime round the quadrangle . . . very reverently done: very simple and moving. No words, but commentary by GF (archdeacon) with hymns in between stations and a slow drum in the background.' Negotiations over school handovers followed on 25 April, and the next day the only British politician to share his view of apartheid, Barbara Castle, arrived, described by Huddleston as 'very vivacious but suffering from sinusitis and deafness'. They had a useful discussion, and the following day, she gave 'an excellent talk on Economic Aid – followed by questions, which she dealt with brilliantly.' Later that year, at the prompting of the Organisation for African Unity, Tanzania, along with several other African nations, was to break off diplomatic relations with Britain over its handling of the Prime Minister Ian Smith's Unilateral Declaration of Independence (UDI) in Rhodesia. It was a principled stand destined to lose Tanzania substantial British aid in the years ahead.

On 27 April Huddleston talked at length to Nyerere and Mrs
Castle. 'In the end I saw for the first time quite clearly the next
step with regard to S. Africa – the need to put pressure on
Portugal at every level' (Portugal was the last colonial power in
Southern Africa, other than Britain. A South Africa surrounded
by pro-ANC independent African states would be severely weakened. However, Mozambique and Angola were not to win independence from Portugal until 1975). This had now become ANC
policy, in reaction to the unholy alliance between Salisbury,
Pretoria and Maputo (capital of Mozambique); Nyerere 'greatly
reassured me about my own position. No other African, to me,
has the same deep charm and drawing power.'

Despite these reassurances though, deep depression struck on
3 May. 'What is the matter with me? Or Masasi?' he pleaded.
Successful negotiations over the handover of schools from Church
control to that of local authorities changed his mood slightly, and
on his parish rounds he found more happy than disappointing
shauris. Nonetheless by 25 May he was feeling very unsure about
his future. 'I wish I had more real love for this place, but there is
so very little love *in* it, in my opinion.' His round of managing
and visitations continued without interruption until his retreat on
23 August, after which he resolved 'to be strict about my hour of
mental prayer before mass: rising at 5.30 am: to try to say some
part of the Rosary daily: to be faithful to my resolve about daily
language-study whenever possible: no despair! Great generosity
with my people with their demands on me: no self pity.' Troubles
continued at the secondary school at Chidya and Huddleston had
to face down forty boys who were out of class and refused to
apologize.

On 14 October a TV crew headed by Erskine Childers arrived
to make a documentary film about Huddleston in Masasi. Hud-
dleston's old friend Bloke Modisane dropped in and stayed.
Chidya loomed large, reflecting the growing politicization of
Tanzanian youth under Nyerere, but a visit to the Ministry of
Education at Dar es Salam helped the process. Huddleston wrote
an article for the *Observer* which was published on 19 December.
Though addressed to 'my kith and kin', it condemned British

public opinion for allowing UDI in Rhodesia. He wrote about Tanzania: colonialism had been "removed" – a very courteous process' and this had been followed not by greater efficiency, rather the reverse, but by a sense of social power and purpose: 'the sense of having a freely chosen direction in planning for the future ... To me it is an immense privilege to be part of this moment in African history, even if only for a while until my African successor is chosen and takes over.' He always felt part of the new Tanzania, whereas in South Africa, though the battle against apartheid was far more exciting, described in his own words as 'the most exhilarating activity imaginable', there could be no sense of belonging. However much a European sought to identify himself with the African people 'in their humiliations and degradations', Huddleston knew that he could never succeed simply because he was white and oppressive power was white. 'Even in jail apartheid prevented this.'

Tanzania's breach in diplomatic relations with the UK brought an active year to a close. The logbook is very specific on the intentions of his daily masses, giving a glimpse of the interaction between Huddleston's interior and exterior lives. Other references are less easy to track, but the unexpected death of the Superior at Mirfield, Jonathan Graham, must have led many of the brethren to consider Huddleston should be their next Superior; and one of them, Augustine Hoey, may well have been deputed to sound him out. There could have been little doubt, however, what his answer would be, and his friend Hugh Bishop was elected unopposed. Another message arrived on 23 November with 'strange rumours about Liverpool' and his going there as bishop. Archbishop Michael Ramsey, himself a High Churchman with a fondness for Mirfield and for Huddleston, may have had a part in this, though there is no evidence for this in Owen Chadwick's biography; but certainly many hoped Huddleston would succeed Ramsey at Canterbury in 1974. He would have been a wonderful Archbishop of Canterbury. He would have made the international dimension of the Anglican Communion a force to be reckoned with and a voice – particularly for those in the Southern Hemisphere – to be heeded. He would also have provided direct, unequivocal and inspiring moral leadership to which Britain would have responded, thus improving incidentally the public image of the Church of England. He may not have been so good at the paper and committee work, but even here I believe he would have quickly silenced his critics, remembering other occasions on which he displayed surprising adaptability. In fact Ramsey believed missionary bishops with leadership qualities – pre-eminently Beecher and Huddleston – should be kept where they were as long as possible, so he would not have sought an episcopal see in England for Huddleston. But the appointments secretary would anyhow have debarred Huddleston for his disestablishment views.

The new Superior CR visited Huddleston in late January 1966. A few days later, mass was said for the success of the BBC TV film due to be broadcast in England, and fan mail started to pour in soon afterwards. On 15 March the diocesan synod in Masasi abolished public penance, genuflection and drums in church; the most important item on the agenda was, rightly, lay leadership within the Church. Nyerere was calling for lay leadership across the new nation. But it was proving difficult to extricate good potential leaders from the temptations of power and persuade them to concentrate on the common good at the expense of their own personal enrichment. As with the future leadership of the Church in Masasi, this was a source of worry to Huddleston.

News of Verwoerd's assassination in early September came to him as 'a most ghastly shock to Africa and no help at all – except, perhaps, as a warning against *all* forms of violence.' In November, Joe Rogaly, who had been commissioned by Collins to write Huddleston's biography, arrived.[18] His presence added a new dimension to Huddleston's routine. Maurice King was around for much of this period, and Masasi was playing an important part in the forming of his views on primary health care in the developing world. Rogaly's account of Huddleston's lifestyle is interesting, for in addition to transcribing some of the logbooks, he was intrigued by Huddleston's close following of the Church's year and the daily intentions of the mass. On 6 December, the end of his third week in Masasi, he typed a lot of letters for

Huddleston, many of them pre-occupied with the stand-off in Rhodesia: he was 'very friendly now and very excited about [Ian] Smith's refusal to accept [Harold] Wilson's terms, padding across with his torch to my hut so that he could have someone sympathetic to talk about it . . . If you are with [Huddleston] he's never still – always jumping up to see someone or fetch something or drive off somewhere . . . He never seems to tire. He's got this fire on the inside all right. On so many things he is a man of immediate action, and his energy is formidable.' He discussed Huddleston with one of his closest colleagues: his love of praise and dislike of criticism. 'He is always with children and says they keep him sane. He has plenty of cause for anger or depression . . . The real lesson,' Rogaly observed shrewdly, 'which [Huddleston] knows, is that this mission plus the Benedictines (which is ten times as big an employer) makes up the only decent target for young trades' union men – and, I might add, government officials – to work on; the rest is bush.'

Rogaly, with Dr Maurice King, the primary health care pioneer, attended one of Huddleston's high masses. 'A great deal of High Church this and that, much incense swinging . . . [Huddleston's] jewelled mitre, with its two pointed golden peaks . . . is red between, like a great open jaw to the sky . . . the communicants on their knees, heads back, tongues out for the Master bird to place the wafers on their fledgling beaks . . . Critics say he's substituting one set of mumbo-jumbo for another, but even if you deny the religious truth of what he's doing (which I feel unable to do) then at least he is giving people a reason for some more structure – social and political morality . . . in the midst of tribal morality's decay . . . and giving an essentially bored people – with little to do or see all day in the dust – some great colour and excitement and emotional experience and, perhaps most important, he's giving himself the best possible reason for being here and it is undoubtedly good for him and those like him to be here owing to the good material and physical work they do in health and education.' Huddleston told Rogaly: 'it's services like this that make me know, when I'm in a depression – which I often am – that everything is all right.' That mass was followed by a confirmation: '[Huddleston] put his thumb in holy oil (held out in a small silver box for him) made the sign of the cross on the forehead, then put his enormous white hand on a tiny black woolly head, practically obliterating it from sight as he said the prayer, in Swahili . . . eyes tight shut; forty-four other little pairs of eyes straining round to see what would happen to them.'

Huddleston's frustrations had induced him to tender his resignation; but on 16 December, at a clergy meeting, a deputation of three, including Hilary Chisonga, his eventual successor, came to say how sorry they were to have heard his words about resigning. They asked him never to talk of such things again. 'Very comforting!' reported Huddleston.

Rogaly left in the New Year, by bus for Mtwara, Lindi and Dar es Salaam. Life resumed its customary pattern – heat, cold, rain, mud, trips with children, meetings, visitors, safaris to outlying parishes, letters, *shauris*, periodic tiredness; above all the diurnal Christian year with its catholic calendar; a retreat in late February. On 18 May he had a two-hour talk with Julius Nyerere, with whom he raised the possibility of becoming a Tanzanian citizen. Nyerere tactfully dissuaded him. Days later he asked himself, 'will this gloomy tunnel never end?' and on 23 May, 'simply overwhelmed with depression . . . I get more and more alone. I wouldn't mind if I felt I was doing the diocese any good. But I don't and I'm *not* . . . I am wholly and unreservedly depressed.' On 28 July his benefactors, the Ramptons, arrived for a ten-day visit. They wished to see how their money had been used. In late August he took a holiday at a retreat house near Nairobi. That autumn Nyerere visited Mkomaindo hospital, talked to each of the blind children in turn, then reproved his Masasi audience: although there was a high literacy record, its record for *maendeleo* (development/self-reliance) was bad. 'He also reproved our drinking habits!' On 1 December: 'I still *feel* depressed almost consistently and I can't believe this is right. So *wish* I could get a clearer lead, but the Lord obviously doesn't intend it. I don't want to go on, and on, and on, in this dreary way for I know I can't do my best work. I also don't want to run away because things are hard.'

Huddleston's tendency to swing from satisfaction to deep depression continued into 1968. Evelyn Baring's visit early on in the year got it off to a good start, but by 20 February a 'most distressing meeting' had left Huddleston feeling desolate once more. 'It seems to me *almost* hopeless to try and convey my own feelings of despair over the lack of real love in the diocese.' He told Archbishop Beecher of his decision to resign 'AT LATEST by *November 30 1970* and earlier if any right and suitable job was offered'. The promise of £40,000 from Holland and a wonderful letter from Oliver Tambo cheered him somewhat, but depression had set in, and on Easter Day he wrote: 'The darkness deepens, Lord with me abide – a strange sentiment but only too true of my present state of soul. When *will* a break come? Is it entirely my fault?' Three weeks later a glorious bathe 'with six of our kids' and an excellent day's talk with the historian Adrian Hastings restored his spirits, and on 28 May he was invited to become Bishop of Stepney. A letter from Beecher some days later encouraged him to accept, and on 13 June a message from London confirmed that the Queen had approved his appointment. That same day he addressed the clergy assembled at Mtandi. This is what he said:

I wish to explain to you as simply as I can why I feel it right at this time to leave Masasi, for I realise my decision must seem to you all a very sudden and unexpected one. Perhaps you may think that some new circumstance has arisen to make it necessary; or perhaps you may even think that I no longer love the diocese or its people. No! Nothing new has happened, except an invitation from the Bishop of London to help in his large diocese (the largest in the Anglican Communion in terms of numbers) as Suffragan Bishop of Stepney. But long before that invitation reached me two weeks ago I had been trying to discover what God's will for me and for the diocese really was.

(1) When I came to Masasi eight years ago I knew, and I said publicly many times, that I would be the ast English bishop of the diocese; that my work must be to prepare in every way

possible for an African to follow me. It seemed to me that preparations meant three things:

First – that the diocese should have no more debts and that its buildings (St Cyprian's, Chidya, the hospitals, Mtandi itself) should be put into good repair so that they could not be a burden on the bishop or the Diocesan Finance Board.

Secondly – that the diocese should really be part of the Church of the Province of East Africa and that its Synod and constitution should be strong.

Thirdly – that there should be African leadership throughout the diocese and that this should be a real leadership, not one in name only.

But all three of these aims depend, of course, on increasing the extent of Self-Reliance in the parishes.

How far we have succeeded in realising these aims you must judge for yourselves. I certainly do not think I have done enough, and I would have liked very much to stay a few more years and see more accomplished. But, again, there are reasons why I feel it would be a mistake to do so.

(2) It is clear to me today that SELF-RELIANCE is the key to everything else; that unless the diocese can be *really* self-reliant it cannot make progress in any other way at all; it will die. You all know the ways in which we have tried during the past four years to increase *Ada ya Kanisa* [church giving], and also the extent of our failure. It is not that we have failed entirely (*Ada ya Kanisa* is double what it was four years ago) or that we must think *only* about money when we talk of Self-Reliance. But we *have* failed. And, as your bishop and father in God, I believe this failure is my fault at least as much as yours; and the responsibility for this failure is my responsibility before God. And so I have examined my conscience many times to try to see how I can do better. At first I thought it was because, owing to the difficulty I had in learning Swahili (I was forty-seven, remember, when I started) I could not make you understand: and that this would improve. Then I thought it was because I was able to get large sums of money from my friends in America and England – and to re-

build hospitals etc. and that our Christians felt there was no *need* to give. The Bishop would provide. (I do indeed believe that, in Masasi, we have depended far too much on help from UMCA, USPG etc. but in the diocese of Central Tanganyika, Bishop Alfred has brought far more money into the diocese than I have! And yet they are self-reliant.) But in the end, I came to see that it was my own leadership that was wrong; that somehow even though in England, America, Zambia, Nairobi, I could move people to give me their trust, I could not do so here in Masasi.

In October 1966 I wrote to President Nyerere for his advice. I said I was doubtful whether *any* English bishop ought to lead an African diocese. I asked what he thought I should do and he replied: 'I ask you to accept my assurance and to know that if staying is not an embarrassment to you, I want you to stay.' So I stayed.

But, as the days passed, I still felt the same deep doubts about my ability to win your trust and your love. I think there are some men who can lead and direct others without worrying about such things. I am not one of them. I need to know that in what I am doing, or trying to do, the people who are working with me (the clergy in this case) are really whole-hearted in their trust and in their love. Increasingly I felt that this was not the case here in Masasi and that I could no longer, as an Mzungu [European], hope for it to be so.

In February of this year I wrote to Archbishop Leonard to say I thought I ought to resign *not later* than 1970, but that if any suitable work was offered to me in the meanwhile I must be free to consider it on its merits. I also wrote to the Archbishop of Canterbury explaining that I was sure it would be right for an African bishop to take over not later than 1970.

(3) When the invitation from the Bishop of London reached me two weeks ago I knew I must make a decision; but it was not at all easy to do so and I felt I needed advice. I asked the help of the Archbishop, of Bishop John Sepeku of Dar es Salaam, of the Superior of my own Community and also of

four senior priests who had all worked in Masasi for many years. All except one felt I would be right to go. In fact I went to Dar es Salaam especially so that I could give my answer to the Bishop of London and so that the appointment could be made public as soon as possible. I am very sorry it has been so long delayed: but that is because of events I cannot control.

So I come to say goodbye and I do so with a very heavy heart. I came to Africa twenty-five years ago. Therefore nearly all my work has been with Africans and for the African Church. Africa is where my heart is and where it always will be. But sometimes, I believe, God does call men to show their love for people, for places and for the work even of his church, by leaving all these in His hands; by not holding it fast oneself. I truly believe that God cares for the Diocese of Masasi and its people much more than I do, and that it is in His hands.

He will over-rule all my mistakes and all my failures and sins since I came here. I ask your forgiveness, each single one, for anything I have said or done to hurt you. And I assure you of my prayers every day in the years that lie ahead.[19]

There is little to add by way of comment on this fine statement. Huddleston found himself in a position of significant social and economic power when all he had wanted was to serve the UMCA-taught Christians of the area, and the policies of the new national government encapsulated in Nyerere's Arusha Declaration of 1967. He found implementing the financial aspects of Self-Reliance dispiriting work, and his frustrations built into sometimes unreasoning anger against his own colleagues, white and black. But his real authority arose from the fact that education, at both primary and secondary levels, had been mission-led and mission-sourced: and he was the head missionary. He inherited a job replete with power and authority: he had had not only to manage and superintend the schools, but also to finance them out of funds from USPG in Westminster. The UMCA tradition was for bishops and priests to practise and share the poverty of their flocks, and so a little money went a long way. But whether or not they behaved like rich people they were all regarded as sources of wealth procured from rich backers at home. The poverty, to which they and Huddleston aspired, paradoxically, was at odds with the riches to which they had access. Huddleston found a similarly ironic situation where the standard of education raised unfair and unrealistic expectations in school leavers. For him, the concept of appropriate education, unlike appropriate technology or medicine, was a sinister one, used a decade earlier to justify the passing of the Bantu Education Act. But whereas black South Africans' expectations were limited by the white minority government's *diktat*, South Eastern Tanzania was constrained by the endemic and unalterable poverty of the region. Apart from the bright few who could be trained elsewhere to become doctors or teachers or work in government offices in Dar es Salaam, school leavers had little to look forward to other than subsistence farming. This was one cause of Huddleston's growing depression as the principles of Self-Reliance post-Arusha began to be put into practice, often with disappointing results.

Julius Nyerere and Trevor Huddleston could be considered politically naive to have assumed that the principles of respect, commonality, honesty and self-sufficiency embodied in Arusha would solve all problems without producing new ones. Previous attempts to bring wealth to the region included the disastrous ground-nuts scheme, financed and managed not by the British government, but by Unilever. Evidence of its failure was apparent only a few miles from Masasi, in ruined buildings, roads leading nowhere. Later several other countries offered capital and expertise: the Italians built a fine metalled road, Dutch and Scandinavians were generous and asked few questions, Americans sent dollars and students to study tribal customs and write theses on African anthropology. Huddleston had always been a good fundraiser, and through his American trips and British friends, brought funds for capital and maintenance projects in the diocese. But he knew that this could only ever be but a short-term answer, and he resented being regarded as a 'holy cash cow'. Receiving foreign aid did not fit easily into the new rules and routines of Self-Reliance. Even with no strings attached, successful beggars cannot be choosers. While hospitals and clinics developed during his time as bishop, and Maurice King's health-care schemes produced cost-effective results, the conflict between an educational system run with foreign management and money via the missionary society and the country's dedication to self-sufficiency and autonomy produced tensions which proved nearly unbearable for anyone seriously involved in both. Though Huddleston had influence and power, he knew he should use it only to tide affairs over until local authorities could take over, and that his job should be quite different – to serve, to facilitate and then to fade away. Thus he spent many months convincing the diocesan synod, the teachers' union, the education department that responsibility for church schools should be handed over, and by 1967 he had achieved this. By then he had plumbed the depths of loneliness and desolation, saved by his appointment to Stepney, and that of his successor, Hilary Chisonga, to Masasi in his place.

The education hand-over was the focus of Professor Terence Ranger's contribution to *Trevor Huddleston: Essays on His Life and Work.*[20] Ranger discovered correspondence revealing how Huddleston managed the change, in a store-shed in Masasi in 1975. At first sight it is 'a tedious story, narrowly focused on "church responsibilities" and light years away from the drama of the South African townships. On second reading, though, it is the story of a necessary emancipation ... Huddleston's policies, which had led to many clashes with local officials in the years before 1967, ended up magnificently in harmony with the ideals of ... Self-Reliance.' Determined to hand over the Church schools to the education authorities early on in his episcopate, he had a difficult balancing act to perform. Too rapid a process of Africanization risked damaging the schools' ability to function in the best interests of the pupils. He demanded that the hand-over took place through a planned process involving full consultation between the Church and education authorities. This provoked resentment among many of the increasingly articulate male African teachers and obscured the real barrier to the implementation of a unified education service which brought together church and government schools: a lack of cash. Huddleston grew impatient with excuses and demanded that the government authorities

compel the local district councils to pay the subventions it owed
to church schools. He failed in this consistently over the next two
years and by September 1965 his patience was exhausted. He had
already alienated more than one district education officer, including an ex-UMCA teacher who figures in his daily logbooks,
George Kasembe. Kasembe found it difficult to understand Huddleston's apparent unwillingness to hand over Church schools
immediately. From this time on Huddleston's attention began to
shift from education to the other urgent needs to be met from the
funds at his disposal, in particular improving clergy pay and
conditions, as they were relatively much worse off than the
teachers. Moreover, since his arrival the Church had spent
£75,000 on improving and extending Mkomaindo Hospital,
building new dispensaries, building and equipping an agricultural
school and providing a tractor and plough for a local farming co-
operative. By 1966 he was pointing out, in a letter answering a
request from the Masasi District Council for money to improve
teachers' housing, that 'it is impossible for us to help in every
area of development at once'. By January 1967 he longed to be
free of the schools altogether, and publication and implementation of the Arusha Declaration gave him his chance. 'I personally
have no desire to continue with the management of schools and
feel that it is a quite disastrous waste of time and money,' he
told a district council. Julius Nyerere's statement on Education
for Self-Reliance came just in time for Huddleston: it could
validate his policy, it commanded (at first) countrywide support,
and Huddleston himself enthusiastically endorsed it for its egali-
tarianism, acceptance of poverty for all as a fact rather than
a condition to be escaped from, and insistence that outside
aid, in whatever form was only a short- or middle-term solution;
the long-term solution lay with Tanzanians themselves. He called
a teachers' meeting on 15 April at which he pressed that 'we
hand over control of virtually all our primary schools at the
earliest possible moment. I feel that this is in line with virtually
all that the President has said.' Three months later he addressed
the diocesan synod, determined to resign if his recommendation
was not accepted. But it was accepted unanimously by the synod,

which agreed with Huddleston 'that the Church is here to serve in any way it can, but no longer to *manage* or govern . . . This, as I see it, is the logical consequence of the Arusha Declaration.'

Huddleston had played a difficult hand brilliantly, taking advantage of the trump card his friend the President had given him. In other respects he was the first to blame himself for failure, poor work, lack of love. Certainly his management style was more autocratic than that of some other bishops in the area, but it is difficult to see how he would have achieved as much as he did without leading from the front. Lay leadership was lacking; clergy wages were too low; local employment possibilities too restricted; the Christian religion did not dominate the area or provide viable alternatives to subsistence farming. Hindsight suggests that Huddleston blamed himself for much that was inevitable while overlooking the considerable achievements of his episcopate at Masasi.

Bevis Cubey, a distinguished eye surgeon who worked with the three other missionary doctors personally recruited by Huddleston at Mkomaindo Hospital, wrote: 'He did not spare himself, this radical, single-minded man of prayer who managed on five hours' sleep. He mastered his insulin-dependent diabetes over several decades which included . . . uncertain journeyings on Land-Rover-shattering "roads" to remote outstations for pastoral visits and confirmations where carbohydrate intake was critical to him, and heat, thirst, and the risk of infection ever present. But however hard he was on himself, he was habitually gentle with others . . . His greatness was that he combined almost paradoxically not only dignity with humility, and eloquence with boyish enthusiasm but crucially the cold steel of uncompromising idealism with the warm humanity of caring about the individual whatever the colour of his skin.'[21]

Cubey added that Huddleston left a permanent legacy. Although Mkomaindo Mission Hospital, that had been developed under his aegis to District Hospital status, was taken over by the government within two years of his departure and deteriorated in terms of staff, morale, fabric, equipment and drugs availability, the training of local nurses and Rural Medical Aids, into which longer term investment and effort had been concentrated, continues to bear fruit in surprising ways. The star trainee nurse of thirty years ago, Patrick Mwachiko, is now the fourth bishop of Masasi to have succeeded Huddleston. He recently agreed, after much deliberation, to the government's request that the diocese should take back the running of the hospital. Other trainees from the 1960s are now the trainers and leaders of Tanzania's health service. Huddleston's African achievements are significantly enhanced by his work in Tanzanian health care and education. His love of children, of all colours, became another part of the folklore of the region.

CHAPTER SIX

STEPNEY

1968–1978

This book was originally entitled 'Father Huddleston – his biography' to emphasize the primary importance of his years in South Africa. He was 'Father Huddleston' to a generation of black South Africans. His sudden, unexpected and glorious growth into maturity started in 1943 in Sophiatown where he found his calling fulfilled in an immensely testing job and discovered the gifts to do it outstandingly well. His career as leading opponent of the South African government's racial policy continued in drastically altered form after his enforced departure in 1956. He was not to return until 1991: the massacres of Sharpeville in 1960 and Soweto in 1976, the escalation of the ANC's armed struggle all took place while Huddleston was in, what he always termed, 'exile' from the land and people he loved. The liberation of South Africa remained his central vocation and ministry – its early growth, establishment, nourishment, expansion, enforced diminishment, unimpeded strengthening and eventual achievement of much of what he sought – is the outward and visible sign of the strength and greatness, not just of what he did, but of what he was, his potential fully realized. In early April 1998 a distinguished Oxford academic asked me whether I thought that, *mutatis mutandis*, Huddleston personally overthrew apartheid as Pope John Paul II could be said to have brought down Communism. Of course, apartheid was brought down by the black Africans, in or out of the ANC, who devoted their lives to this necessary cause, and not to any white individual or group, however committed, however determined and eloquent; and of course the Holy Father was a great deal more than simply a mega-anti-Communist. But I said yes to the questioner, because all those I have interviewed who fought and won the armed struggle against Pretoria's policies have testified to the unique difference Huddleston made to their lives, and to the struggle.

After Huddleston's departure in 1956, Pretoria intensified the implementation of its apartheid policies. Shortly after the Treason Trials had begun in 1959, 40,000 African commuters from Alexandra township boycotted the buses so successfully that Pretoria unilaterally reduced the township in size. By 1962 it was inhabited only by working adults, living alone. This was social engineering on a remarkable scale. March 1960 saw the tragic failure of a major political offensive against the Pass Laws, where bitter internal divisions within the ANC leadership and between the ANC and the radical, Afro-centric but anti-Communist, Pan-Africanist Congress (PAC) culminated in the deaths of sixty-nine unarmed civilians protesting at Sharpeville, near Alexandra. A state of emergency was imposed and the ANC and PAC joined the Communist Party as illegal organizations. The number of Africans convicted for pass and other minor offences exceeded 1,500,000 by the end of 1960. In 1961 Pretoria withdrew its application for re-admission to the Commonwealth after the Nationalist votes for the country to become a republic narrowly beat the pro-Commonwealth white vote. By the end of 1963 the Minister of Justice could confine without trial for one or more periods of 90 days anyone he chose. For opponents of white supremacy, darkness descended.

By 1968 a certain pattern in the development of Trevor Huddleston's career was emerging. His first two moves to and from South Africa were not of his volition but those of Fr Raynes. By the time of his re-call, he was already in middle age and his experiences had left him temperamentally and empirically unprepared for normal Church work: he could not put Africa behind him, and even if he wanted to, his audiences forbade it. His next career move – and indeed his subsequent ones – were also engineered from the outside: it would be very surprising were it otherwise, for no Anglican religious brother (monk) or prelate brother (bishop) would have much thought of personal ambition

and achievement – and Huddleston was both, a rare and awk-
ward combination. He made no secret of his delight at becoming
a bishop, something he had always wanted to be from his early
childhood days in Golders Green and Hampstead Garden Suburb.
He tackled the problems and opportunities of Masasi with energy
and enthusiasm (not always diplomatically), so much so that he
effectively worked himself out of a job. What he could do, what
he had to do there, he had done. Just as he longed to escape from
Britain back to Africa in 1958, so in 1968 he knew he had to
leave Masasi for England again, much though he loved its people,
much though he had done for the education, living standards and
religious awareness of thousands of South Eastern Tanzanians.
Job opportunities were few and far between, and a major See –
London, Durham Winchester, still less Canterbury or York – had
been ruled out by the establishment's branding of him as a rebel
and a nuisance, essentially unclubbable and possibly unreliable
too. His expressed view of Rhodesian UDI in the late 1960s was
only the most conspicuous of his public stands, and derived
directly from his anti-apartheid commitment.

Archbishop Michael Ramsey may well have played a part in
Huddleston's translation to Stepney, but it was Dr Robert Stopford, the Bishop of London, who invited Huddleston to take the
job. He could not return to Mirfield in any capacity; he could not
return to his first love, South Africa; he could not return to
Britain except as a prelate brother. The Stepney offer arrived in
the nick of time, as Masasi had done in 1960 and as Mauritius
was to in 1978 – as indeed did heading the Anti-Apartheid
Movement in 1981. The only problem was an ecclesiastical one.
Stepney was not a diocesan see, but only a suffragan – co-equal
with Kensington, Willesden, Edmonton, under London, whose
authority itself remained north of the Thames, Southwark being
in charge in South London. It was a step down from Masasi,
noted a *New Statesman* profile from 1968, but 'he is the last
person to worry about his own status,'[1] which anyway included
pastoral responsibility for three of London's most testing boroughs – Tower Hamlets, Hackney and Islington; and ninety-four
churches many with a resilient, sometimes congenially Anglo-

Catholic life, inspired by earlier generations of great East End priests and pastors. The move from Africa to England was made through the prayers and schemes of his well-wishers and seems to have come as a welcome surprise to Huddleston himself. According to Alix Palmer in the *Daily Express*, Huddleston had 'left his heart in South Africa . . . I am now fifty-five and if I were to do another big job I had to do it now.'

On 14 June 1968 Geoffrey Moorhouse in the *Guardian* noted that 'the monk of Mirfield, opponent of Apartheid and now Bishop of Masasi . . . is leaving Africa for good . . . At the age of fifty-five he is leaving the continent with which his name will always be identified in the history books.' Quoting Huddleston's statement that 'England is no longer my home and never will be. I am an African', Moorhouse perceptively commented that 'eating those words will be the hardest thing that has ever happened to him', adding that 3 July, the day of his departure, 'will be a day which history ought to mark well because then the native people of that continent will lose the fiercest and most genuine friend they ever had from the world outside.'[2]

He had arrived in London on 4 July 1968 where he stayed with the Deaconesses of St Andrew's in North Kensington, one of his favourite boltholes. Later in the month he met his predecessor at Stepney, Everard Lunt, a former vicar of the famous evangelical parish of St Aldates in Oxford, and renewed friendships with the Denniston family, and with Jack Linscott, an elderly unreconstructed Communist then living at Morden College, Blackheath, with whom he enjoyed companionable evenings and political talk – in pubs, at the theatre. He dined with the Ramseys at Lambeth Palace and with the Canon John Collins at Amen Court. To mark Human Rights Year, then in progress, he attended a dinner at the Mansion House. He visited his old school, Lancing College, and his step-mother in Devon. By early August he was caught up in the Lambeth Conference, a once-a-decade gathering of Anglican Bishops. Ramsey asked him to chair the committee on 'The Varieties of Unbelief', despite his lowly status as a suffragan: he was not invited for that reason to the opening reception 'for *some* bishops' and instead spent the

evening with Oliver Tambo.[3] A fine photograph of Huddleston
with a group of Tanzanian children graced the front cover of the
brochure setting out the episcopal agenda – 'The Church for all
races, all ages' – that was still paternal rather than fraternal. In
early August he stayed with his friends near Richmond and two
days later addressed a meeting at Central Hall, Westminster,
thence to Mirfield and a holiday with the Howicks in the Scottish
borders. Installation took place on 3 October, by which time he
had moved to his new house at 400 Commercial Road, E1.
Previous Bishops of Stepney, including his immediate predecessor,
Everard Lunt, whose sudden resignation had precipitated Huddleston's appointment, had lived in Amen Court with the canons
of St Paul's, a world and several miles away from the East End.
To live in the midst of where he worked had always been an
important part of Huddleston's ministry and he persuaded the
Church Commissioners to buy a small four-storey house in the
heart of his patch. He loved it there, got to know his neighbours,
lunched with publishers in the West End, saw old friends – the
Horans, the Wyndhams, the Greenways – and made new ones:
Tom Driberg, Frank Longford, who, rather misguidedly, got
Huddleston onto his anti-pornography committee. He was reunited with his niece, Anne Mary Jarvis, who had married the
Conservative politician, Cecil Parkinson in 1957. He went to
Ireland on speaking engagements, spoke on Africa at the Cambridge Union on 20 November and was soon fulfilling a busy
diary of episcopal engagements – confirmations, clergy meetings,
church gatherings of all sorts. Anecdotes abound about his good
neighbourliness. When the father of one local family died Huddleston called round after the funeral: the widow was still in her
nightie when her children brought him in. Both quite unembar-
rassed, he explained he always went shopping in the market at
this time of the week, and offered to do her shopping, which he
did for many weeks thereafter.

His nine years at Stepney were successful in that Huddleston
carried out his episcopal duties with flair and energy, care and
thoroughness which characterized his ministry at every stage
and was warmly appreciated by the clergy and people of the East

End. In addition, he enhanced his office by his spontaneous and
natural identification with many sections of society in the area.
But he would never trade on his reputation. On 3 October 1968
he preached at St Dunstan's, Stepney, at his installation:

> Today I come among you as a newcomer . . . I have everything
> to learn . . . My experience as a bishop has been the glorious
> one of caring for part of the great African Christian com-
> munity. The diocese I have just left (and I know you will
> understand me if I say that my heart is still there) is different
> in almost every respect from the diocese to which I have now
> come – vast in area (the size of England): sparse in population
> (about the same as Stepney). Entirely rural with no sizeable
> towns: its people for the most part earning no salary at all
> but living on what they could grow . . . a typical part of the
> undeveloped world . . . I need emphasize the contrast no
> further. I only make it clear because it would . . . be foolish
> to look at the work which you and I are going to do together
> until I have had time to understand our common problems
> and opportunities.[4]

There are at least four strands in Huddleston's Stepney years
that need to be both unplaited and then re-integrated: his day-to-
day work in the diocese; his public speaking against racial and
other prejudices in Britain, making him a controversial national
figure, hated by white East Enders as well as professional anti-
Communists; confusion in his private life, culminating in his
temporary collapse in 1974; and his reciprocal personal and
pastoral friendships and relationships in and outside the Stepney
area. His engagement diaries for the whole period reveal something of the first two, but are chiefly made up of the fourth; of
the third, there is no mention.

Huddleston's early Stepney years were dogged by the prevail-
ing public controversy over race relations. His views on race
arose naturally from his African experience of apartheid, but
this took on a rather different meaning in 1969 in London.
While throughout South Africa under Verwoerd and then Vorster
apartheid was consolidating its position and the ANC leadership

was in jail or exile, race relations in Britain were in a different
sort of turmoil. The tide of immigrants from the Caribbean and
East Bengal (later Bangladesh) washed into the East End of
London and many provincial cities, bringing large numbers of
hard-working families who would happily take menial jobs in
order to climb the ladder out of poverty. As a consequence, they
were widely resented by the indigenous working classes who, for
the past decade, were supposed to have 'never had it so good'.
There were genuine fears about job losses, and anxieties over
white superiority afflicted all classes of British society. Enoch
Powell, Conservative Member of Parliament for Wolverhampton,
brought these racial tensions to a head in his infamous 'rivers of
blood' speech in Birmingham on 20 April 1968, which called for
a government programme of voluntary repatriation for Caribbean
immigrants. Despite Powell's subsequent eviction from the
shadow cabinet, the reactions to his speech were depressing and
the violence it unleashed has haunted race relations in Britain
ever since. At the time, Huddleston felt it was a good thing that
this submerged racialism had come to the surface: 'The church
has to make it clear to the Christian community that racial
prejudice is totally anti-Christian.'

Powell's speech was essentially an exhortation to black Afro-
Caribbeans to take the money and return to their country of
origin. But the sweet reasonableness with which Powell urged the
repatriation option was offset by the venom with which he dis-
posed of his enemies: 'Who are these people . . .? Those who seek
to change their fellow men and improve human nature, and who
seize with delight upon such rich material for social and moral
engineering . . . those who indulge the luxuries of pharisaism and
self-righteousness, so long as it is at the expense of others.' It is
difficult not to believe he had Huddleston in mind.[5]

Huddleston was now constantly called upon by the media to
pronounce on racial issues, which he did, refusing to comment
on other issues on which he felt less personally involved. But
Stepney itself contained many white racists who feared for their
livelihoods with the influx of Afro-Caribbeans and East Bengalis
seeking British citizenship and a chance to better themselves.

Huddleston was felt not only to have failed these poor whites but seemed actually to target them for his personal animosity. He was well aware of the beneficial effects of past influxes of refugees to the East End of London and in April 1976 he wrote the preface to a pamphlet published by the Community and Race Relations Unit of the British Council of Churches in which he urged a sense of history and a sense of global geography on those trying for a reasonable approach to immigrant communities whose well-being had become his number one priority. The booklet concentrates on two such communities – the Jews and the Bengalis of the Stepney area. He contrasted the vigour and strength of Stepney in times past – thanks to Jewish and Huguenot influxes following their persecution in mainland Europe – with the white racism fanned by Enoch Powell's speeches.

Huddleston met Powell with Canon John Collins on 10 June 1969. Many years later, Powell's obituarists rationalized his political activities at this time, finding in him and Churchill the only interesting Conservative thinkers of the post-war period. But Huddleston and Collins were appalled, and for the former, memories of fifteen years ago in Sophiatown added emotion to opposition. On 13 June Huddleston wrote an article in the *Daily Express* which provoked massive hate mail. In it he suggested a debate with Powell on television, to cover not only race relations but the relation between religion and politics on which Powell was negative and Huddleston positive. On 14 June *The Times* commented that Home Secretary James Callaghan should rid himself of the taint of racialism. On 15 June Colin Legum, the *Observer*'s leading African expert, admitted that Powell was getting a better hearing than his adversary. He thought a public debate might sort things out, and recommended, in retrospect rather bizarrely, that the Duke of Edinburgh should capture the public imagination 'as Mr Powell has done, on behalf of the immigrants'.[6] *The Times* of 18 June carried a letter from the great and good, noting that Mr Powell's emphasis on the need to appease widespread fear by ever more stringent controls on immigration and by activating generous repatriation grants, had helped to articulate and extend that fear. The *Catholic Herald* of

20 June contained an article by Norman St John Stevas, MP, asking Powell about the reality of the danger from black immigrants: 'Or is it only that they contribute to our society by driving our trains and buses, and working its hospitals and nursing homes?' But public response was mainly pro-Powell, whose slightly Hitlerian features and moustache and staring eyes demonized a man of power and original, if eccentric, thought who was articulating the fears of many of his fellow citizens. He and Huddleston wrote to each other in mutually respectful terms: Powell admired Huddleston's courageous stand on South African racial matters, Huddleston always reacted well to praise, however unlikely the source, but their published positions are separated by an unbridgeable gulf.

Huddleston's already considerable volume of hate mail grew heavier in the wake of his very public confrontation with Enoch Powell on a BBC televized 'Great Debate' on 12 November 1969. Huddleston could not shrug this off. It may have induced several serious depressions in 1969 and 1970.[7] He was deeply hurt by his rejection, as he saw it, by his own constituency – fellow high Anglicans, fellow workers in East London. His hatred of the spectre of black inferiority on a permanent basis never wavered, but it was now offset by an apparent anti-white prejudice which marked him out for continual and long-lasting hostility and vilification.

Reactions to the growing racial crisis resonated throughout the year. On 29 November Edward Heath rejected Powell's views and eased him out of the shadow cabinet. Despite this, Huddleston's personal vendetta, played up by the media, led him into serious stress, and a year later he announced he was considering bringing his involvement in public affairs to an end. 'Perhaps I overstate my comments but they come from the heart and because I want to be heard.'[8] He loved his Stepney work 'which I share with very good clergy' but life outside Stepney was difficult. 'The demands of mass communication are dangerous to me spiritually. I have little private life.'[9] But he wanted to continue to speak on human rights. The *Church Times* reported his words: 'During the past two years I have received more consistent abuse because of my well-known attitudes to race, colour and the arms issue than ever I received in my twelve years in South Africa . . . I have often thought of returning to those parts of the world – the hungry world – than to remain here if one has to accept this kind of profitless abuse.'[10]

He contemplated renouncing British citizenship over the issue of arms to South Africa. On 16 November 1970 he spoke, supporting Dennis Healey against arms trafficking with South Africa at the Cambridge Union, starting from the premise that 'What is morally wrong cannot be politically right'. He was by now battling with the new Conservative administration over its African policies. He quoted from a letter he had written to *The Times* earlier in the year[11] protesting the government's insensitivity and indifference to black African opinion, 'so that it can have no claim to *moral* authority in this country', thereby attracting the wrath of Lord Hailsham and other high-minded Conservatives. Huddleston agreed with Nyerere's analysis of British governmental motives: 'Tanzania is not saying that members of the British government are racialists. What we are saying is that the British government is proposing to arm racialism. And because we are men, not God, the states of Africa . . . have to respond to the actions of governments and nations, not to their motives.' Huddleston declared that Tory ambivalence about the racial crisis in Africa made him sick: 'I can no longer bear to live with this persistent self-delusion . . . I would be much happier if our leaders would declare openly that apartheid and all that goes with it is an acceptable, indeed a preferable, alternative to any form of democratic socialism. For that is what they really mean.' He challenged his audience and government ministers with the words of Leo Tolstoy: 'I sat on a man's back choking him and making him carry me, yet assure myself and others that I am sorry for him and wish to lighten his load by all possible means – except by getting off his back.'

Throughout this controversy Huddleston kept in touch with the struggle against apartheid. In 1969 he became a Vice-President of the Anti-Apartheid Movement, after almost ten years of association with it after the Sharpeville massacre. But

AAM was not to become his overriding priority for another
decade and, in the meantime, problems and opportunities nearer
home preoccupied him – in his public life, his Stepney pastoral
and episcopal life, and in the growth and nurture of the friendships which meant so much to him. One of these was with Jenny
Leggatt.

On 16 February 1996 she wrote: 'When I was 18 I read
Naught for Your Comfort and was so impressed with it, com-
pounded by my own wish, perhaps, to become a missionary' and
sent Huddleston a fan letter. 'He responded in an encouraging
way and asked if we might meet ... at All Saints', Margaret
Street ... Trevor striding in a black cassock and beret. He put
me at my ease and we had a good talk.' In fact he found her a
job at the Africa Bureau. 'Trevor was a constant source of
inspiration to me in my religion and also as a person. He was
wonderfully warm and friendly, hugely enthusiastic and had a
charming "no nonsense" air which was completely unstuffy and
un-priestly.' They became good friends over the years. Visiting
Soweto after Sharpeville, 'I was smuggled into townships and
mission stations. I went into tiny shacks where Trevor's photo
was an endless decoration on the poor walls. He was loved by
all Africans and by quite a lot of whites too. . . . Trevor was
unstintingly generous in helping me to understand Africa.' After
a life-threatening illness she spent six months in St George's
Hospital:

> Trevor, at the height of his fame and busy as could be, always
> found time to visit me. He would stride down the huge long
> ward and make for my bed at the end ... He wanted to help
> me and pray with me and give me communion. Once, when I
> was almost at death's door, he came and performed the
> beautiful service of anointing. . . . I recovered but largely
> because Trevor, who was certainly now my friend as well as
> my hero, encouraged me, prayed for and with me and was
> always there, visiting, writing letters, truly with me in a way
> that has to be impressive, generous and large-hearted. . . . He
> has remained, throughout all my life, my dearest and most
> loved friend. I admire his strength and energy, his warmth

and generous way of giving himself. I love him for his entirely non-judgemental attitude to everything. When I let my faith slip he never interfered or said anything; when I asked for prayers he gave them willingly; when I asked for anything he gave it, if he could. When my husband was having a serious operation Trevor insisted I stay with him because my husband was in the London chest hospital nearby. I wandered around London all day not daring to telephone in case the news was bad. Eventually I called Trevor who yelled down the phone, 'He's fine, Tim's fine. It all went as well as it could, I'm waiting for you. Jump in a taxi and come NOW.' And I did and he greeted me at the door . . . with a large gin and tonic in one hand and big arm to hug me with in the other. . . . Trevor is magic with children – they all adore him, whatever age. He puts them at their ease, he talks to them as ordinary human beings, and they respond to his warmth and genuine interest in them.

I feel that Trevor's passionate nature and his sexuality is there for all to see, has been brilliantly channelled into his work against apartheid and for Africa. He has made lots of very important friendships, many with women who are probably in love with him, but so what? If he can use his amazing charisma and sexual charm and get people to do things for his causes, all credit to him. And he knows this and has used his gifts wisely. . . .What is abidingly brilliant about this man of God is his warmth, laughter and generosity, his kindness in taking such care and time to help someone through their life, especially at difficult times . . . the way he is passionate about what he believes in – so passionate that he gets angry with others who cannot see the vision! He is a man who loves life but loves God and prayer more. If he hadn't been a priest and monk I think he would not be who he is today and all of his life . . . I love Trevor with all my heart for the human being that he is and for sharing himself with so many.[12]

I cannot say for how many other people Mrs Leggatt speaks. I know of several others – less articulate, equally whole-hearted. These friendships provided solace to Huddleston through letters or meetings, they formed a part of his daily prayer life; they included men as well as women, the old quite as much as the young, and no class or background feature reduces the world of his friendship. To ask whence this talent came is to invite speculative and tendentious answers. Did the absence of his parents in his early life foster his ability to make strong friendships outside the family from an early age? The evidence is rather the other way, in that relations with his sister, aunt and parents were also very close, while lifelong non-familial friendships only developed towards the end of his schooldays. Were they a sublimation of his strong sexuality, restrained but not nullified by his vows? Presumably yes. Did the lonely life of a monastic bishop create a powerful need for strong supporting secular friendships? Yes. But is it not enough to acknowledge and celebrate his love of friends and friendship without looking any further? Yes.

As to the rest of 1969, he preached on race at Westminster Abbey (9 February). On 8 May he went on holiday to the monastic seclusion of Caldey Island off the Welsh coast, well known for the louche Abbot Aelred and his community.[13] On 22 November he preached at the West London Synagogue. He dined with Norman St John Stevas, holidayed in Naples and Devon in August and spent December at Mirfield. He regularly met the Howicks, Mother Joanna, the Horans (where he stayed), Mischa Scorer, Donald Chesworth, Joe Rogaly, and his clergy, especially Ted Roberts. In 1970 the same names recur, together with Hugh Bishop CR, his friend Rob Towler, the Sampsons, Oliver Tambo, Hilda Bernstein, Tim Yeo (whom he married to Diane Pickard on 30 March), Father Mario Borrelli, an Italian Catholic priest with whom he stayed close friends. Borrelli's lifework was with the poor of Naples, celebrated in a book which won fame comparable to *Naught for Your Comfort*, called *Children of the Sun* by Morris West. He was studying at the London School of Economics and became Huddleston's guest at Commercial Road. Here he was joined by Tim Horan, another LSE student and son of Forbes Horan, Huddleston's friend and contemporary in Yorkshire who had been appointed Bishop of Tewkesbury at about the time

Huddleston went to Masasi. The two of them, together with Jill
Thompson, who latterly had been Huddleston's secretary in
Masasi and now Stepney, would regularly enjoy endless radical
talk with him on contemporary issues.

1970 saw the tenth anniversary of his episcopate, for which
Alan Talbot organized a field day in a local school playground
with mud huts and other evidence to celebrate the far-flung
nature of his career. Also in 1970 he visited Downing Street
several times to protest the proposed resumption by the British
government of arms sales to South Africa. On 15 March the 10th
anniversary of Sharpeville was remembered and he preached at
the shrine at Walsingham on 20 May. Each year he would holiday
in August – with his friends, the Ramptons or the Howicks. He
attended bishops' meetings at Fulham, and visited Barbados on
Community business. On 20 October he attended the bishops'
meeting at Fulham Palace and in November appeared on *The
Frost Report*. Christmas was spent as usual, first with the prisoners and warders at Pentonville prison, then with the Ramptons.
His domestic arrangements improved after the arrival in Commercial Road of Winnie and Edward Bottomley, an Anglo-
Catholic couple from Huddersfield who cooked and cleaned for
him, and big Ben, a driver employed by the Ramptons, who was
made available to drive him to and from appointments in and
out of London. Two new friends made were Ivor Smith-Cameron
of London University's Anglican chaplaincy and Robert Birley,
former headmaster of Eton and a tireless campaigner against
apartheid.

Another important friend to Huddleston during this period
was David Sheppard, eventual Bishop of Liverpool. The two men
had first met at the House of Lords in 1956. Sheppard was
impressed by Huddleston's conviction that apartheid must be
brought down and that a sports boycott would help bring this
about. He became enthusiastic about encouraging cricketers to
boycott South African tours. In the early 1960s South African
teams had always been all-white and the whole sports system,
according to Peter Hain, was riddled with apartheid.[14] Teams
were selected on the basis of race, not merit. And whites in South

Africa were sports-mad. The effectiveness of the boycott, one of whose leaders was Peter Hain, was immediate and long-lasting. In 1958 Huddleston and others formed the Campaign Against Race Discrimination in Sport and challenged South Africa's participation in the Empire and Commonwealth Games in Cardiff. In 1960, following his talks with Huddleston, David Sheppard, then an international cricketer of the greatest distinction as well as an up-and-coming cleric, refused to play in the current series. In 1965 the Anti-Apartheid Movement (AAM) organized pickets with placards outside each ground on the South African cricket tour. By 1991 one of the world's greatest sporting nations in the world had achieved pariah-status in many fields of sport. The AAM had proved it was easier to achieve success through practical protest against sports links than to reduce international investment, still less to implement military intervention against the apartheid regime. But just as Huddleston had urged a cultural boycott in the mid-1950s, so his initiative over the sports boycott a year or so later proved to have been original and farsighted as well as effective. Sheppard and Huddleston both drew strong moral support from the friendship they established during the latter's years at Stepney.

Huddleston's diaries for 1971 reveal another full and productive year. He joined the International Commission for Justice and Peace, preached at the Catholic Cathedral in Liverpool (20 January), Queen's University, Belfast (31 June), St Paul's Cathedral and Great St Mary's, Cambridge. He sat on Lord Longford's Anti-Pornography Committee, making clear his strong, though not particularly enlightened views of the effects of pornographic images on impressionable young minds. On 3 May 1971 he had an appointment with a persistent right-wing critic of his, Dennis Delderfield. There is no evidence as to what transpired, but three years later a personal crisis erupted in which Delderfield may have played a part.[15] He holidayed in Scotland, visited Delhi and the CR house in Barbados, went to the opera at Covent Garden five times, befriended the wives of John Robinson (former Bishop of Woolwich and author of the controversial work of radical theology, *Honest to God*) and Geoffrey Fisher, who gave him Fisher's pectoral cross and some much-needed pullovers. In December he visited Tanzania where he resumed his friendship with Julius Nyerere.

Towards the end of 1971 he was to give vent to his frustration with the continuing stream of hate mail in a sermon preached at Great St Mary's, Cambridge on 21 November: 'I would be so thankful . . . not to be expected to preach about [apartheid, the Third World, pornography] subjects which form the basis of almost all the public letters I receive.' On the text 'Why does this generation ask for a sign?' he found an answer in the Saint Mark's account of the feeding of the five thousand, where: 'a vast crowd of people who had come out of the villages to hear Him, had found themselves on the hillside without food and yet they all ate to their hearts' content, and seven baskets were left over'. Huddleston identified his own predicament with that of the 'young Nazarene' who, according to Saint Mark, 'sighed deeply to himself'.

. . . It was a sign of anger with a generation too obstinate, too self-concerned, too parochial to recognize the sources and implications of the wonders done in it. And here you see he touches at the very heart and core of the mystery of faith. 'I tell you this, no sign shall be given to this generation'.

> Why? Because first and foremost everything becomes false as soon as a sign is demanded, and 2) because it is not for clever and sophisticated man to decide on his own standard whether God has acted or not. And 3) because God's signs are either freely given and summon man to strengthen faith, to fan a flickering flame of love and fire, or they are not signs at all. They cannot be demanded as proof because the signs demanded by man are the signs which always, inevitably, inescapably destroy the proof they seek to find. To one coming back from Africa there appears here to be a generation bored with the trivialities of affluence, a generation disgusted by the deviance of party-political attitudes . . . we wear mankind as our skin and yet we are prepared to tear one another apart on behalf of this nationalism or that, of this idea of race or that.

He offered his congregation some glimpse of a vision which 'was central to Holy Scripture, to the Catholic tradition and to any acceptable Christian proclamation of the Gospel in our day.' We belong to one world, we should recognize our interdependence and fight our attitudes to race and wealth: 'it is God's world ... He is involved in every single movement and change and subtlety. It is one world ... and the Church is called to be the sign and sacrament and focus of that Unity. This is far deeper than any institutional or structural unity that we can imagine. And the Church is called to be the witness of that transcendent, all-holy, all-knowing, all-loving almighty God.'

He ended by quoting an unnamed French priest: 'Now is the hour of the garden of the night, the hour of silent offering; therefore the hour of hope; God alone. Faceless, unknown, unfelt, yet undeniable God.'

He had used the same text as the basis of a sermon he preached at Mirfield's Commemoration Day earlier that year. 'Why does this generation ask for a sign? I tell you this: no sign shall be given to this generation. With that He left them [the disciples].' A sense of his despair at the Church is here matched with a deeper perception: Jesus as a critic of existing institutions. 'Why does this generation ask for a sign? They are seeking security rather than faith. Why does the Church ask for a sign? Success, increased church attendance ... 'The Sign,' Huddleston declared, 'is the Lord Jesus Himself, the Living Lord who called Mary Magdalene "Mary"; who called Thomas, "Touch me"; who called Simon Peter: "Do you love me?" '[16]

This memorable insight was echoed in his Easter sermon preached at St Mark's, Victoria Park about race and 'the Power which finds definite expression *where we are*'. 'From time to time,' he told his congregation, 'from within the institutional Church and from outside it, men are raised by God whose sole purpose appears to be to demonstrate the meaning of power as a spiritual reality.' He pointed to Martin Luther King Jr assassinated on that day three years earlier. 'To accept a situation and to do nothing about it – as if God's will were only to be found in what is *static*: this is profoundly un-Christian.'[17]

The beginning of 1972 was marked by a number of important visitors to Commercial Road: Desmond Tutu, Jenny Leggatt, David Sheppard, several members of CR, Terence Ranger, Jonathan Dimbleby – and a young unknown called Peter Mandelson, then a very bright schoolboy from Hendon County Grammar School, close to where Huddleston had spent his own formative years. Mandelson wrote to him 'and to anyone else I could think of' to raise funds to get him to Africa to undertake field study in the changing tribal and social *mores* of Rwandan and Tanzanian Africans before taking up his place at St Catherine's College, Oxford. He required the costs of travel, limited expenses and pocket money. He had virtually given up all hope of financing his year off when he received a call from Huddleston, whom he had met once before (he was one of the many schoolboy fans of *Naught for Your Comfort*). 'I've got some good news for you,' he was told: Huddleston had persuaded a diocese in Northern Tanzania to employ him and had located sufficient funds to cover what was needed. He spent a useful and interesting year in East Africa, in three different locations, writing monthly letters to Huddleston reporting his findings and state of mind, on political as well as sociological matters. In his last posting, while sorting diocesan files, he came across a file with his own name on it. This, he discovered, contained Huddleston's letters arranging his trip and also revealing that Huddleston himself was funding him, on condition that the identity of his benefactor remained secret. He never told Huddleston he knew, though he visited him regularly during the Stepney years. Subsequently the young man became (in 1997) the most famous Minister Without Portfolio in modern British history.[18]

1973 and early 1974 reveal the same pattern of public, pastoral and personal life. In early October 1973, in his anti-porn mode, he attended a Foyle's literary lunch for Malcolm Muggeridge and in late November he spoke to the International Defence and Aid Fund for Southern Africa conference on 'Apartheid Legislation with particular reference to political trials'. It was a period when the Tambo family relied heavily on him, particularly after Adelaide Tambo suffered a severe accident, breaking her femur in three places jumping from a first-floor window when a fire developed in the family kitchen in their house in Alexandra Park Road, Finsbury Park. Oliver wrote on 19 September: 'I need hardly say how very much Adelaide and the rest of us need your prayers. The doctors describe her condition as "very nasty" and it might be up to six months before she could leave hospital . . . I would love to call on you sometime when your "whirl-wind world" is moving at less than its normal speed – Lots of love, Father: Oliver.'[19]

This was the year in which Tambo said, thinking no doubt of his own country: 'Nationalism hastens the course of liberation.' Huddleston had the traditional socialist view of what he called patriotism, which is perhaps near to revolutionary nationalism, but a great personal admiration for Nyerere and his response to the latter's *realpolitik* – possibly combined with his depression over the hate mail he had received following Enoch Powell's speech – had strongly impelled Huddleston to seek Tanzanian citizenship and cast away his British and South African affiliations. Nyerere gently dissuaded him: 'Even if Tanzania were a racial paradise, and Britain were another South Africa, I would be saying the same thing to you: stay where you are and continue the fight.'[20]

To widen his interest he had become a trustee of the Runnymede Trust, set up by the Ramptons, while within his pastoral concerns, clergy friends and their families proved an unmixed blessing to him, as he to them. At a less conventional level, young radicals like Christopher Searle and Peter Mandelson sought him out. Companionable holidays with the Wyndhams, the Howicks, the Ramptons and the Camerons enabled him to return cheerfully, after making his retreat, to a more austere life. Preaching round the country continued. The Scarborough *Mercury* reported his visit there to address the Scarborough Committee of Feed the Minds on 18 October 1973:

Feed the Minds is not just a slogan, it is a reality, a fact . . . Many people had an image of Africa from the mass media that presented only the upheavals, violence, instability and immaturity, but in a land where some people earned £30 per head per year, there were also developments ... It was this kind of poverty that could give the Western world an understanding of life that has been overlaid and destroyed. Africa had limitless contributions to make. The real deprived countries are those too worried about economic difficulties, and when they wake up it might be too late ... The glory of Africa is that it still sustains and holds onto the meaning of community, and allied to this is the quality of self-reliance. Africa is the continent of infinite riches, the continent awakening like a great giant, the continent able to give back to the world that is dying for lack of it, a spiritual truth. The Christian church is there in every small village, at the grass roots.[21]

He worked hard with Donald Chesworth, Peter Watkins, Mary Dines, Michael Barnes and Monsignor Bruce Kent for 'War on Want'.[22] He saw Oliver Tambo, back in England from his endless attendance on African leaders in the cause of the ANC. With Ruth First he addressed a conference on 'South Africa – the Imprisoned Society' at London University in December 1973, briefed by Hugh Lewin of IDAF.[23] He worked to establish adventure playgrounds for East End children, and in a project with Donald Chesworth proposed the use of the Thames foreshore near Stepney to provide the kind of amenities he had sought and found for his Masasi children some years earlier at Lindi.

Huddleston started 1974 with an all-night vigil with the Sisters at Aylesford and the showing of a television profile by Melvyn Bragg on BBC 2. Press speculation that he was being groomed as the next Archbishop of Canterbury attracted the criticism from colleagues that he was spreading his talents too widely. On 12 January a distinguished Anglo-Catholic academic, Valerie Pitt (who thought Donald Coggan, then Archbishop of York, 'a humbug') wrote to warn Huddleston against 'frittering away ... your moral authority from your witness in South Africa and your media charisma which carries conviction even when you're talking nonsense.' It was a powerful warning letter. But for

Huddleston a more immediate problem was a severe outbreak of laryngitis. This may have been linked to his diabetes, as it had occurred before at moments of crisis and was to recur several times later on. He was diagnosed diabetic in the early 1950s when he developed a bout of laryngitis that he could not shake off. He explained it to a journalist some years later: 'I felt generally run down so a doctor friend gave me a full check-up. Suddenly I was on insulin and I've been on it ever since.' On 10 April 1974 Huddleston's secretary confirmed that 'he was recuperating after a bad attack of laryngitis.' His get-well mail swelled.[24] The *Guardian* reported that 'the reformers propose as Mr Harold Wilson's first choice [as the next Archbishop of Canterbury] Dr Trevor Huddleston . . . one of the most uncompromising, most militant and most magnetic of men in a mitre.'[25] But by 22 April Victor Chapples in the *Sun* was able to announce that Huddleston, 'one of the most popular figures in the Church of England, is no longer being considered as a successor to the Archbishop of Canterbury because of his health. He was suffering from stress and strain with a virus infection . . . His doctors have told him to take a complete rest and he is staying with friends in the country . . . Dr Huddleston is best known for his stand against apartheid. As a priest in Johannesburg he challenged the South African government's policy. As a result he was treated by black Africans as an equal but by the government as a trouble-maker.'[26]

Laryngitis notwithstanding, the breakdown Huddleston suffered in early 1974 appears to have been as much psychological as physiological. It was prompted by two letters of complaint about the same incident: both were from the mother of two schoolboys who used to play regularly upstairs at 400 Commercial Road. One letter went to Huddleston, the other to the police. What exactly was the substance of the complaint is not known. That it involved sex is certain. The press got to know about it and Huddleston rang close friends who lived near Richmond in a state bordering on hysterical collapse. In the presence of a solicitor the police interviewed him for half-an-hour in his office. When the police left they indicated that the matter – whatever it was – would remain on the files. Much folklore has accreted round the episode, much hearsay and innuendo. Huddleston's love of small and beautiful boys had never been a matter he had kept to himself, and indeed it was to continue undiminished and unashamed well into old age. But it seems undeniable that press interest in the potential prosecution of a leading cleric and public figure was what precipitated Huddleston's collapse.

For several months after the breakdown in early March, Huddleston recovered at a friend's holiday house in Scotland. He had been seen by a psychiatrist who said that if Huddleston were admitted to a psychiatric institution (which would be the normal practice) he would never be the same again: but if, during a period of withdrawal and rest, he could rediscover himself all might still be as before. His condition was certainly serious enough for psychiatric intervention. He was in a state of collapse: scarcely able to speak, eat or sleep or do the simplest chores. He went for long daily walks in Scotland, accompanied by his hostess. He spoke on the telephone every evening to the wonderfully supportive Bishop of London, Gerald Ellison. His appointments diary for 1974 shows blanks and crossings out in March, April and May, as well as the whole of August blanked out (which would have been normal practice). But the support of close friends and colleagues seemed to have worked its magic and by mid-September he was back at work, busy and engaged as ever. It was a remarkable recovery by any standards, with Commercial Road soon full of children, and Huddleston arranging trips to the pantomime for them at Christmas. And although his breakdown might have put paid to any further speculation about his future as Archbishop of Canterbury, there was no lasting damage done to his reputation: only four years later he was deemed capable of tackling another major episcopal job.

The 1975 diary was as full as ever, further proof of the speed and extent of his recovery. There were outings with boys, visits to friends old and new, hearing confessions, taking part in consecrations, synods, episcopal and ruridecanal meetings; dinners with the great and the good of the left: Tom Driberg, Nadir Dinshaw; opera at Covent Garden; Buckingham Palace on 26 June, the CR festival at St Katharine's on 7 June, preaching at St

Paul's on 8 June; concerts at the Festival Hall; visits from Peter Mandelson, Fr Aelred Stubbs CR, Donald Chesworth, Naomi Mitchison; parish visitations, dedications, a farewell to his great friend Canon John Collins on his retirement; an American visit in August, a three-week Canadian trip in October; the state visit of Julius Nyerere (including a state banquet on 18 November and a private audience on 22 November); visits to doctors, triple doses of cold cure . . .

In 1976 the Soweto massacres brought the anti-apartheid struggle back into the forefront of Huddleston's life. Nearly 500 young blacks were killed in the troubles which lasted from June 1976 till January 1977. Historians of apartheid recognize in the atrocities of Sharpeville in 1960, only four years after Huddleston's departure, and Soweto in 1976, half a generation later, two crucial events in South African postwar history, but are divided as to their long-term effect. One school asserts that despite their traumatic impact at the time they were both turning points where South Africa did not turn; the other and more convincing analysis shows how the first is based on an incomplete and inadequate understanding of events on the ground, relying too heavily on secondary sources (particular the media) and thereby restricting the assessment of the complex nature of internal African resistance to what is reported, such as the sporadic outbreaks of collective protest or the apparent status at that time of the main opposition group, the ANC. In *After Soweto: An Unfinished Journey*, John Brewer restores much of the complexity while demonstrating just how significant Soweto was for both whites and blacks in South Africa. He concludes that the uprising 'helped to initiate liberalisations which have implications far beyond those which the government intended,' while simultaneously changing African protest and resistance 'in such a way to strengthen it'.[27]

After Sharpeville in 1960, Huddleston was stripped of the South African citizenship he had obtained in 1952. During his Masasi years and for much of his time in Stepney, the ANC leadership was exiled or imprisoned, the movement banned, its supporters harassed, while the continuing effect of apartheid legislation – especially in education and social engineering – produced a whole new generation lacking self-assurance, self-awareness, adequate education or work opportunities, without even the will to strive for racial equality. At the same time, there had grown up a small but growing cadre of applicants for military and guerrilla training in the Eastern bloc who were prepared to fight in the armed struggle when the time came. The same pressures and divisions accelerated after Soweto, in the final years of Huddleston's Stepney ministry and during his time in Mauritius, and were firmly entrenched on the international agenda by the time he assumed the presidency of the Anti-Apartheid Movement in 1981. Pretoria had gone some way towards accommodating non-white demands, and Soweto, according to this interpretation of recent South African history, influenced policy towards the reformation of apartheid, and the African response to it.[28] In 1982 the government founded the Centre for Black Advancement and created the new Ministry of Constitutional Development. But the years after Soweto were fraught with new dangers for those Huddleston sought to help from Commercial Road. A difference in degree between the incapacitated majority and the militant minority became a difference in kind in which militancy grew out of despair and so became inevitable. The armed struggle was the only way to beat apartheid. After Soweto, passive resistance and occasional mass action were transformed into a war of independence 'fought with bombs and bullets . . . industrial strikes, poetry, religion, political organisation, examination boycotts, classroom disruption, newspaper copy, street riots, the theatre and mobilisation in the factories . . . detailed party manifestoes, pavement daubings, patient organisation, and spontaneous collective action, calculated negotiations and strategic boycotts, stones, bricks and pens.'[29]

None of the South African governments concessions impressed the international community. Brewer quotes David Watt's comment in *The Times*: 'Things are changing, yes, but the more they change the more they stay the same. And the more they stay the same the more they go backwards.'[30] Brewer distinguishes 'three complicating factors in the equation: the interests of the right wing in South Africa which seeks to reserve a major power bloc for whites; the demand of racial opposition forces against which attempts to satisfy these interests must be set; and lastly the involvement of external forces, like the world powers, who can apply international economic and diplomatic pressures.'[31]

In 1976 Huddleston knew that while apartheid might eventually crumble at the periphery, at the centre it was alive and kicking. In the same year he preached against it in the aftermath of Soweto, but he was losing the sort of direct contact with events on the ground which would enable him to play his full part in the evolving anti-apartheid struggle. And meanwhile he had a busy life to lead, with two more years in Stepney before a chance encounter took him to the Indian Ocean. By early 1977 he had decided to leave his Stepney job on his 65th birthday – 15 June 1978. Bishop Ellison replied to his request on 8 February 1977: 'I am sure you will appreciate with what deep regret the news will be received . . . in the Stepney area to which you have made such a profound contribution . . . For the last three-and-a-half years you have been a constant stay and support to me, and your wisdom and loyalty have been of immense help to me.' Though different in temperament the two remained close friends until Ellison's death. They had come through testing times together. Huddleston's diary remained full – the month of November 1977 listing forty-eight meetings, services, preaching and lecturing engagements, six confirmations, work to promote local East End ministries, and attendance at the Evangelicals' conference at the retreat centre at Scargill in Yorkshire. In South Africa, political protest had exploded once more in August, after Steve Biko, leader of the influential Black Conciousness Movement, was beaten to death by his police interrogators. On Christmas Day the prisoners at Pentonville received their annual Christmas visitor – Bishop Huddleston.[32] The early months of 1978 are not recorded, but by 3 April Huddleston was on the other side of the world.

So a decade of London church life – more like Swindon than Sophiatown, Mirfield or Masasi – left its mark not only on him but also on many East End Christian worshipping congregations of many levels of churchmanship. His friends and colleagues from his Stepney years may feel scant justice has been done to his considerable achievements there: his organizational work with Archdeacon George Timms, his initiatives for post-ordination training, the setting up of team ministries and the Bethnal Green Ministry Project with his close friend Ted Roberts. Within the Church he was a tireless visitor to sick clergy, a relentless campaigner in committees whenever he felt the Stepney parishes were overlooked, while outside the church his work with MPs like Harry Greenway (Conservative member for Ealing North) will always be remembered. He supported Greenway through a period of difficulty and taught him how to speak effectively in public, while steadfastly cherishing his friendship with the whole family.

All of these things demonstrate his creative response to what he found at Stepney but underlying his wide-ranging pastoral, political and personal activities was his unceasing concern for the generation of black South African school-leavers of the 1960s, restricted by the Bantu Education Act to second-rate education for servitude. This concern erupted from time to time – the Soweto uprising; Desmond Tutu's election as the first black bishop of Johannesburg – but it was never far from his mind or heart. A return to South Africa was never an option while apartheid continued, but new experiences in the multi-racial societies of the Indian Ocean would bring it a step nearer.

Once again it was an overseas posting that challenged him to make yet another new beginning, this time to the see of Mauritius, together with the archiepiscopal oversight of the Malagasy Republic and the Seychelles. He left with the prayers and good wishes of hundreds of East Enders, one of whom, Prebendary John Pearce wrote: 'As you go to Africa, be sure that you go supported by the prayers of your people in East London. We are all deeply thankful for your love and leadership and pastoral ministry to us all – in fact for being a reality. I have *never* heard *anyone* in East London do other than thank God for you. We feel a deep love for you and a deep trust. Remember that you are remembered daily in prayer by hundreds and hundreds here at home.'[33]

How did he get the job? Canon James has seen Archbishop French's file on the subject during his stay in Mauritius. Huddleston's predecessor there died on 16 February 1977; this was followed by an indecisive election, to be followed by Huddleston's appearance, the first of three nominations, on 8 September. He must have hesitated about allowing his name to go forward but on 25 October he was duly elected.[34] This is clearly only the bare bones of an interesting ecclesiastical stitch-up.

CHAPTER SEVEN

MAURITIUS

1978–1983

Huddleston left Britain for the third time in his life in 1978, when he had almost reached retirement age. Earlier departures from England were both to Africa – in 1943 to wartime Cape Town and in 1960 to Dar es Salaam, capital of the Swahili-speaking, poverty-stricken, not-yet-independent state of Tanganyika. 1978 gave a very different picture. Huddleston's remarkable ability to rise above his depressions and gloom over much of his lifework has already been noted and deserves recapitulation. He took on the novice guardianship at Mirfield in 1956 with every intention of doing a good job: he was not to know that his personal charisma would actually militate against him: too many unsuitable novices, attracted by his presence at Mirfield, tested their vocations to the dismay of many in CR, while his constant absences to visit and speak to school and other audiences all over Britain about South Africa interrupted the relationship he had to establish with the postulants. He was still under obedience as a member of CR, but the only acceptable career move would be to become a prelate brother, suspend his oaths and enter the Anglican episcopate. But he was too famous, too controversial, too much 'a bit of a nuisance' (as he himself put it to his brethren), to expect much of a welcome from those designated to appoint bishops to senior Sees in the Church of England. But a new job with new challenges had to be and was found. Despite the tragicomedy of his arrival and early pre-consecration time in East Africa he was to achieve much for the indigenous clergy, schools, hospitals and people of that remote area. He learnt to preach and write, though not to think, in Swahili. He tactfully continued the strategic withdrawal of the missionary church from a significant part of the African continent, preparing local Christians for a new world in which independence, self-sufficiency and the community spirit replaced the Anglican attitudes favoured by missionary societies in Britain. He succeeded, by a mixture of diplomacy and forceful action, in transferring complete responsibility for education and schools in South East Tanzania to the government, at both local and national levels; identified his own successor, Hilary Chisonga (an African); and withdrew. Few had any inkling (apart from noting his irrational bouts of anger, which were quickly forgotten) of the deep periodic depressions which left him totally 'in the dark', their only evidence in his logbooks. To most colleagues and friends he remained an active, forthright and devout leader and bishop for the area's 50,000 Christians, who were taken aback at his determination to leave them. Some thought his management style arbitrary and autocratic, but it is difficult to see how otherwise he could achieve the best in whatever pastoral or administrative situation he was confronted with; and other missionary bishops were equally eccentric in their styles and much less effective. By 1967, his depression had struck more deeply; he was convinced that he had nothing more useful to contribute, and indeed remained doubtful whether his coming had achieved anything to spread the good news of the Christian gospel in action in Masasi. His longing for change was more a reflection of his despair at the results of his work than any clear picture of what he would like his next job to be. Stepney came along out of the blue. So, a decade later and after damaging attacks on his integrity had left him 'not a happy man' in Alan Paton's words[1], did the see of Mauritius, and the wider seas of the Indian Ocean, sailed so vigorously by his father seventy years earlier.

On 3 April 1978 Huddleston arrived in Mauritius at Plaisance airport, proceeding the next day to Bishop's House, Phoenix ('no servants! no nothing!') Enthronement at St James's Cathedral followed on 9 April, and his first bishop's meeting took place on 15 April; the next day saw his election as Archbishop of the Indian Ocean, a high and lonely Anglican office which he seems to have relished. His predecessor had been a Mauritian, and some thought that Huddleston's appointment at such a politically sensitive time inappropriate – he may have thought so himself – but his opposition to racism and love of African socialism worked in his favour. He was soon in a fresh ecclesiastical and social round of a very different kind from those he had previously experienced in the townships, Tanzania and East London. In Mauritius there was a small expatriate colony to be bonded, local schools and churches to superintend, two new languages to learn – French and Creole, because English was rarely spoken or understood except by the expatriates. In Madagascar, part of the Province of the Indian Ocean, a third language, Malagasy, was required; but he was too old to make much progress and didn't get far with his Creole lessons. Heroically he buckled down to learning French, as seventeen years earlier he had learnt Swahili; but none of these activities prevented the regime at Bishop's House, keeping scrupulously the discipline of daily mass and the Offices, either at one of the churches or the house chapel.

In June he made his first visit to the island of Madagascar where most of the Christians of the Indian Ocean lived. His impact on them was muted by the politeness with which they agreed with everything and understood almost nothing of this gaunt and famous old Englishman suddenly in their midst. A curfew was still in force following violent civil disturbances. He and the bishop of Antananarivo, Ephraim, drove through that diocese in the dark, 'very steep hills like Kampala and Assisi, and the Cathedral and Bishop's House are on the top of one of them.'[2] He preached on 4 June in a mass lasting two-and-a-quarter hours. The next day he inspected the local theological college, St Paul's, Ambatoharanana, designed by Butterfield – 'Six students, Fr Benzies, and two priests . . . All lecture in Malagasy. Very few books because students don't use French. Magnificent lunch with vino etc.' There followed a visit to Diego where he was met by a delegation and taken to 'a *great* crowd in small pro-cathedral. Party afterwards at Eveche – African dancing (crocodile) and lots of young people. The next day he set off for Ambilobe with Fr Gabriel and Mr Simon, 'full of kindness and

humour'[3]. They travelled through beautiful country which
reminded Huddleston of Masasi. A large lunch was followed by
the confirmation of seventeen candidates: 'very strong, vigorous
singing'. A bad night followed: 'some tummy trouble – so, lighter
suppers for me! No sleep – baby crying all night at intervals and
v. hard bed!' Visits followed to two local agricultural projects, a
shopping trip in the market at Tananarive followed by several
church meetings including 'a very strange discussion about the
use of the chalice and a specific request for another method of
Holy Communion for reasons of health and because the intellec-
tuals were offended'. On 11 June, after another sleepless night, a
two-and-three-quarter hour mass took place with three psalms,
eight hymns, two anthems and a very full cathedral. 'Many young
people.' After an excellent lunch he was driven sixty kilometres
to a seaside spot where the first Christian missionary to Madagascar had landed. A small building commemorated the event –
'looks very dilapidated already with broken doors and windows.
Heavy rain at times . . . visited very interesting old fort with
George III cannon.'

He returned to Mauritius on 13 June, celebrated his sixty-fifth
birthday two days later, and had daily meetings from then on.
His house was not as congenially placed as in Masasi or Stepney,
but it was a fine example of colonial architecture, with a great
verandah and plenty of large rooms, so that when Bishop George
Briggs[4] came to stay in 1981 they were able to co-exist harmoni-
ously for eighteen months. Inevitably, children started to come
and were given Coca-Cola and biscuits and went swimming with
him and whoever else was staying. A new life developed, similar
but not identical to his previous ones, for despite the regular stream
of visitors, Huddleston was often lonely at Bishop's House.

On 1 July 1978 the Mothers' Union, a body for whom he had
developed considerable respect since his Sophiatown days, held a
mass meeting, followed by a confirmation and reception at
Bishop's House. He visited the US embassy on 4 July for Thanksgiving and from 10 July to 16 August he attended his second
Lambeth Conference at Canterbury. He was back in Phoenix for
a patronal festival at St Louis' Cathedral on 25 August, preaching

at St James's Cathedral and conducting another confirmation on 27 August. The American navy visited the island later in the month and he enjoyed a welcoming reception at the embassy. A talk on 'racial conflict' on 1 September was followed by a third confirmation; a meeting of the Bishop's Bazaar committee (an annual fundraising event, efficiently organized and of long standing); lunch on 10 September at the Divine Life Society Ashram; farewell parties; the Annual General Meeting of the Mauritius Society of Social Service on 14 September; daily meetings with government ministers and organizations, the Church Commissioners, and the Committee for Indian flood relief. On 1 October he delivered his first sermon in French and the next day attended a Requiem for Pope John Paul I at St Louis' Cathedral. Two days later, he and other clerics sat down to agree a reduction of the number of public holidays from well over twenty to twelve. The intention was twofold: to boost economic productivity and to be fair to the different faiths and their feasts. Local Christians agreed that they could manage with only one – Christmas – but Easter Monday still continued to be observed.

Summer was approaching: 'Already it's beginning to warm up, though mornings and evenings are still beautifully fresh and cool. It's beautiful and noisy with birdsong. I usually have my breakfast on the verandah and look across a great circular sweep of lawn with a tall palm tree on one side, a clump of banana on the other and a lovely mixture of tropical and ordinary green foliage in the middle, This garden is a great delight, but never more so than when there are children running about in it.'[5] Quite close to him in Phoenix were two schools, 'institutions pre-scolaires', one with a percentage of handicapped pupils. The Cathedral authorities in Phoenix had been planning to hand over a large hall to enable the school to cope with these children, and another church not far away in Beau Bassin was working on a similar plan: 'It makes all the difference . . . to have twenty little creatures in red pinafores chasing each other and popping balloons as they go.'

He was gradually getting to know the fourteen parishes, and celebrated in French, in one or other of the local churches most weekdays. He could now also preach in French but 'very badly and often, I'm sure, very ungrammatically: but unless I make a start I know I shall never do any better at all. How wonderful it would be if, like Pope John Paul II, I could speak five languages (there are at least that number in Mauritius) and switch from one to another at will.' He wrote often of the diminishments of age, especially memory loss.

As at Masasi, fund-raising was a priority: the Diocese had been unique in the Anglican Communion in receiving a forty per cent government subvention, about to be withdrawn, so that an extra £12,000 a year had to be found from the generosity of the 7,000 Christians of the island, half of whom were teenagers and only recently confirmed. 'Religion,' he concluded his 1978 report, 'is a major and all-pervasive influence, and respect for one another's faith and culture is the only basis on which the island can hope to prosper and be at peace.'[6] That respect, learned among the Muslims of Masasi and the Hindus of Stepney, became the dominant theme of the next eight years of his life. Pauline Webb, Chairman of the BBC Community & Race Relations Unit in her essay, 'The New Ecumenism', describes its developments and fulfilment in action.[7] She picks out one particularly memorable example: 'Every year the whole community in Mauritius, whatever their faiths, shared one common pilgrimage . . . to honour the tomb and memory of a folk-hero who had once been a village priest, Père Laval. He had come to Mauritius from France just after the Napoleonic Wars . . . and made his home among the indentured Indian labourers working in the sugar fields and there lived a life of such transparent saintliness that the love of God shone through him onto everyone he met.' On 19 May 1979 a mass for his Beatification was held on a high open-air site overlooking the town of Port Louis, attended by over 150,000 people – many of them Muslim, Hindus and Buddhists whom the bishop invited to take part in the liturgy. Huddleston read the Old Testament lesson. Presiding at the Mass was Cardinal Bernardin Gantin, Chairman of the Pontifical Commission for Justice and Peace, a French-speaking African from Benin who had several friendly meetings with Huddleston during his stay. 'Every language and cultural group took part musically, and, before the crowd dispersed, each of the non-Christian faiths, represented by their leaders, contributed some kind of public prayer ... The whole marvellous eucharist was symbolised for me at the kiss of peace when a dozen or so young children brought baskets full of white pigeons and released them over the crowd. As they wheeled and circled above us the setting sun caught them ... "their feathers like gold". So the day ended, and as far as I could see from my seat on the high platform near the altar, the crowd filled the whole curve of the hills, sometimes with music, sometimes with stillness, but always with real worship and devotion.'[8]

He loved Madagascar and visited there again in June and July, in cold, grey weather. His main purpose was to decide the future of the theological college at Ambatoharanana. Should its functions be transferred elsewhere and its buildings used for the school? The struggling Christian churches of the fragile democracy of the island were hardly central to Huddleston's main mission in life and his lack of Malagasy meant that communication and decisive action were limited. He was glad to return from the visitation to a blazing wood fire and excellent meal with the daughter of one of the priests. The next day he and his party visited the Roman Catholic Seminary: 'vast place, magnificent library ... whisky at 10.30 am! But still exceedingly cold and windy.' He was impressed to find a very large university with many facilities open to young students and, at the heart of it, an excellent 'chaplaincy centre' which is served by an ecumenical team. He later wrote: 'The queen of England may have had Calais written on her heart, MADAGASCAR is inscribed on mine.'[9]

After Madagascar came a visit to the Seychelles to consecrate the first *seychellois* bishop, Archdeacon French Chang-Him, in St Paul's Cathedral, Victoria. 'And a great occasion it truly was. The cathedral, now enlarged by a hundred seats, was packed, and an overflow in the hall was able to watch the service on closed-circuit television. In the end the Bishop of Antsiranana was sick and unable to come, but Bishop George Briggs (first bishop of the Seychelles) was flown out from England at the government's expense so we had the necessary three, plus one, consecrating bishops. And in the sanctuary was the Roman Catholic bishop and the Papal Nuncio who happened to be visiting the island . . . I was the chief celebrant.' He stayed a week and used the opportunity for meetings of the Provincial Standing Committee, making progress on a customised experimental liturgy and with the production of a provincial journal, in French, Malagasy and English. 'The most important thing was to meet each other and share our problems . . . The Anglican Communion is precariously but truly represented here and it is my job to make it a more living, related and caring part of the Christian family. Distance, language and culture all have to be transformed from barriers to bridges of communication.'[10]

Back in Mauritius he started what becames known as the 'Phoenix Parties' to develop friendly relations with his 'Pelagian' neighbours (mostly non-churchgoing expatriates). On the last Tuesday of each month there was a buffet supper, a subject, a speaker and a question-and-answer session. Speakers in the first two years included Alan Paton and Naomi Mitchison. On 9 September he organized a service of rededication and renewal for the whole diocese. It was held in the Cathedral and attended by over 800 people. The new experimental liturgy was used, assisted by a mass choir of the Youth Fellowship. Less than a fortnight later he flew to England, to brief the Friends of Mauritius in Hampstead Parish Church, to visit the Community and College of the Resurrection at Mirfield and to spend an afternoon in the Huddleston Centre for Handicapped Children in Hackney, which he had helped to establish while at Stepney. The last full week of his visit was spent at the Primates' Meeting at Ely where he was impressed by Archbishop Gregory Hla Gyaw of Burma, the first bishop allowed to leave his country for seventeen years.

A fortnight after his return and three days before Christmas, Cyclone Claudette hit Mauritius: all churches were closed, water and electricity supplies were cut off and many trees were blown down. Just after Christmas he developed serious eye problems and the local ophthalmologist diagnosed a retinal haemorrhage. He knew that laser-beam treatment was the only hope, so flew to London on the next available plane and saw his Harley Street surgeon within two hours of arrival. He had to stay for a month of complete rest, but by early March 1980 was back for three weeks in Mauritius, returning to England for the enthronement of Robert Runcie as Archbishop of Canterbury on 25 March.

Despite these fatiguing journeys and a demanding lifestyle his stamina seemed endless and on his return to Mauritius he immediately plunged himself back into local activities. The theological college was flourishing, with thirteen ordinands, four from Rodrigues – as many as the diocese could pay for. The staff was ecumenical and he himself gave a course of lectures on spirituality. He also benefited from a visit by John Martin of the Anglican Communion's central office and an expert in how to use the mass media. His Phoenix parties were addressed by Jack Jones on trades' unionism and by Muslim and Hindu laymen, and the college laid on a three-month course to teach Sunday school teachers ('in such a religious country as this, whether Christian, Hindu, Muslim or Buddhist – developing the expertise of such teachers proved useful in developing the cultural life of the island').[11] He asked the readers of his newsletter to help in his failed attempts to induce the Foreign Office in London to re-instate university grants to foreign students as this virtually excluded Mauritians from attending British universities or medical schools, even though English was the medium of education. And he rediscovered the delights of sea bathing: 'six of my young neighbours (four Muslims and two Seventh Day Adventists) drop in very often to play "Caromme" (a kind of snooker played with draughts) on my verandah and football in my garden . . . As Low Sunday was a glorious sunny day, after two morning services, I took them off for a swim and found about 1,000 other people had had the same idea. But there was room for all of us and to spare. Room too for a colossal meal, washed down with Coca Cola at the beach cafeteria. I find I am emotionally deprived if I don't have children somewhere around.' In fact many children came and played in his house and garden. At least one of them, Gilles, he adopted, cared for and later saw through school and university. Gilles would be found sitting on his knee at the Phoenix parties with his brother Nino close by. From 9–11 May

1980 Huddleston also presided at 'the most worthwhile confer-ence I have attended in my two years here' of the Mothers' Union at 'Le Foyer de l'Unité', Souillac, attended by ninety delegates.

'I am . . . now in my *third* year as Bishop and I can already feel "Time's winged chariot hurrying near" – there's still an awful lot to be done.'[12] Visits from Donald Chesworth, his goddaughter Dr Susanna Everitt and Alan Paton and his wife punctuated his round of pastoral care. Paton later wrote that Huddleston didn't like Mauritius: 'I don't think there is any doubt that his heart is still in Sophiatown.'[13] His workload increased in this period because his archdeacon was away and Huddleston had to depu-tise at St Thomas's, Beau Bassin, becoming directly involved in pastoral work: sick communions to the old and ill, and con-fessions. He visited the Seychelles in July and Madagascar in September. At a confirmation for seventy children and adults followed by a sung eucharist in a packed church 'the singing lifted the roof and everything that *could* be sung *was* sung'.[14] He loved the service 'with its enthusiasm and wholeheartedness: and it's an encouragement too for a minority church like ours to find itself growing and to see how many young people are part of the family'. Afterwards he sat in the shade of a great tree and listened to a reception committee's words of welcome: 'it reminded me so much of many similar visits in Masasi – a glorious mixture of courtesy and friendship, simplicity and generous hospitality'. Africa recurred to him in his Madagascar visits – 'always such a tantalising place to me because of its African-ness', and on his return to Mauritius he took the blind boys of St Hugh's school for a grand picnic at Blue Bay, not just 'down to the sea but into it'. This experience reminded him of the blind children in Masasi whom he took swimming at Lindi. At the end of November he celebrated forty-three years in the priesthood and twenty as a bishop.

1981 opened with a cyclonic storm which kept everyone at home in darkness, though this did not interfere with his baptism of the (episcopalian) American ambassador's granddaughter or long-awaited arrival of Bishop George Briggs. On 16 January he made the eight-hour flight to Western Australia for the first of

several fruitful visits to the Archdiocese of Perth, where he was
to strike up a long-lasting friendship with Archbishop Peter
Carnley. His main job was to lead the Anglican Summer School
for the Province of Western Australia. He loved being in a large
country like Africa again and stayed with the Bishop of North
West Australia, Howell Witt, an ex-Mirfield student now working
in the largest land diocese in the Anglican Communion – as far
from end to end as London is to Moscow. He visited Madagascar
at the end of March and on 19 April attended his first Primates'
meeting in Washington DC. The best encounter there was with
the Archbishop of Central Africa, Walter Makhulu, who had
been chosen to preach the sermon at the closing service of the
conference. They first knew each other when Makhulu was seven
years old and served Huddleston as altar boy every Wednesday
morning in Sophiatown. The American visit concluded, Huddleston flew east for a holiday in Scotland and to visit many English
friends, including the Bottomleys, who had looked after him in
Stepney, en route to Mirfield. He returned to Mauritius in July.
While in London he resumed contact with leaders of the Anti-
Apartheid Movement. He also presided over the amalgamation
of the Friends of Mauritius and the Seychelles with the Madagascar Missionary Association: problems had arisen from divided
loyalties and 'stem from the basic problem of communication
over long distances: over cultural and linguistic differences: over
a shortage of cash to make meetings possible'.[15] He looked
forward to another 'Partners-in-Mission' Conference in 1982,
bringing together at least five Anglican Provinces to discuss 'the
Mission of a Minority Church'. But his eyes were set on other,
more cosmic, boundaries, bringing together not Provinces but
whole monotheistic religions. Phoenix parties with multi-cultural
speakers fuelled this enthusiasm, where 'religious themes can be
discussed so frankly and openly across all the cultural, genera-
tional and social barriers of our fascinating country'.[16] His Creole
lessons did not yield great results, for which he blamed old age.
In November – just after ordaining four deacons, two of whom
were soon to take up their studies in Western Australia, thanks
to his intervention and the generosity of the United Society for

the Propagation of the Gospel (USPG) and Archbishop Carnley –
he suffered another retinal haemorrhage, another swift visit to his
London eye surgeon ensued followed by an equally swift return
to Mauritius. He considered founding a diabetic association: there
were many highly skilled doctors but one of the highest per capita
figures in the world for diabetes.

1982 had its share of surprises. After a Parliamentary visitation which included his devoted friend the former MP for Ealing
North, Harry Greenway, and the worst flooding in Madagascar's
history (65,000 people homeless in Antananarivo alone), he
spent March in England, mostly on anti-apartheid business. The
previous year he had succeeded Bishop Ambrose Reeves as
President of the Anti-Apartheid Movement and he co-chaired
the conference in London which turned out to be the most fully
representative one ever held. Press coverage was poor but the
subsequent agreement of Nigeria to make funds available from
its oil revenues proved vital to the Movement's viability. Ambassadors and High Commissioners from the five Front-Line African
States and great crowds of anti-apartheid delegates from all over
the world were there. The conference ended with a march and
mass rally in Trafalgar Square 'that nearly finished me. It was
bitterly cold and I had already picked up a virus . . . so I spent
my last week in bed instead of visiting Dublin to deliver the
Albert Luthuli Memorial Lecture as planned.'[17]

Back in Mauritius he witnessed on 11 June a General Election
in which the existing government was wiped out and a new one
put in place. He paid another visit to Perth, travelling via Bombay
to avoid using South African Airways. Carnley asked him to
conduct two retreats, one for clergy and one for 'pastoral assistants'. Huddleston's impact on Australia's growing opposition to
apartheid was profound, according to Archbishop Carnley. 'I
remember [Huddleston] delivered a really great oration from the
Cathedral pulpit. He talked about the horrors of apartheid but
also expressed some very clear criticisms of Mrs Thatcher. In the
course of the oration he recounted some conversations he had
had with her, when he went to try and persuade her to take a
more clear anti-apartheid stance . . . His visits were very widely

covered in the press and certainly his oratory made a huge impression. He was able to deliver a quite long address of at least forty-five minutes at the Cathedral Anti-Apartheid Rally, apparently with only a few notes but in the manner of an old-style orator. He delivered his words with plenty of punch and graphic imagery. This brought the anti-apartheid cause squarely into our lives at the time. Consequently, the friendship which I developed with Trevor and the impact of his commitment to working against apartheid prompted me to introduce resolutions both to my own Dioceses and to the General Synod of the Anglican Church of Australia, declaring apartheid a form of heresy. His influence thus penetrated the decision-making structures of Australian Anglicanism. I think from this point of view his visits were of quite enormous importance in clarifying an Australian mind on apartheid.'[18] It is worth noting in this context that during the early 1980s Perth became a popular refuge for political exiles from South Africa.

After some short but much-needed holidays, Huddleston was back in Madagascar in July on theological business. Mrs Indira Gandhi paid him the privilege of a visit on 23 August, but an attempted coup in the Seychelles, with South African compliance, only served to reinforce his concerns over the vulnerability of the Indian Ocean in the ideological conflict between East and West. The 'Partners-in-Mission' consultation on 'The Role of a Minority Church' duly took place in September as planned, despite considerable logistical difficulties, and with the help of finance from USPG and a charitable trust in London.

In November a 'quite unexpectedly long telex message arrived from the United Nations to say I had been nominated for a "Gold Award" for my work against apartheid: it was to be presented on 5 November.'[19] Huddleston was required to attend and address a plenary session of the General Assembly.[20] He flew first class to New York and thence to London for Anti-Apartheid Movement meetings with Pauline Webb, Hilda Bernstein, Abdul Minty and Michael Terry, followed by a further meeting with the executive of the International Defence and Aid Fund. Cold weather brought on symptoms of another diabetes-related attack and he was back in Mauritius on 16 November. A month later, on 31 December 1982, his great friend and fellow traveller in the vanguard of the struggle against apartheid for more than thirty years, Canon John Collins, died. Huddleston was elected to follow him as Chairman of the Trustees of IDAF. He confessed in his newsletter of that month that he was finding the divisiveness of the world depressing and disturbing and looked for a different kind of patriotism from the bitter nationalisms most governments mean when they use that term. What we shall never know, for he kept no journals of these years, was how his inner life was altered by these huge journeys, these small and great achievements, his isolation, in the midst of a vast ocean, from the world he longed to change – the world of apartheid South Africa. His newsletters, blandly episcopal for the most part, reveal occasionally a glimpse of his loneliness and his despair at how the politicians were taking over. The departure of Bishop George Briggs back to England after his lengthy sojourn at Bishop's House was a sad moment. There must have been many others.

1983 was the year of the culmination of his inter-faith efforts, so central to his time in Mauritius. It was also the year in which he resigned from the archdiocese of the Indian Ocean in order to return to London to head both the Anti-Apartheid Movement and the International Defence and Aid Fund for Southern Africa. 'So much to do: so little done,' he reflected, along with Cecil Rhodes, a somewhat unlikely source of inspiration for Huddleston. 'The little death of saying farewell is not made easier by realising how the past five years have flown by with so little accomplished . . . It has always taken me longer than it should to adjust to new challenges and new situations. And when . . . the adjustment has to be made rather late in life and has involved coming to terms with the cultures, religions and languages of three separate island-states, it has been just that much more difficult. It is only now that I am leaving that I feel myself confidently at home . . . I have been fortunate to have had such a bonus at this point in my life and I am more thankful than I can express for all the encouragement I have received here.'[21]

The Inter-Faith Conference held in Mauritius over ten days in

January 1983 was an event of more than ecumenical importance, as Pauline Webb testified.[22] Huddleston 'used his enormous house to convene a conference of distinguished leaders from all the various communities of faith, inviting them to answer the question, 'What is man? What is the meaning of life?' and in the light of their answers to consider together the kind of society they wanted to create in Mauritius that would enable everyone to attain the fullness of their humanity.' It led to Huddleston proposing Mauritius as the place for a World Council of Churches sponsored inter-faith consultation in preparation for its Sixth Assembly. 'It was that consultation, drawing its members from fifteen different countries, which brought a global dimension to [his] growing concern for inter-faith dialogue.' It was a great life-changing event for many of the participants, who had shrunk initially from the idea of worshipping together. After witnessing the Hindu Kavadi festival and watching the worship of other faiths in action, after sharing, arguing, eating, living together, 'we were finally unable to resist worshipping together . . . There was an overwhelming sense that we were standing together before a mystery too great for any of us totally to comprehend, a glimpse of that heaven beyond our horizons, and yet made real for each of us through the graciousness of divine revelation and the humility of human response.' It was Huddleston who led the delegates from this contemplation to acting together to work for peace and justice, and specifically against apartheid. He told the consultation of the next step in his ecumenical journey: he would spend the rest of his life in the struggle for the soul of his beloved country. He invited participants to meet again a year later in London at an Inter-Faith Colloquium which he was organizing under the auspices of the United Nations Special Committee against Apartheid.[23] As conference Chairman Huddleston 'imparted an intensity and urgency to the proceedings, which on occasion even burnt into anger with anyone who tried to pass off pious platitudes or make virtuous claims for their own particular communities.' Four resolutions were adopted: better information on the effects of apartheid on its victims; more inter-faith groups to provide aid to such victims; drawing to the attention of religious leaders and groups the sufferings of apartheid's victims; organizing boycotts, calling for sanctions, opposing arms sales, praying for apartheid's victims and for their oppressors.

One curious result was that having found allies for his own cause, Huddleston was now courted for his support for the projects of the other participants. He became Chairman of the Friends of the Pagoda in Battersea Park. He became Provost of the Selly Oak Colleges, one of the main centres of inter-faith ecumenism in Britain. He broadcast frequently on BBC's external services, including a marathon series of reflections on the creed – later published in book form.[24] Muslims say religion is a matter of knowing where you have tied your own camel, and Huddleston's was still tethered to the orthodoxies and unorthodoxies of the Oxford Movement. As to his own recollection of the Phoenix consultation, words, for once, failed him; but he listed the presence of two Jewish rabbis, a Muslim leader from Siberia, a Christian Arab from the West Bank; three Buddhists from Native American groups; Catholics, Lutherans, Quakers, Sikhs, Muslims as a sufficiently eloquent testimony to what they had achieved.

It was an amazing bridge between the multi-racial world he was leaving and the sharply re-focused London life to which he was returning. His achievement in Mauritius, as in Masasi, was the result of his ability to determine priorities. In Madagascar he did not attempt to master the details, but once he had worked out the way ahead he drove ruthlessly towards his goal. This concentration on essentials was to mark his London life and work.

But his return was marked by a sense of loss. He no longer knew who he was or where he was. He had ceased to be a diocesan bishop after 23 years (exactly half his ordained life). He dreaded retirement at Mirfield as he told his contemplative brethren at CR's daughter house, Emmaus, in Sunderland in June 1983.

CHAPTER EIGHT

LOSS AND GAIN

1983–1991

As if Huddleston's achievements to date were not sufficient for a post-colonial bishop and monastic Anglican pushing seventy, he never ceased in his efforts to support the victims of apartheid among whom he had grown to maturity in Johannesburg thirty years earlier. In 1981, on the death of Bishop Ambrose Reeves,[1] he was elected President of the Anti-Apartheid Movement (AAM), speaking and writing with undiminished passion and conviction of how apartheid must die before he did. It was his address to the General Assembly of the United Nations,[2] which helped bring the idea of sanctions against South Africa to public acceptance throughout the West, and to some in the Eastern bloc as well. He was re-elected President of AAM unanimously from 1981 onwards and his annual calls to action to AAM activists were remarkable for their clarity and controlled anger. By the 1980s the AAM was established in many countries as the struggle in South Africa intensified. Huddleston travelled to meet many government leaders, his influence helping to inspire the worldwide campaign.

Like the ANC, the Anti Apartheid Movement had a prehistory.[3] In the late 1950s international attention was focused on Africa, then emerging from the colonial era. AAM was a direct result of this period of rapid change. Its origins can be traced to the Committee of African Organisations (CAO) which met during the mid-1950s in the basement flat of Dr David Pitt at No. 200, Gower Street, London. He was joined in 1958 by a very young student who had attended the Congress School in Fordburg – Abdul Minty. Minty, a tireless supporter and friend to Huddleston for more than thirty years, now holds high office in the Department of External Affairs in Pretoria. Also involved in CAO was Canon Collins's Christian Action which raised funds to help defendants in the Treason Trials of 1957–61. Inspired by Chief Albert Luthuli's international appeal for an economic, cultural and sports boycott of South Africa, CAO launched the Boycott Movement on 26 June 1959 (Freedom Day in South Africa) and a vigil was held outside South Africa House in Trafalgar Square. Huddleston, Julius Nyerere and Michael Scott spoke later at a public meeting. The committee's links with the South African struggle were further strengthened by the arrival later in the year of Tennyson Makiwane (ANC's Youth League leader and a treason trialist). CAO's early supporters crossed the political divide: Barbara Castle was the most significant British statesman of either major party to identify totally with its aims, though others – David Steel, Jeremy Thorpe, Tony Benn, Fenner Brockway, David Ennals, Jo Grimond and Harold Wilson were all involved. John Grigg, an unorthodox Conservative, played a major part in its early development and there were a number of high-profile sympathizers from show-business and academia. At a meeting on 29 December 1959, the Movement identified three priorities requiring immediate attention: the Treason Trial and the banning of black leaders; the extension of the Pass Laws to women; and the poverty-level wages paid to Africans.

17 January 1960 saw Huddleston in the chair for a conference on boycotting South African goods, attended by 250 people from 168 organizations. Its activities resulted in an acute financial deficit, guaranteed personally by the movement's treasurer, Vella Pillay. 28 February inaugurated a month of intense activity with a march and rally, led by Huddleston, from Marble Arch to Trafalgar Square.[4] After Sharpeville (21 March 1960) the Boycott Movement gained still greater momentum. On 22 March 400 people stood in silence outside South Africa House. Other marches and rallies followed. Sharpeville turned the Boycott Movement, which began as an offshoot from CAO, into the Anti-Apartheid Movement and determined its future direction.

Huddleston had for years believed in boycotting as the only effective non-violent means of drawing the world's attention to the evil of apartheid and had proposed a sports boycott of South Africa in 1956 in *Naught for Your Comfort*. But the massacre at Sharpeville brought a new urgency to AAM and a new chapter of violence and oppression in South Africa. The rioting that followed, and even more the government's declaration of a state of emergency, forced the consequences of apartheid onto the world scene and provided a new long-term purpose for AAM. During the 1960s the Liberal leader David Steel was the Movement's President but its policies did not chime with the more pragmatic Africa policy of the Wilson administration. AAM stood for support of all liberation movements (often suspected of being tools of the Kremlin) and economic sanctions. In April 1964 AAM sponsored an international conference to examine the feasibility of applying economic sanctions against South Africa, and in the same year the new Prime Minister, Harold Wilson, announced a qualified arms embargo. But by the late 1960s the government in Britain had relaxed its stance.

Huddleston himself was slow to re-enter AAM during his early years at Stepney, despite having been made Vice-President as early as 1961. He was already committed on so many fronts at this time and there was a certain *froideur* between him and Bishop Ambrose Reeves, AAM's President, perhaps connected to Huddleston's celebrity and Reeves's relative marginalization by the Church hierarchy after his expulsion from Johannesburg. This seems to have disappeared entirely by 1975 when Huddleston willingly took on Reeves's presidential responsibilities after the latter had suffered a severe stroke.

The Soweto uprising of 1976 was provoked by Pretoria's imposition of Afrikaans as the sole language of instruction in Bantu secondary schools. With Abdul Minty, AAM's Honorary Secretary since 1963, and Michael Terry, AAM's Executive Secretary, Huddleston led a delegation to both the Foreign Office and the Ministry of Defence to press for an immediate arms embargo against South Africa. Soweto was followed in 1977 by the banning of the 'Black Consciousness' movement and the appalling death in police custody of its founder, Steve Biko, for whom, and for the ANC, AAM organized a Central Hall rally at which Huddleston was one of the main speakers. 1978 was the UN-designated International Anti-Apartheid Year for which Huddleston addressed a meeting to promote it, shortly before he left Britain for Mauritius.

During his years in Mauritius, Mike Terry updated Huddleston on AAM progress on a monthly basis, and met him at the Ramptons' on his home leaves. By the early 1980s the Anti-Apartheid Movement was beginning to have an impact. Hitherto neither public opinion nor government policy had been supportive. The calls for more pressure on Pretoria, United Nations involvement, support for the ANC, the priority of the peaceful transition to majority rule throughout those parts of Africa still important to Britain were never on the British government agenda. That AAM's policies were vindicated, as Zimbabwe, Mozambique, Angola, and eventually Namibia floated free of the imperial yokes, was of little consolation.

In March 1982, AAM organized a three-day conference in London under the banner 'Southern Africa: The Time to Choose'. It ended with a rally in Trafalgar Square at which Huddleston addressed an audience of over 20,000. That same weekend the ANC's London offices were blown up by South African paramilitaries under Craig Williamson: it was widely expected that ANC's President-in-Exile, Oliver Tambo, would be in the offices and therefore this can be counted as just one of the many unsuccessful attempts of BOSS (the South African Bureau of State Security) and allied organizations to assassinate Tambo. In fact, he had been detained in Maputo at a meeting of the Front-line States called by President Samora Machel of Mozambique.[5] After this the Foreign Secretary, Lord Carrington, met the AAM leadership. Carrington was impressed by Huddleston's convictions and prepared to recognize the significance of AAM's role in African affairs: Pretoria was sufficiently impressed by the new strength of the ANC to bomb its London headquarters.

Now seventy years old, Huddleston induced a new flow of blood into Anti-Apartheid Movement's affairs and into his own life, from a tiny flat above the Rectory in St James's, Piccadilly, offered to him by Donald Reeves, the Rector. His sitting-room sofa turned into his bed at night. He received daily press reports faxed from AAM's offices in Mandela Street. He knew of the situation on the ground in Soweto and throughout the country from the reports back by his many African visitors, now in exile and often having served long prison sentences. He knew that African opinion on change, stimulated by the concessions of Pretoria in the early 1980s, had hardened. 'Once change develops dynamics of its own, it only excites African expectations for more. Thus the repeal in 1985 of the Mixed Marriages Act and the Immorality Act increased pressure for the repeal of the Group Areas Act – the kernel of apartheid. Allowing people to marry across the colour bar is meaningless if they cannot live together . . . Political co-option had not brought economic *embourgeoise-ment* or the relaxation of restrictions in social life. Improved educational facilities for Africans were creating a new professional and managerial class which produced strong new support for African nationalism, and a more militant refusal to take up sponsored platforms.'[6]

Huddleston regarded the liberalizations with suspicion. Determined and obstinate, but once again fully abreast of what was happening in the country he loved, Huddleston fought his own fight with the British government in general and Mrs Thatcher in particular. The new Prime Minister listened to him but took little notice of what he said, regarding the ANC as 'just another terrorist organisation'. On 9 October 1983 Huddleston, answering a question after his university sermon at Great St Mary's, Cambridge admitted that his 'forty years' involvement in the struggle [against apartheid] had made very little impact, not only in South Africa but in this country and the West . . . Apartheid . . . is a challenge to the conscience of the whole world: and it is a challenge which the West consistently refuses to meet; and I say that *ex animo*, without reservation because I believe it to be true.'[7]

Summing up the year to December 1983 in the first of his annual reports for the Movement,[8] Huddleston wrote:

All of us involved in AAM recognise that we have moved into a new and critical phase of the struggle. South Africa today is more aggressive both internally and externally towards those who oppose its racist philosophy. The new constitutional proposals, designed to deprive the majority of South Africans of their birthright and to entrench the present government in power, the continued uprooting of hundreds of thousands from their homes, the increased police surveillance and brutality, the legislation designed to limit press freedom everywhere – all of these express the internal threat to human rights and human dignity. In foreign policy the aim of destabilising its African neighbour states is pursued relentlessly: the attack on Lesotho, the occupation of the southern province in Angola, and even the support for a mercenary assault on the Indian Ocean state of Seychelles are examples of South African ruthlessness. In the meanwhile, no settlement of the Namibian war is in sight. Every attempt to implement Security Council resolution 435 [declaring the South African occupation as illegal and calling for an immediate withdrawal of troops] has been blocked and the illegal occupation of the whole country continues with tacit support from the Western Powers – including Great Britain. Never was there a time when AAM so greatly needed the support of all who care for human rights and for justice and peace in our world. But the Movement cannot act effectively if it is hampered by lack of resources. We have found fine new premises. Already we have a magnificently dedicated and committed staff. But we urgently need more money if – in face of the challenges – we are to act effectively. As I begin to engage myself much more actively in the Movement I appeal to all our supporters to make the coming year an even greater advance on all fronts than was 1983.

The need for fund-raising recurred for the third time: for a man who had incorporated poverty as a vow into his life, his willingness to raise money for causes he backed – AAM, the pay of Masasi clergy, IDAF deficits, projects in Mauritius as well as Masasi – is particularly striking.

But now he was back in daily contact with South African affairs he wanted to restore his authority to speak on African subjects from personal experience. By the end of 1983 he decided to visit the Front-line states with Abdul Minty. In January 1984 they went to Zambia, Zimbabwe, Mozambique and Tanzania, staying at Nyerere's residence where the two renewed their long-standing friendship just as Nyerere was preparing to retire. It was a historic visit as the two moving spirits of the international Anti-Apartheid Movement were respectfully received by heads of state and foreign ministers of the five countries most directly subjected to South African interference with their internal affairs in the interests of maintaining white supremacy in the region. Huddleston also visited Botswana, which proved to be a meeting ground for his old friends: he was reunited with streams of well-wishers, now living in exile, whom he had known in Sophiatown in the 1950s.

After the trip Huddleston reported to the AAM executive:

I've come back from the visit feeling that we really are at a most critical moment in the South African scene. There is nothing like getting back to the grass roots of the struggle to make you realise that there just isn't any alternative to complete commitment on this issue. The main point that I wanted to discuss with the front-line governments was the South African foreign policies of destabilisation and aggression. I want to be certain that I'm saying on behalf of the AAM what the governments of the front-line states want us to be saying. This is terribly important because things are changing so rapidly at the moment. Although we were only there for two-and-a-half weeks I did meet those in control of every one of the front-line states we visited. All the governments bent over backwards to see that we had access to all the people we wanted to see, that we had transport and that public relations were well-organised. I found that there was total and complete unanimity on the issues of South African destabilisation and aggression. This came through particularly clearly when one of the Presidents said that the front-lines states' organisation is top priority – always. If there's an emergency meeting the top people will drop everything else in order to be there. In Zambia President Kaunda and I agreed that Zambia has already had to make quite considerable concessions to South African economic pressure, but there is a concerted effort to create a new balance of trading partners which will enable Zambia to step-by-step reduce its dependence on South Africa. Obviously this is something that will take a good deal of time – and it's not only that time is lacking, but the fact that the economic situation for so many of these countries is a downward spiral. The South Africans are playing on this with everything they've got and it does make these countries terribly vulnerable. Even so, we felt that there was a buoyant feeling in Zambia, not at all defeatist. We learned that South Africa is using Botswana as a way through to Zimbabwe for destabilisation purposes, in a very massive way. Meanwhile, South Africa is claiming that Botswana is allowing infiltration by guerrilla fighters. Whenever it wants to be nasty to Botswana it picks up on this and accuses Botswana of supporting the South African resistance. In Zimbabwe Robert Mugabe told us in great detail how the South Africans are infiltrating and where. He finds himself in an incredibly difficult situation. Mozambique turned out to be in many ways the highlight of the tour. It was quite extraordinary for me. Maputo is such a beautiful city – so orderly, clean and disciplined. The people stand tall and the kids are well set up. You feel there's a kind of commitment to making the country what it ought to be after all their years and years of struggle. They suffered more from South African destabilisation than any except Angola and are still suffering, bitterly, through South African support for dissident groups, the 'bandits' as they call them. And yet they are totally confident. I do not believe that South Africa is winning that battle on the ground. If South Africa is negotiating, it is not negotiating from strength as it likes to appear to be doing. As far as Mozambique is concerned, apartheid itself is the enemy, there can be no peace in Southern Africa until apartheid itself is destroyed and therefore there is no question of the Mozambique government selling out on that issue. This was spelt out to us clearly and specifically . . . In

Tanzania during discussions with President Nyerere we felt this was the worst situation economically. They are fairly up against the wall. There are so many shortages in vital areas, medical supplies, spare parts, everything is at rock bottom. Yet there is extraordinarily high morale. So what can we in AAM do? The front line states are facing the most critical moments – we just can't afford *not* to be totally committed at this moment.

1984 was the first of several years of successful campaigning. In March, Huddleston wrote a long piece, which he submitted to *The Times*, deeply deploring the Accord of Nkomati signed between South Africa and Mozambique. It was a serious setback to African political aspirations as it deprived the ANC of a base for guerrilla incursion and went far to legitimizing apartheid:

Friday 16 March 1984 should be remembered by all who care about peace in Southern Africa as the blackest day since the Treaty of Vereegning which ended the Boer War. And for the same reason. It marked not the magnanimity of the West – those champions of 'Christian civilisation' in Africa – but a further step in the consolidation of institutionalised racism known as 'Apartheid' – of course it is not recognised in these terms by the governments of the Western powers nor by the media which so cheerfully hail the Accord of Nkomati (to be signed by President Machel of Mozambique and Mr Pieter Botha of South Africa on Friday) as a major advance towards 'peace'. Of course, too, it is confidently expected that a similar accord will be signed between the Angolan and South African governments in the near future.

In case it should be assumed that I write these words as an armchair critic I shall state my credentials: I spent most of the month of January this year visiting five of the Front-line States of Southern Africa – Zambia, Botswana, Zimbabwe, Mozambique and Tanzania . . . I have been actively involved in the Anti-Apartheid Movement since its inauguration 25 years ago. But for 12 years my parish was what is now known as Soweto – the largest African town in South Africa. I learnt the meaning of apartheid by daily contact with its victims. The purpose of my visit in January was to discuss with the governments concerned the impact on their countries of the twin policies of South Africa: massive *aggression* and continuous *destabilisation* ... the constant attacks by a highly trained South African army and air force, equipped with the most sophisticated weapons; the support by South Africa of each and every subversive movement in these States: the occupation – in defiance of international law – of Namibia and large areas of Angola: all of these together have resulted in compelling Mozambique and Angola to negotiate on the best terms they can get. The bully, if he is strong enough, can always win the first contest and force surrender by his muscle. But the bully cannot win *any* contest if he is restrained by his equals or superiors.

Behind all the negotiations and manoeuvrings and deceits of the past three years lies the deliberate policy of 'constructive engagement' with South Africa pursued by the Reagan administration and tacitly supported by the West. It is this that has allowed South Africa to pursue its act of aggression and destabilisation without protest and unhindered.

It is this, too, that has encouraged (if indeed they need encouragement) the Western Powers and particularly Great Britain, to invest billions in South African industry and commerce.

It is the double-talk of Western governments who profess abhorrence of apartheid and condemnation of violence but who totally refuse to use the only alternative – an effective sanctions policy – that constitutes their moral depravity and their acceptance of evil.

At a meeting of delegates of most of the world's religions – Judaism, Buddhism, Islam, Hinduim, Sikhism, traditional religions and Christianity – the first of its kind to address the problem – apartheid was described as ... 'evil – deeply disastrously evil ...' and all its manifestations (including specifically those *inside* South Africa and Namibia) were condemned in these terms: '... there is a fundamental and unanimous moral and religious opposition to apartheid ... this opposition calls for *action* ...'.

As one leader of the Front-line States expressed it to me: 'There is only *one* enemy: that is apartheid itself. Until apartheid is destroyed there can be no peace in Southern Africa.' And I would add – no peace in God's world either.[9]

Mrs Thatcher had proposed an official visit in June by P.W. Botha, then trawling European capitals as part of a new damage-limitation exercise. The visit was dramatically shortened as a result of Anti-Apartheid Movement activity and eventually he had to be transported by helicopter direct from Heathrow to Chequers and back with no overnight stay, on 2 June. On the eve of this meeting Huddleston led a delegation to meet Mrs Thatcher to protest at the visit and a mass protest was held the next day: the biggest ever AAM march through the centre of London. New issues were raised – most notably the visit of P.W. Botha – and old ones refurbished: the arms embargo and forced removals. Glenys Kinnock, wearing a black sash, delivered a document to Downing Street which established the legal basis for African freehold property ownership (denied by the apartheid regime) signed by King Edward VII. At a deeper level AAM had helped the world see how desperate Botha was not to lose further international support. His short and unhappy visit caused a sea-change in attitudes towards the implementation of sanctions. And Nelson Mandela had begun to take centre stage as the primary focus of press and public interest. Huddleston took a petition for his release to the United Nations in New York. His identification with the campaign for Mandela's unconditional release personi-fied his contribution to AAM's own struggle for authority and a hearing, as its annual report for 1984 made clear:

Our Silver Jubilee year has certainly been a year to remember . . . Clearly the visit of Prime Minister (and President) Botha hard on the heels of the Nkomati Accord and then the implementation of the new consitutional arrangements, followed by the farcical election and the inevitable protests were the events that hit the headlines. And – more recently still – the occupation of the British consulate in Durban and its consequences. All of this – and so much more – is an

indication of three things: first that the situation inside South
Africa is one of ever-increasing turbulence: secondly, that the
attempt to deprive of their citizenship 4/5ths of the population
is not only doomed to failure but is the determining cause of
the massive support for the United Democratic Front, and of
the great upsurge of resistance to apartheid at every level: and
thirdly, that our support in Great Britain and wherever in the
world AAM exists, has to be far stronger, far more vigorously
expressed and far more persistently organized for action than
ever before. We know that we have the duty and the privilege
of expressing the true meaning of solidarity with the African
people at this crucial moment in the struggle. We also know
that another and vital task for us here in Great Britain is to
keep the conscience of the public alight in the fact of government apathy and double-talk. Now, if ever, is our chance to
make sacrifices of time, of energy and of money on behalf of
the Movement.

AAM's work for Mandela's release was a key to international
support for the ANC and Huddleston turned it in the lock. Four
years later all involved knew there would be no solution without
his unconditional release – a concession eventually made by Mrs
Thatcher. In Huddleston AAM had a credible, influential, even
magisterial spokesman who could make these things possible and
open doors.[10] In September 1985 he scented victory. He wrote to
Mrs Thatcher about his recent visit to Australia and New Zealand and to the firming up of anti-apartheid attitudes he had
encountered among government ministers in both countries. He
also urged her to stand firm on the implementation of Resolution
435 and criticized the government's present policy of opposing
effective sanctions: 'Events in South Africa, South Africa's
renewed aggression against its neighbours and its intransigence
over Namibia, all underline the pressing need for effective international action.'[11]. The sea-change in attitudes towards South
Africa was clear and unmistakable:

It reaches us every day through the media: in television
newscasts from all over South Africa: in the press reporting of

government statements concerning the economy: in the reaction to speeches here, there and everywhere: in the frenzied efforts of President Botha to present a 'reforming' image to the world whilst using massive repression against the African people. Above all this crisis-point in the history of the struggle has been marked during the past year by a massive change in the attitude and in the actions of the international community. For the first time the Commonwealth countries are discussing not the evils of apartheid but the positive, practical and immediate measures needed to abolish it. And (although these words will be published after the Commonwealth Heads of Government meeting in Nassau) the position of Great Britain will be the unenviable one of having to stand alone against both the old and the young member-states. And it will stand alone because of its refusal to act against apartheid: its obstinate and indefensible rejection of the use of effective sanctions in support of the African people at this crucial moment in their fight against tyranny. Whatever the outcome of the Conference, the AAM will have achieved a mighty triumph in bringing the international community to a true understanding of this 'moment of truth'. We have worked hard in the past 12 months to arouse the conscience of our country and of our friends throughout the world. This report tells of the efforts we have made. I am truly proud to be the President of such a Movement and to have been able to represent it in its approach to government: in its great public demonstrations: in its responses to the lies and propaganda of the South African regime: and in the vast expansion on its membership.[12]

Important though AAM was in bringing to the attention of peoples and governments the total unacceptability of the apartheid regime, there was another organization which Huddleston was appointed to lead from 1983, the International Defence and Aid Fund for Southern Africa (IDAF). He succeeded Canon John Collins as Chairman of the Trustees upon the latter's death, occupying the post alongside his AAM activities for the crucial final decade of anti-apartheid.

The Defence and Aid Fund for Southern Africa, as it then was, was created to cover the legal costs and support the families of the Treason Trialists in 1959. John Collins, Chairman of Christian Aid, a Canon of St Paul's Cathedral and a founder of the Campaign for Nuclear Disarmament, had visited South Africa in the mid-1950s to meet members of the white business community who wanted to defend themselves against the 'unfair' attacks on the racial policies of the government. Collins also met many prominent black leaders and white liberals and as a result became a life-long opponent of apartheid. When Nelson Mandela and his colleagues were arrested and threatened with the death penalty, Collins quickly established fund-raising offices in Johannesburg, Durban and Cape Town as well as one at his own home in Amen Court in London. DAF was internationalized in 1961 with the three-fold objective of defending political prisoners on trial, supporting their families and publicizing their cause. IDAF, in existence until 1991, functioned as a humanitarian non-governmental organization working for 'constructive solutions to the problems created by racial oppression' in the area.[13] Its international office was in London and by 1991 it had national committees in Sweden, Norway, Finland, Ireland and the Netherlands, Canada and New Zealand. Denmark, Switzerland, Australia and the United States also had national committees, which disbanded before the IDAF wind-down took place post-apartheid. The Fund had consultative status with the Economic and Social Council of the United Nations and UNESCO, and related closely to the United Nations Trust Fund, of which it was a beneficiary, and the United Nations Centre against Apartheid. It was also a beneficiary of the European Economic Community's Fund for Victims of Apartheid. Fifty-two governments supported its work directly or indirectly, of which Canada, Scandinavia and the Netherlands were most prominent. Despite such blue-chip backers, IDAF's wide-ranging commitments in South Africa regularly outstripped its income. A committee channelled proceeds directly to the recipients until the Fund was banned in South Africa under the Suppression of Communism Act in 1964, and from then on, all payments were administered by IDAF in London. The ban was lifted in 1990. As the Fund's full name suggests, its work was not strictly limited to South Africa and at one time it ran programmes of defence and aid in Angola, Mozambique, Rhodesia (Zimbabwe) and Namibia as well as South Africa. Thanks to skilful fund-raising IDAF was able to distribute substantial amounts of money to pay for leading South African lawyers to defend hundreds accused of treasonable activities in opposing the apartheid regime. Much more difficult was the provision of support to the accused families, particularly where a long sentence of imprisonment had been imposed. To do this without incriminating the families in receiving aid from a proscribed organization, the Fund's General Secretary, Horst Kleinschmidt, helped set up a network of unpaid volunteers who every two months received through the post, by registered mail, the cash sums they were to transmit with full details of what to say to each family involved, including particular messages which were kept deliberately ambiguous. These volunteers would in turn buy registered envelopes, with money supplied from the centre and, after posting the packages to recipients, forward the Post Office documentation to IDAF headquarters.[14] The whole archive is now at the University of the Western Cape; it consists of many thousands of letters between those who received assistance from IDAF and the network of correspondents through whom the remittances were sent. The correspondence dates back to 1961 and in the Archive's own estimation provides: 'a valuable account of black people's daily lives under apartheid over almost three decades. It is a rich vein of South African history . . . an enormous collection which is unique and of great historical value to future historians.' How the volunteers came forward and were selected, screened, briefed and managed is also testimony to the organizational skills and resourcefulness of Kleinschmidt and the other executives. Those close to the IDAF committees had friends, and those friends had friends. Discretion and a reasonable level of clerical competence were the main qualifications. At the time of writing the exact workings of the process are confidential, and the speedy winding down of the operation in 1991 probably ensured that they will remain so. Microfiche copies of the archive are held at the Institute of Commonwealth Studies in London University.

Any account of the work of IDAF must acknowledge the vital role of Horst Kleinschmidt. For him, Huddleston was – and remains – a hero and their partnership in IDAF released in each potentialities and qualities that served the victims of apartheid consistently well over the key years of the 1980s. It was not at all predictable that Huddleston could co-operate so fruitfully either with subordinates or with his superiors, his experience of the latter being limited to Geoffrey Clayton, Raymond Raynes and Julius Nyerere. This limited experience and the high standards he set himself might have led to an arbitrarily dictatorial or unforgiv-ing attitude to those working directly under him – teachers and pupils at Rosettenville, novices and students at Mirfield, clergy and government officials in Masasi, parish clergy in Stepney and Mauritius, as well as the executive officers of AAM and IDAF. However, the testimonies of all who accepted and thrived under him – especially Abdul Minty, Michael Terry and Horst Kleinsch-midt – were unanimous. To both organizations Huddleston brought charismatic leadership, intuitive management skills and tact and sensitivity in executing his authority. Throughout the turbulent years that saw their winding down and transformation, Huddleston's role was of the utmost importance and without it the jobs of the others would have been impossible. With him they could tackle and overcome difficulties, think up and implement fresh ideas, inspire others and gain precious experience for post-apartheid challenges.

By 1982, IDAF was in serious trouble – financial, political, organizational – and Kleinschmidt was given a probationary six months, after other jobs in AAM, to get it back on the road and save it from being closed down by its Scandinavian paymasters. His job was complex and multi-layered. He had to run a largely secret, banned, fund-raising organization in order to secure good defence lawyers for the hundreds on trial for treason, support their families and research and monitor the situation in South Africa without being able to set foot in the country. He had to be so well informed on South African human rights abuses as to identify arrested and charged campaigners in the armed struggle. He had also to identify suitable lawyers without revealing the source of his funds; getting this wrong could, and sometimes did, lead to IDAF's work coming to Pretoria's attention. Lives, not only of defendants, were at risk.

There was yet another layer to his work. Some of the human rights lawyers approached by IDAF might also be police informants, prepared not only to take the money and then sell their clients down the river but to incriminate IDAF activists in the process. This was a world closer to John le Carré than to Franz Kafka, and required the skills of a spymaster to distinguish and commission those who could be trusted not to betray under pressure. Both Huddleston and Kleinschmidt learnt these skills the hard way. Kleinschmidt was thought by the ANC to be tarnished by some of his IDAF contacts, and this suspicion made his subsequent career working for the new South Africa difficult. By the time of Nelson Mandela's release in February 1990 the ANC had more important and much more political priorities than paying lawyers' fees and succouring the families of those in prison for sedition – including the Sisulus and the Mandelas. The African National Congress was at last on the march, and all priorities other than taking up power faded. So when Huddleston and Kleinschmidt offered to wind down IDAF and transfer the operation and the ongoing funding to South Africa they received only a qualified welcome from the ANC and outright hostility from the Western governments who supported the Fund. Strong doubts were expressed in London about funding Winnie Mandela's defence, in particular: was this to be a political or a criminal trial?

There were many reasons for Western concern, most emanating from perceptions of the Communist 'menace' posed by the ANC and connected organizations. Some in the ANC, including one of its leaders, Walter Sisulu, were Marxists, and had been since the early 1950s and would continue to be so. In AAM and IDAF there were card-carrying Communists at many levels, which worried the social democrat paymasters in Northern Europe, where the Kremlin with its thousands of nuclear warheads was still perceived to be a potential global threat. Pretoria made much of its being a bastion against Communism in the Southern hemisphere, and this won it support among conservatives throughout the West. The ANC's Communist leanings were thus easily portrayed as being a potential threat to democracy and Christian values. This vitiated ANC's profile in the minds of those who, like Mrs Thatcher, maintained until well after she must have suspected the truth, that it was just another terrorist organization; and that therefore the support it derived from AAM and IDAF endangered Western security. Moscow's relations with its client organizations in all non-aligned countries showed a rather different picture: it supported the ANC but its advice was restricted to a suggestion that the Freedom Charter adopted in 1955 went rather too far on nationalisation. Essentially Moscow supplied paramilitary and tertiary educational facilities to the ANC leadership to do with them what it would. Outside South Africa Cuban forces effectively neutralized South Africa's war against Angola but this was implementing a decision made in Cuba, not Moscow. Such were the unreasoning fears of the final pre-Gorbachev years that the Krelim factor (non-existent though it probably was) played its part in maintaining the apartheid regime and its ban on the ANC.

At all events Kleinschmidt, backed by Huddleston, restored IDAF fortunes and improved its performance; funded many defences; made life-saving cash payments to the families of detainees in a clandestine and highly efficient programme organized by Rica Hodson, now head of Walter Sisulu's office; and tried and failed eventually to transfer the operation to South Africa. In addition, it was Kleinschmidt who in 1986 thought up the seminal idea of a conference, to be held the next year in Harare, on 'Children, Repression and the Law in South Africa'. He travelled five times to Zimbabwe to organize it. He also travelled with Huddleston on several fund-raising trips – including one to Malaysia, where one evening Huddleston tripped and fell, cracking his skull and losing much blood. Fortunately an English-speaking Malaysian doctor was found almost immediately to stitch the wound (and Malaysia agreed to contribute to IDAF). They visited Namibia together after its liberation in 1990 and were entertained by the new President, Sam Nujoma, with cups of cocoa, the official residence having been stripped bare by the departing South Africans. Dennis Herbstein vividly recalled Huddleston in Vienna at a regular United Nations' international conference on Namibia:

> Representatives from every member state, lots of rhetoric, though South Africa was in fact piling on the pressure in its war in Namibia and Angola. Sam Nujoma was the star of the occasion . . . Trevor introduced him in a speech which turned into one of those seemingly effortless, but no less passionate for all that, exposés of the evils of apartheid and colonialism . . . He talked for perhaps twenty minutes . . . The Third World and Eastern Bloc delegates were spellbound . . . They could sense the passion, made the more effective in a contra-dictory way, by the austere style of his delivery. The East Europeans should . . . have been sceptical about the credibility of this man of the cloth, even though none could match his track record in fighting apartheid on the ground. Afterwards they crowded round, shaking his hand and asking for his autograph. Sam . . . was almost forgotten.[15]

They made a successful trip to Japan and to Switzerland for the shareholders' meeting of one of the leading Swiss banks. Here Huddleston's protest against investors who tacitly supported the apartheid system was angrily and ignominiously rejected. In London they worked together with visiting exiles and ex-detain-ees, including Thabo Mbeki, then Oliver Tambo's chief protegé and now President of the Republic of South Africa.

Huddleston's career in IDAF began with his first annual address on 11 May 1985, in which he quoted the words of Lloyd George to Sol Plaatje, the Secretary General of the ANC, and his colleagues on 21 November 1913: 'I was greatly impressed by the ability shown by the speakers. They presented their case with moderation, with evident sincerity and with power . . . The contrast between the case made by these black men and by the deputation headed by your Prime Minister was very striking . . .'. Huddleston then pointed out that seventy-two years – 'exactly my lifetime' – had elapsed and 'the only difference today is that the British Government is not even willing to meet us'.

In 1986 the Commonwealth Secretariat sent an Eminent Persons Group (EPG) on a fact-finding 'Mission to South Africa'. The authority and determination of the co-chairmen, President Obasanjo of the Nigerian Federation and Malcolm Fraser of Australia, led to a thorough-going visitation and a concluding report that was well-informed, serious and committed.[16] The Commonwealth Secretary-General – Sir Shridath 'Sonny' Ramphal – believed there was little chance of a negotiated settlement, agreeing with the report's conclusion that 'the cycle of violence and counter-violence has spiralled and there is no present prospect of a process of dialogue leading to the establishment of a non-racial and representative government'.[17] Pretoria reacted to the visit by bombing her neighbouring states in reprisal. After the publication of the Eminent Persons Group report, AAM staged a huge rally on Clapham Common in favour of sanctions and confronted the government – principally Malcolm Rifkind and Geoffrey Howe at the Foreign Office – in a series of distinctly unfriendly meetings attended by Huddleston, Bob Hughes, Abdul Minty and Mike Terry. Interviewed on BBC Radio 4's *Today* programme Huddleston's attack on government policy was played back to Rifkind in his car and he responded by a blistering personal attack on Huddleston. Later that day, at a stormy meeting, he maintained that Alan Paton, Helen Suzman and Chief Buthelezi were all against sanctions and thus supported government policy. Huddleston shot this to ribbons with devastating effect and Rifkind threw the AAM delegation out, pointedly not shaking hands with Huddleston. 'There was blood on the carpet,' the Foreign Office's press office later commented. Rifkind may well have known by then that the policy was flawed; Huddleston had got under the skin of this eminent Scots lawyer attempting to defend a brief he was uneasy with. Geoffrey Howe perhaps knew that holding out against sanctions was not good for the United Kingdom and not, in the long run, good for South Africa. From now on, South Africa was seen as an issue that Thatcher had to deal with. She had to get some movement out of Pretoria; she had to get the State President to talk to, and later release, Mandela. Huddleston conceded, of Thatcher, that 'she listened'.

AAM had helped get South Africa on the international agenda. But it was the passing by the US Congress of the Comprehensive Sanctions Bill in 1986 that told Pretoria the game was up. It was a world crisis. In September Huddleston wrote:

Without any doubt the past year has been the most eventful and the most significant in the history of AAM in Britain and elsewhere. This, of course, has been due to the escalation of the crisis in South Africa and Namibia and the tremendous response from the people of this country to what we in AAM stand for. The great rally in June was perhaps the largest ever seen in London since World War Two and was the clearest possible demonstration of the fact that the Tory government is totally out of touch with the mood of the vast majority in this country. It was in fact a demonstration of a determined and vigorous support for the policy for which we have always stood: mandatory economic sanctions as a way by which we can hasten the end of apartheid and support to the full those at the heart of the struggle. However, it is not only in demonstrations that our activity as a movement is shown. I have personally led delegations to the Foreign Office during the past year to make clear to the government our position, and, as a result of those delegations, I believe I can speak with far better authority. Indeed, it has become clear that the government has no real policy for ending apartheid because basically it has no desire to have one. The Commonwealth initiative and the Report, *Mission to South Africa*, of the Eminent Persons Group was of the utmost importance. Just because the authority of the representatives of the Commonwealth was unquestionable, the strength of their recommendations carried immense weight. The Movement once again demonstrated clearly and openly its position to the attitude of the British government at the mini-summit at Marlborough House. One of the most encouraging developments during the past year has been the response of local authorities throughout the country to our appeal to commitment to the 'apartheid-free zone' concept ... We are at a crisis point in the struggle to end apartheid with all deliberate speed. We simply dare not allow those who are directly involved in the struggle to be left to the non-event of unending dialogue, which is what the governments of Great Britain, the United States and West Germany particularly offer as their solution to apartheid. We are a 'movement', that is to say we live and grow and at the same time move forward to the goal we have set ourselves: but it is you, the individual members of the Movement, who really will achieve that end if you have the will to do so.[18]

The Harare Conference followed in September 1987. Though this was sponsored by BART (Bishop Ambrose Reeves Trust) rather than IDAF or AAM, Huddleston wrote to AAM members in September:

I am just off to a major international conference on repression in apartheid South Africa, with particular reference to the detention and imprisonment of children. . . . I have every hope it may be successful in again mobilising world opinion on the basic issue which is a moral issue, namely that apartheid, being evil in itself, is irreformable: abolition, total and complete, is the only course. Certainly, the AAM has never wavered in its commitment to this end.

It is sometimes deeply frustrating after so many years of solidarity with the struggle inside South Africa and Namibia, to find it necessary to repeat such an obvious truism. Nevertheless, the most powerful vested interests in the Western democracies constantly return to the theme that 'nothing must be done to hinder the progress of reform'. This is, of course, the easiest way to relieve governments of any obligation to *act* ... Since last year the report of the Eminent Persons Group Mission to South Africa, the British government has continued to refuse to recognize what the report so positively demanded on behalf of the rest of the Commonwealth. In this way, although limited sanctions of one kind or another have been or are being imposed, mandatory sanctions, which would have a really effective impact, have been blocked. This ill serves the peoples of South Africa and Namibia, and also those of the Front-line States in their constantly dangerous situation from South African aggression . . . We know now that governments do, in fact, take notice of popular opinion. We have shown over and over again by our rallies, by our media coverage and by the sheer moral weight of our arguments that public opinion can have a massive impact. We must not slacken our efforts at any level, and above all we must be united in our planning and in all our actions in this crucial year.[19]

The Harare Conference, postponed for five months, proved extremely difficult to organize. Many feared South African reprisals against the conference participants, its readiness and ability to hit ANC targets in Harare having been demonstrated frequently in recent years. Apart from Huddleston himself, then seventy-four and in uncertain health, participants from inside South Africa included academics and church nominees while the external wing of the ANC nominated outside participants. The host was the law faculty of the University of Zimbabwe.

Those four days . . . were a watershed in the politics of the region . . . and the meeting gave a foretaste of the strengths and talents of a South African post-apartheid society . . . Encounters between those inside the country and the political exiles set the tone . . . Their political lives depended largely on their trust for each other, built up by a network of internal organization, high-risk meetings and messages through go-betweens . . . The South African children and mothers, victims of repression and torture, called for peace, but on their terms. Those terms were dictated by the . . . level of suffering and sacrifice which it meant. To them, one person one vote in a unitary state which saw the end of the apartheid regime and

its Bantustans was not a negotiating position but an achiev-
able goal.[20]

Few of the priests, doctors, lawyers, social workers, journalists
and community organizers from South Africa who had come with
statistics and affidavits and in some cases the actual child victims
of torture and their mothers, knew that the ANC would be there
in strength, or that its President-in-Exile, Oliver Tambo, would
himself be present.

The conference papers contained massive documentation of
police torture of children, some as young as nine. The Conference
rapporteur was none other than Beyers Naudé, the Afrikaans
religious leader whose personal commitment to anti-apartheid
ranks with that of Huddleston himself. He founded the Christian
Institute of Southern Africa and as a result of his radical stance
on race and religion had been banned from all public life in 1977.
Thabo Mbeki, then ANC's publicity secretary, paid tribute to
them both, and Naudé concluded with his deep fears for the
safety of those returning to South Africa with nothing to protect
them from the consequence of their presence in Harare: 'I hope
that nothing will happen. I pray that nothing will happen. But
those who do pay a price will pay it for all of us.'[21] Everyone
knew that the price he meant was detention, torture, or even
death.

Naudé and Tambo both praised Huddleston in their addresses
to the Conference, the latter thanking 'our old friend and fellow
combatant . . . for taking this important initiative. In you the
children of our country have always found a protector and a
second parent'. Robert Mugabe, Zimbabwe's head of state,
extended a special welcome to Huddleston, 'one of the pioneers
and an ally in the anti-apartheid struggle'.

Frank Chikane, Secretary General of the South African Council of Churches, who had himself undergone detention and severe
and repeated torture, lifted the veil from some of the more
atrocious cases detailed by the young victims of police torture
who were attending the conference. In some instances they had
only been recently reunited with their families and the evidence

of their maltreatment was still obvious: 'the police attacks on children weren't simply the actions of over-zealous security forces but were actually part of a deliberate policy of terrorising the youth ... During the 1986 emergency, of the 22,000 detainees, 8,800 were children under eighteen.'[22] The subsequent plight of the tortured children, physically and psychologically unable to resume normal life, is a particularly harrowing feature of the subsequent press comment, none of which, however, induced the British government to change its attitude to sanctions on South Africa. Huddleston said at Harare: 'the thing that sickens me from all these Western politicians I have been talking to all these years is the appalling assumption that it doesn't matter if it takes five, ten fifteen, twenty years to end apartheid, and meanwhile hundreds of thousands of children are destroyed.'[23] He may have underestimated the degree to which the United States Congress had moved towards comprehensive sanctions by 1986. With this in place Pretoria was effectively isolated and though much blood was needlessly shed between then and 1994, world leaders knew that the end of apartheid was in sight. In 1987, European AAM activists could be forgiven their scepticism.

Trevor Huddleston was the least self-satisfied person I have ever encountered. It would be wrong to think that his single-minded concentration on child victims of South African police torture, which helped to bring the Harare conference into being, was instrumental in ending the apartheid regime; it ended when international public opinion, and international capital joined hands in blackballing the regime from the international community. But this crucial *rapprochement* arose directly, and quantifiably, from the work of the Anti-Apartheid Movement, the International Defence and Aid Fund and the Bishop Ambrose Reeves Trust, and Huddleston was at the head of all these movements. He knew at first hand that the non-whites of South Africa had suffered repression, loss of self-respect, the destruction of family life through violence, trauma and police action over several generations and that some of the victims and martyrs to the cause of liberation had come from his own and other branches of the Church. He may not have known that it would require

America's Congress commitment to comprehensive sanctions to make that liberation – so long hoped for, so remote until the last moments – a reality.

The years between 1987 and 1991 showed no signs of Huddleston easing up. In January1987 he was in New Delhi attending the International Youth Conference against Apartheid and celebrating the seventy-fifth anniversary of the ANC. It was here that he first met Rajiv Gandhi, with whom he immediately formed a strong friendship, lasting until Gandhi's assassination in 1991. In February he was in Moorfields Eye Hospital again. In April he flew to the United States on AAM business. After Harare in September, October was filled with a conference at St Katharine's, Stepney, a visit to Great Tew and a holiday in Devon, finishing with a press conference under AAM auspices for Sam Nujoma, President of the South West Africa Peoples' Organisation (SWAPO) on 23 October, followed the next day by a demonstration for sanctions, which he addressed. In November he had important meetings with Frank Chikane of the South African Council of Churches, and with Geoffrey Howe at the Foreign Office. The year ended with award of a doctorate at the City University; and on 10 December, the presentation of an AAM petition in favour of sanctions to Downing Street.

1988 continued in the same vein. He was in Moorfields Eye Hospital in early February but was able to take part in the launching of the press conference for the Mandela release campaign – the subject of a mighty flow of correspondence between St James's Piccadilly, the Foreign and Commonwealth Office and Downing Street – and to visit Australia, Malaysia, India and Nigeria. In May he attended the annual general meeting of IDAF, paid a flying visit to the USA in late May, and enjoyed one of the most exciting events of his life on 11 June – the Free Mandela Concert at Wembley. The noise was tremendous, and at its height, two old men acknowledge the rapturous applause: they were Oliver Tambo and Trevor Huddleston. It was a huge success, the BBC giving over ten hours of prime time to it. Right-wing Conservatives were enraged. Huddleston gave it a moral authority across the whole of the television network:[24] he understood how important mobilizing international celebrities was for raising awareness. The AAM team, with Oliver Tambo and Mandela's lawyer representing the imprisoned leader, then flew to Glasgow to launch the Freedom March on London, accompanied by the SWAPO Secretary-General, Andimba Toivo Ja Toivo.

Later in June came celebrations for his seventy-fifth birthday, the launching of his *Festschrift* published by Oxford University Press and a grand AAM party at London University's Institute of Education. An OUP reception and dinner followed on 16 June. The next month he received an honorary doctorate from Warwick University and on 17 July, Huddleston and Archbishop Desmond Tutu addressed an AAM mass rally in Hyde Park. Mandela teeshirts and badges were worn conspicuously by London's primary schoolchildren as a direct result. Three generations were now engaged – those who knew him and his work in the 1950s, Michael Terry's and Peter Mandelson's generation, now in their forties; and children of twelve and upwards for whom Nelson Mandela's name was becoming a mantra.

July 18, 1988 was Mandela Day, marking the seventieth birthday of South Africa's future President. About this Huddleston wrote in September:

> The past year in AAM has been dominated by one event, the seventieth birthday of Nelson Mandela . . . It is literally true that virtually the whole world knew of this event as a result of the great pop concert at Wembley in June which was the preparation for it. A billion people saw on their television screens some of the greatest stars in the world who gave their services free for this event. In spite of considerable pressure from our opponents, the BBC transmitted the whole event live for over ten hours. This marvellous concert was followed by another almost equally significant event, a rally in Glasgow attended by over 30,000 people to launch the Freedom Marchers on their way from Glasgow to London. Twenty-five marchers, each representing one year of Mandela's life imprisonment, walked 600 miles and finished their march on the day of the great rally in Hyde Park. All of this got

considerable press coverage, at least in Great Britain, and the rally itself was the largest that the Movement has ever attempted. It was addressed by President Oliver Tambo, Archbishop Desmond Tutu and many others. As a result of these efforts, it is reckoned that the membership of our movement has doubled during this past year. There is no need to add my own thanks to all who have taken part in these events, for the success of them is a thanksgiving in itself. As I write, events in Southern Africa are once more in a critical stage. Talks involving Angola, South Africa, Cuba and the United States, centring on the withdrawal of South African troops from Namibia and the implementation of the United Nations' Security Council Resolution 435, have created vast shock waves through the continent. At the same time, the South African government has been launching various diplomatic initiatives aimed at gaining support from various African states and so creating for itself a return to a recognized position in the world community. Again, as I write these words, the results of the municipal elections in South Africa are not known, but it is very clear that President Botha is by hook or by crook trying to show that he has sufficient black support to influence favourably world opinion. There have been very strong reactions to the initiatives over rugby football and soccer with regard to the sports boycott. Again the final picture has yet to emerge. We have to recognize that AAM is a solidarity movement whose aim is quite simply to give its fullest possible support to all those who are working for the immediate end of apartheid. We are not attempting to dictate what is the best manner in which this struggle could be brought to a successful conclusion. Inevitably, however, because we are now a world movement and because our title is what it is, people turn to us for guidance. It is by no means easy in such a turbulent moment of history to give effective guidance and to take the appropriate action. Perhaps next year the picture will be once more clearer and we shall find ourselves again moving rapidly forward to the climax of all our efforts when apartheid will be no more. In the meanwhile, the watchword is 'Never relax: always press on'.

He ended on a personal note of thanks about his seventy-fifth birthday celebration. 'This was something totally unexpected in its magnitude and was most deeply encouraging because of the hundreds of messages I received from governments (our own excluded) and individuals all over the world. I do recognize that there are limits to what I can usefully do and I certainly do not intend to become a burden to the movement because of the diminishments of old age. However, I also intend to give all I can in this next critical period of the struggle, and it is wonderful to know that we are so united.'[25]

On 3 October he flew to Mauritius where he spent two-and-a-half weeks, and later returned to London for a follow-up to the Harare Conference on the position of children in occupied Namibia. He attended an EU meeting in Bonn on 8–9 December where sanctions were discussed. On 14 December 1989 the United Nations General Assembly issued a declaration of all-round support 'to secure a speedy . . . end . . . no relaxing by the international community to achieve profound and irreversible change.' Huddleston later wrote: 'No-one would dare to claim, and I would not even wish to, that it was the voice of the Church in South Africa that aroused the international community, through the UN declaration, to effective action. It was the long, heroic struggle and endurance of the black majority inside South Africa which brought us all to that great moment of decision.'[26]

In January 1989 he was again in Australia, and in April flew to Nigeria as a guest of President Babangida for a week-long tour of the country during which he was given Nigeria's highest award, the Grand Commander of the Order of the Niger, for his commitment to the anti-apartheid cause. In May he was in the US receiving another honorary doctorate, but was back in time for a banquet at Claridges for the state visit of the Nigerian Federal President, and a week's visit to Sweden in late May. In June he was in Edinburgh attending the Scottish Miners' Gala, and at Mirfield at the end of August to attend the requiem for his lifelong friend Mark Tweedy, followed in October by another, for Hugh Bishop, in St Paul's Knightsbridge.[27] AAM visits to Belfast, Oslo and Switzerland followed and on 13 December he

was part of a delegation to Downing Street in support of sports
sanctions, returning there on 12 January 1990 with a petition on
the subject. The rest of January was spent on AAM business in
Japan.

On 11 February 1990 Mandela himself was released from jail
in a ceremony few will forget. On 3 February Huddleston lunched
with Jesse Jackson, pursuing American public opinion. On 12
March he flew to Sweden to meet Mandela, Tambo and other
leading members of the ANC. On 9 March Douglas Hurd, then
Foreign Secretary, replied to Huddleston about political prisoners
in South Africa, developing the distinction between ANC's and
Pretoria's definition of such persons. 'This problem can only be
resolved by the parties directly concerned . . . But we are doing
what we can to urge both sides to find a mutually acceptable
solution as quickly as possible. I am encouraged by press reports
which suggest that progress is being made.'

Such insouciance was not matched by the Prime Minister, Mrs
Thatcher, who wrote to Huddleston on 17 April in reply to his
letter of 25 March: 'The accusation that Britain supports apartheid is absurd . . . The sanctions issue belongs to yesterday's
debate . . . It is for the South Africans themselves, all of them, to
determine the future constitution for their country . . . It is a great
pity that the ANC cancelled their exploratory talks with President
de Klerk planned for 11 April.' If progress in Pretoria showed
signs of hope, the British government's progress towards a real
understanding of what was happening did not. With the ANC
now unbanned, a second Mandela concert took place at Wembley
under AAM auspices on Easter Monday (16 April 1990).
Huddleston was there and Mandela attended. He introduced
Mandela thus:

> Tonight I have the great honour to introduce to you and to
> millions all over the world the Deputy President of the African
> National Congress of South Africa – Nelson Mandela. But
> this is more than an honour. It is the fulfilment, after so long,
> of a commitment to see *good* triumph over *evil*. Behind me
> you see unfurled the colours of the ANC – black, green, gold.

Those same colours fluttered behind me thirty-five years ago at Kliptown near Johannesburg, on one of the proudest days of my life, when at the Congress of the People in June 1955 we adopted the Freedom Charter which sets out the vision for a new South Africa – a united, a non-racial and democratic South Africa, which belongs to all who live in it. For having this vision of a new South Africa Nelson Mandela and 155 other leaders were charged with treason in 1956; for seeking to make this vision a reality Nelson Mandela served twenty-seven years in the dungeons of apartheid. His courage and fortitude in prison inspired millions of ordinary people across the world into action against apartheid. Today, as we celebrate the release of Nelson Mandela and his compatriots we also celebrate the independence of Namibia from over a century of colonialism and apartheid. But today's international tribute is much more than a celebration and an opportunity to express our appreciation to the countless millions the world over who have striven to secure the release of Nelson Mandela. It is dedicated to the on-going struggle to free South Africa itself.

He paid tribute to Tambo and ended: 'Nelson Mandela has been released but he still is not free and cannot vote in his own country. There are still thousands of political prisoners. The apartheid system is still alive. We must not relax – nor must we allow our governments to relax their pressure – indeed we must intensify our campaigns for boycotts and sanctions – until all the people of South Africa are free . . . It is now my great privilege and honour to invite Nelson Mandela to address you.' Mandela's own speech, which gave a moving tribute to British AAM campaigns, ended with a timely impromptu encomium of his friend Tambo's achievement during those thirty years in exile.

Before the concert, Mandela met the heads of the international committees of AAM, and this helped to sustain them during the difficult four years that followed. For Huddleston, business continued as usual with the annual general meeting of IDAF in Oslo in late May, a celebration of AAM and the Freedom Charter in late June, the visit of Winnie Mandela on 3 July, and her great welcome in the Central Hall, Westminster; and later in the year a visit to President Sam Nujoma in Namibia. His stepmother Lorna, Lady Huddleston, died at the beginning of November and he travelled twice to Devon for her funeral on 9 November, and the commitment to earth of her ashes at St Andrew's, Tavistock on 20 January 1991.

CHAPTER NINE

NOW IS THE TIME

1991–1998

Trevor Huddleston was deeply unsure whether and when to return to his beloved country. He often said that this would not be until apartheid was dead and buried, and came to believe it would outlast him. Certainly in 1991 it was still firmly in place. He agreed with his long-time anti-apartheid co-worker Hilda Bernstein:

> So the ANC is unbanned, Nelson Mandela is released, and we are back to where we were thirty years ago . . . except that Nelson Mandela was then forty-one, except there was no State of Emergency, no Terrorism Act, except that Victoria Mxenge, Ruth First, Joe Qali and hundreds of other anti-apartheid militants inside and outside South Africa were not murdered, except that tens of thousands had not fled into exile, except that four million had not been uprooted from their homes and dispersed in desert lands to fit with apartheid policy, except that all the wisdom, all the abilities, the energies, the constructive idealism of thousands of Nelson Mandelas had not yet been thrown away, confined to Robben Island, or killed and lost for ever.[1]

1991 had started with a mass protest organized by the Anti-Apartheid Movement outside South Africa House on 1 February, and Huddleston's attendance at the Southern African Coalition Conference at Church House Westminster later that month. In April he was inducted as a Fellow of Queen Mary and Westfield College and on 25 April met Nelson Mandela at Oliver Tambo's home. No doubt on this occasion they discussed the wisdom of him returning to South Africa. Tambo was recuperating from the effects of a stroke he had suffered the previous year and Huddleston regularly brought him Holy Communion at his home during this period.[2] On 1 May Huddleston addressed the 10th and final IDAF annual conference. Later that month, his friend and colleague over three decades, Donald Chesworth, died. They had worked together on several important projects, not least providing playgrounds for East End children on the Thames foreshore and bringing the world's attention to the plight of the Kurds in Eastern Turkey, who were enduring massive persecution, including gas attacks, by their Turkish overseers. He had originally been alerted to this project by Richard Rampton QC, son of the Ramptons, who had aided his many causes since 1962. After Chesworth's funeral at St Botolph's, Aldgate on 3 June, he met with former President Kenneth Kaunda of Zambia, now a firm and lasting friend. On 12 June he dined at the Astors with Oliver Tambo.

In the end, his closest friends advised him to return. He had written to Tambo on 4 March asking for his view and Tambo had replied that he felt it was essential that Huddleston attend the forthcoming ANC conference as a full delegate to ensure that 'what remains of apartheid is totally destroyed.'[3] Tambo then consulted Walter Sisulu who raised it with Mandela. As a result Huddleston was invited as a full delegate and also asked to make the opening speech. In accepting, he wrote: 'I do not regard my visit as a cause for celebrating the end of apartheid but for taking part in the final stages of the struggle.'[4] On 22 June he left Britain for Johannesburg with Abdul Minty to open the first ANC annual conference to be held on South African soil since the movement was banned thirty years before. It was held at the University of Natal, Durban from 2–6 July and was attended by 2,250 delegates from all over South Africa. The ANC National Executive's letter of invitation made plain their enthusiasm for his attendance: 'We think it is absolutely crucial that those stalwarts of the Freedom Struggle, such as you are, who have given their wisdom, energy and determination to the cause of liberation would . . . take their honourable and rightful places at the conference

... The ANC and the people of South Africa have benefited enormously from your selfless and unflinching devotion and contribution to our struggle for freedom, human dignity and social justice.'[5] Without Abdul Minty to accompany him he would never have managed such a demanding schedule. Taking Minty, 'was the wisest choice I have ever made, and the most rewarding'.[6]

His description of the conference and his visit form the major part of his second autobiographical book, *Return to South Africa: the Ecstasy and the Agony*.[7] He wrote it in ten days, urged on by Abdul Minty, immediately on his return and believed he had succeeded in his aim – to update *Naught for Your Comfort*. Given his age and the stress he was under it was a considerable achievement, but reviews were few and far between and sales were unspectacular.[8] Nevertheless, it is a remarkably honest and well set out account, which logs the agonies as well as the ecstasies, and the experiences that embraced both.

'It would have been better had you come at the release of Nelson. There is a sombre mood here because of the carnage.' Archbishop Desmond Tutu was the only one of Huddleston's close friends in South Africa who had tried to dissuade him from coming. The 'carnage' he referred to was the tide of black against black violence that was engulfing the townships. While Huddleston was there the government and police provoked atrocities by the Inkatha Freedom Party (IFP), responded to in kind by the ANC's militant wing. These were commonplace and widely reported in the press, particularly in Huddleston's favourite paper the Johannesburg *Star*. A committee of enquiry found that 3,697 people had been killed or injured in the attacks launched by hostel dwellers on local people in Soweto and the Johannesburg townships, particularly Alexandria.[9]

Foremost among the ecstasies was 'the dear love of comrades', most eloquently realized as Walter Sisulu welcomed him at the airport and brought him back to a regional ANC meeting called to elect delegates to the Conference.[10] Here he was to meet again many of his 'creatures' who remembered him from the mid-1950s – 'Chinkie' Modiga, Samuel and Abel, Tom Dakile, 'Sally Maunye, beautiful always but never more so than in her uniform

as a Girl Guide and "Brownie" (called, as I remember, "Sun-
beams"?) leader'. Meeting them caused him to reflect on his love
of children, often and openly expressed throughout his life and
always and increasingly subject to misunderstanding and innuendo. Those he named here[11] 'each so incredibly responsive to
the love I had for them and to the relationship which that love
created across all barriers of colour, age and status. I have no
doubt that, for me, it was my vow of celibacy, depriving me of
the possibility of having children of my own, of being the father
of a family, which made such love for so many children the most
powerful force in my ministry. There is far too much inhibition
about the relationship between adults and children in Britain,
and, I suppose, there are all kinds of reasons – child abuse,
whether physical or sexual, one-parent families, the divorce rate
and economic and social deprivation.' And he quotes one of his
'creatures', Pulé, now a handsome man of fifty or so: 'You knew
he was like a father, and he had love you know, love, love, love
. . . Saying "Father" meant real Father.' And another, trained by
Huddleston to play the part of Mary in the Ekuteleni nativity
play: 'and he used to say to us in order for the play to succeed
we must pray with him. . . .' Huddleston continues: 'I quote Pulé
and Sally to try to convey what I cannot say in my own words:
only in theirs. But when I met them both, and many others of my
children, I knew the ecstasy, and for those precious moments the
agony was not there. And so it was with so many personal
reunions: the reality of a love that does not fade or decay or
disappear with the years. And a love that was deeply, wildly
reciprocated.'

His 1991 visit marked the highpoint of his personal crusade
against the continued existence of apartheid. He was to make
other visits to South Africa – in 1992 to mourn the victims of
the Boipatong massacre; in 1993 to speak at Oliver Tambo's
requiem mass and attend his funeral, and in November of that
year to give the first Oliver Tambo memorial lecture. But his
final visit to South Africa in July 1995 was a disaster. He longed
to be buried by his friends, and they longed to have him: but
practicalities supervened. He was too old to live on his own,

even with a full-time nurse in a house in Soweto – his preferred option. Archbishop Tutu was too involved in the Truth and Reconciliation Commission hearings in Cape Town to be able to guarantee the sort of twenty-four-hour nursing Huddleston now needed. An old people's home was found for him by CR but inevitably it was full of old white people, nursed by black people – a rebarbative reminder of all the race barriers he had fought so hard against, and his reaction was predictably furious and hurtful to all. It ended in his tears and a resentful return to Mirfield where his younger brethren took up the burden he had hoped not to inflict on them.

He and Julius Nyerere had helped launch the Anti-Apartheid Movement in 1959, to bring to the attention of governments and media the full horrors of apartheid in action. By the mid-1980s AAM's exclusive focus on Southern Africa was somewhat defracted when groups of far-left activists saw in it an opportunity to express their protest against a variety of social and economic problems not all associated with racism, nor even Southern Africa. In time AAM thus acquired a somewhat suspect public aura which made it far easier for a government still determined to keep trade links with South Africa open to marginalize its initiatives and influence. Even so, by 1991 its achievements far outweighed its controversial aspects. Branches had grown up all over Britain and in Scandinavia, Holland, the USA and Canada, and India. Its publications and press provided a vital flow of information about the reality of life in South Africa for the majority of its citizens. It was entirely responsible for the concerts, the marches, the rallies and the television spectaculars. Unsurprisingly, by 1991 AAM was facing a serious cash-flow crisis. Income, apart from government grants from non-British sources, was limited to what the membership could raise. The costs of mounting a major public rally ran into hundreds of thousands, if not millions of pounds: the shortfall was becoming a chasm. A 'Trevor Huddleston-Anti-Apartheid Movement Special Account' was set up. Huddleston, never one to avoid the difficult jobs, wrote to the great, the good and the rich, but the results were disappointing. Two African Heads of State – most notably President Babangida of Nigeria – came to the rescue and by November of the following year AAM's debts had been cleared. Huddleston continued to be identified with its aims, in good times as well as bad, launching the 'Vote for Democracy in South Africa' campaign with Mike Terry on 5 September 1991 at the Trades' Union Congress annual conference. On 26 October he was in Sheffield for a celebration of another of his perennial concerns – Tanzanian self-reliance. In front of the Tanzanian High Comissioner, Huddleston, as patron of 'Tools for Self-Reliance', himself received the 250,000th tool.

The rest of the year was dominated by the emotions of his return visit to South Africa, and drew to a close with a requiem at Mirfield for Fr Martin Jarrett-Kerr CR, who had followed him at Sophiatown; the departure of Horst Kleinschmidt from IDAF on 29 November; his opening address as President of the National Peace Council on 1 December; a visit to Geneva on 17 December to discuss the Kurdish situation with the International Red Cross; the launch of *Return to South Africa* at the Royal Commonwealth Society on 5 December and IDAF's last day on 18 December.

The 'carnage' in South Africa, of which Desmond Tutu had warned, came to a head the following year. On 17 June at Boipatong – an indeterminate township on the Vaal Triangle, next to Sharpeville – Inkatha, inspired by government police, went by night to murder and undermine ANC credibility. Forty-nine people were massacred. A deeply shocked Huddleston flew to the area on 27 June with Mike Terry. He was invited by the Vaal Council of Churches to participate at the funeral service for the victims on 29 June, which had been declared a national day of mourning. Huddleston and Terry, accompanied by Desmond Tutu, drove across the veld to the unidentifiable site of Boipathong, getting hopelessly lost in the process. In the end, Tutu had to commandeer a local schoolchild to navigate. Huddleston was warmly and enthusiastically greeted by everyone but tensions were mounting, with army and police everywhere, and as they walked through the graveyard a black youth kicked out at Terry.

The massacre resulted in a call for mass action across the

country by the ANC. Elsewhere, the international community, aided by AAM, pressurized Pretoria to keep the negotiating process alive. The ANC leadership believed that the only way in which the peace process could preserve its credibility was by involving the international community through the United Nations and by the presence of international observers sponsored by the Security Council. Pretoria and most Western governments were against any role for the UN but intense lobbying by AAM persuaded some Western leaders to support UN involvement and then to work on Pretoria to accept it. Huddleston's Boipatong visit provided a focus for this process, and it was followed by an AAM International Hearing on Violence on 14 July at Grays Inn in London, which was funded by the UN. Huddleston and Terry spent much of their short June visit in arranging for witnesses to come to the Hearing, which took place at the same time as a UN Security Council meeting was being convened in New York. The evidence assembled could thus be presented straight from London to the Security Council via the Chairman of the UN Special Committee against Apartheid. Frank Chikane, Secretary-General of the SACC, was one of those who lobbied with great success, and the Security Council duly sent observers to South Africa and negotiations resumed. AAM did not achieve all this on their own, and its work was now very different from the mass demonstrations of the 1980s, but it provided effective solidarity with the ANC and Huddleston's role throughout was pivotal.

1993 provided some space for his other concerns. On 16 February he was part of a delegation to Douglas Hurd at the Foreign Office asking him to intercede on behalf of the Kurds. In March he attended the AAM seminar on 'The Role of the International Community in promoting Free and Fair Elections in South Africa'. On 13 April he flew to Geneva to see Julius Nyerere in order to plan the AAM international conference which they had jointly convened in June, returning to London for the vigil outside South Africa House on 19 April prompted by the assassination of Chris Hani nine days earlier. Hani, the Secretary-General of the South African Communist Party and former Chief-of-Staff of Umkhonto we Sizwe (the military wing of the ANC), was a young and charismatic leader and his shooting in cold blood outside his home by a white supremacist was both a painful loss and an invitation to violent reprisals. Less than a week later Huddleston received more bad news: Oliver Tambo had died.

Tambo's death took a terrible toll. He and Huddleston had been close friends since the mid-1950s and nothing and nobody could take his place in Huddleston's life, not even Mandela whose unique prestige had brought him powers more sweeping than any Tambo had contemplated. Of Tambo's friendship through good times and bad, he would write: 'How can I ever do justice to the memory of one who changed my life? . . . It was Oliver, in those long lonely years of exile, first in Tanzania, then in Zambia, who held the ANC together: he was ready after the Soweto uprising to receive that great rush of exiles and – at last – to be recognized as the international statesman that he was.'[12] On 28 April he flew to South Africa with Abdul Minty, to deliver the eulogy at Tambo's Requiem at St Mary's Cathedral, Johannesburg on 30 April. The funeral took place on 2 May and the following day Huddleston returned to London for lunch with Nelson Mandela, and Mandela's evening reception at The Dorchester. On 15 May he attended a Memorial Service for Tambo at St James's Piccadilly. Between 14–15 June, he and Nyerere jointly hosted the AAM International Conference at Church House, Westminster, rather as they had helped launched the Movement thirty-four years earlier. The theme was: 'Southern Africa: Making Hope a Reality', and its main purpose was to address the post-apartheid era and to lay the basis for its successor organizations. The conference proved a great success and was attended by Walter Sisulu, Desmond Tutu, Sonny Ramphal, Graça Machel (the widow of Samora Machel, Mozambique's first post-independence President, now married to Mandela) and the foreign ministers of most African states. Huddleston's eightieth birthday coincided with the conference and despite his own reluctance to celebrate, an event was organised at the conference on the evening of 14 June and a eucharist and party at St James's Piccadilly the following day, where Archbishop Tutu preached. The whole week was one of the crowning moments of his life. So much of what he had lived for was close to being achieved. And he was helping to lay the basis for the support that he knew would be so crucial to the new, democratic South Africa.

The rest of 1993 was extremely busy. On 23 June he went to attend Encaenia at Oxford and received an honorary doctorate from his old university. On 2 July there was a lunch party at AAM headquarters for all staff there to wish him happy birthday. On 6 July Mike Terry took him to Birmingham University (where Terry had once been President of the Students' Union) for another degree ceremony. At the end of the month he had meetings and an official Foreign Office dinner given for the ANC's new Executive Deputy President, Thabo Mbeki. On 9 October he was in Glasgow to see Nelson Mandela receive the freedom of the city. On 3 November he flew to Johannesburg to give the first Oliver Tambo memorial lecture at Witwatersrand University on 'The Prospect for Free and Fair Elections in South Africa'. It was a brief visit but he found time to see Walter Sisulu, and to lunch with Adelaide Tambo and Nelson Mandela at the Tambo home. Back in London he suffered a painful foot ulcer and was hospitalized at St George's, Tooting Bec on 5 November. This meant he could not look after himself at St James's, and he convalesced with the Yeo family. He returned to Mirfield on 15 December and, as so often, made a rapid recovery. After staying with one of his goddaughters over New Year, he was back in his Piccadilly flat on 7 January 1994.

The Anti-Apartheid Movement and Downing Street continued to correspond on apartheid, with little result. The new Prime Minister, John Major, took up where Mrs Thatcher left off. Mike Terry observed a change of form but not content in the replies from No. 10, despite the rapidly approaching date for South Africa's long-awaited 'free and fair' elections. On 1 March 1994, Huddleston was in Brussels addressing an international conference on this very topic. He flew back directly to Birmingham, where he had been Provost for many years of the Selly Oak Colleges, an influential ecumenical establishment. From there it was back to St James's, Piccadilly. Here it was on 5 March that he fell and broke his kneecap on the stone step leading from the church to the vestry. He was rushed to St Thomas's Hospital and a few days later was accompanied to Mirfield by Mike Terry. After spending Easter there he returned in June to London to live in a flat at Rivermill rented from the Yeos.

On 26 April he was able to enter South Africa House and vote for the ANC. It was another high-point. He had been deprived of his South African citizenship almost forty years earlier and had refused to re-apply for it since he would never acknowledge the legitimacy of the regime. After representations were made on his behalf in Pretoria he was issued with a passport which would allow him to vote. Despite his health he was determined to vote in South Africa, and only the personal intervention of Nelson Mandela persuaded him to vote in Britain. Mike Terry drove him from Mirfield to London where he was given a hero's welcome as he entered South Africa House. This was all the more amazing since most of those waiting to vote were white South Africans, but everyone wanted to share in the joy of the occasion. After casting his vote together with Abdul Minty, he held an impromptu press conference, much to the annoyance of the diplomats. For a while AAM seemed to be running the place. And because voting abroad was the day before voting in South Africa, this event attracted enormous publicity in South Africa as well as Britain.

May was busier than ever. On 7 May he and Mike Terry flew to Johannesburg for the National Service of Thanksgiving and the inauguration as State President of Nelson Mandela. Now confined to a wheelchair Huddleston was given a room in a top-security hotel. As he was being wheeled down to breakfast, a black bodyguard on each side, he saw standing at the end of the corridor a young Afrikaner soldier with a Kalashnikov. As they came up the solider said, 'I would like to touch the Archbishop', whom he had seen on television the previous day. He said, 'I am an Afrikaner and I represent my people. I also attend the Dutch Reformed Church. I want to say on their behalf how deeply sorry I am for the terrible things we have done to the black people of this country.' Huddleston replied, 'This is now the new South Africa and we must put the past behind us and learn to forget.'

'That isn't good enough,' said the soldier. 'Here is need for penitence.' Then putting his gun down and kneeling on the floor, he removed his cap and asked Huddleston to bless him. Huddleston, who told the story to his many visitors on his return, sometimes with differing details, confessed he was so near to tears that he could hardly speak.[13]

Returning to Britain he preached at Christ Church, Oxford on 19 May and on 25 May flew to California to receive a doctorate from Whittier College. An important Extraordinary General Meeting of the Anti-Apartheid Movement took place at the Friends' House, Euston Road on 25 June to discuss the winding-up of its affairs and subsequent re-emergence in October as Action for Southern Africa, with Huddleston as its founding patron. In July he was honoured with a doctorate from Dundee University, returning via Mirfield to London on 18 July to attend a service at Westminster Abbey to mark South Africa's re-admittance to the Commonwealth. The next day he met Thabo Mbeki with the AAM leadership.

On 13 October he fell in his Rivermill flat and fractured his femur, remaining in St Thomas's Hospital until he was able to return to Mirfield to live. He found hospital conditions intolerable and grew angry with God for allowing the hospital to be so bad – which it certainly was not. He was an extremely difficult patient, rebuking nurses for not paying sufficient respect when a former head of state – Kenneth Kaunda – came to visit out of hours – and eventually discharging himself, as he was to do several times from other hospitals almost until the day of his death. By the end of November he was well enough to visit London to deliver an impassioned attack on apartheid at South Africa House at the launch of Mandela's autobiography, *Long Walk to Freedom*, hosted by the publishers, Little, Brown (Mandela himself had asked Huddleston to preside at the launch). On 19 December, Huddleston at Mirfield took part in a ceremony celebrating his outstanding contribution to the development of the independent state of Tanzania. The High Commissioner, Mr Mchumo, presented him with Tanzania's highest honour, the Torch of Kilimanjaro, in the presence of his good friends from

Tanzania days, Roger and Julia Carter and Joan Wicken, former
personal assistant to President Nyerere.

In January 1995 Mike Terry and Fr Nicolas Stebbing CR
accompanied Huddleston to India where he received the Indira
Gandhi Award in the presence of a great gathering including
Abdul Minty and Nelson Mandela, who was there on his first
state visit. Receiving a large cheque and a heavy stone plaque,
Huddleston made one of his last public addresses:

> I can truly say that for me there is no greater privilege than to
> be honoured in India. I feel deeply humbled to receive the
> Award bestowed on me today. That the Award is in the name
> of Mrs Indira Gandhi has a special significance. For she
> advanced the cause of the poor and the dispossessed in the great
> tradition of her father, Pandit Jawaharlal Nehru, and inspired
> by the great Mahatma Gandhi, the father of the nation.
>
> The Mahatma's unique example of overcoming evil
> through moral actions touched the hearts and minds of people
> across the world and transformed the course of anti-colonial
> struggle in Asia and Africa.
>
> It was in South Africa that the great Mahatma developed
> the philosophy of *Satyagraha* [passive resistance]. As President
> Mandela, in a message smuggled out of prison when he
> received the 1979 Jawaharlal Nehru Award for International
> Understanding, said: 'In twenty-one years of his stay in South
> Africa we were to witness the birth of ideas and methods of
> struggle that have exerted an incalculable influence on the
> history of the people of India and South Africa.'
>
> His profound influence has been manifested throughout
> the South African Liberation struggle by leaders such as Chief
> Albert Luthuli, Walter Sisulu, Yusuf Dadoo, Oliver Tambo
> and especially President Mandela whose presence here today
> means so much to me. Through Mahatma Gandhi, the South
> African and Indian struggles became one – demonstrated so
> decisively by pre-independent India when in July 1946 it
> severed diplomatic relations with South Africa and imposed
> total economic sanctions. It was also India that in June 1946
> first placed the issue of South Africa's racial policies on the

agenda of the United Nations. Having arrived in South Africa
as a young priest in 1943, through my pastoral work I was
becoming inevitably involved in opposing the doctrine of
racial superiority. I personally witnessed the profound impact
of India's solidarity action upon the oppressed people. I can
truly say today that the action served both to inspire and
guide me in all my anti-apartheid activities in South Africa
and internationally. In a real sense, at considerable economic
and political sacrifice, India became the first Front-line State
against apartheid and had remained steadfast ever since.
India's pioneering role resulted in the United Nations taking
up the struggle against apartheid. And in this context, I feel
bound to pay tribute to Mr Enugu Reddy, the former UN
Assistant Secretary General, who personally played such an
important role in this work.

India's unique anti-apartheid role has especial meaning for
me also because of my personal involvement with your great
country. At the time of my birth, my father was away serving
in the Indian navy. And over sixty years ago I celebrated my
21st birthday here in Delhi. I have always cherished the link
with India and have been fortunate to have been able to visit
it so often. This link was given a new dimension when I was
elected as the Anglican Archbishop of the Indian Ocean and
based in Mauritius. This experience also opened my eyes fully
to the miracle of the diversity of human kind which also finds
expression in the multitude of faiths which are practised on
that small island. It was once in Mauritius that I was privileged to meet Prime Minister Indira Gandhi. This was at a
critical period, after the independence of Zimbabwe, when
the major Western powers were making a determined effort
to end South Africa's international isolation. As Chairperson
of the Non-Aligned Movement and host of the 1983 Commonwealth Conference, the Prime Minister Gandhi played a
decisive role in countering this offensive and simultaneously
laying the foundation for effective action to secure Namibia's
independence and to end the apartheid system. Her assassination on that tragic day – 31 October 1984 – robbed not only
India but the world of a great leader.

In devastating and tormenting circumstances, Rajiv Gandhi took over office and was able to give new expression to his mother's values and beliefs. These were challenging times for the freedom struggle in Southern Africa and in my capacity as President of the Anti-Apartheid Movement I was privileged to meet with Rajiv on many occasions. When apartheid South Africa intensified its war of aggression and destabilisation against the independent states of Southern Africa in the 1980s, it was India which was asked by the non-aligned movement to chair the Africa Fund which was set up in 1986 to mobilise international resources in support of the region. I know from our discussions how seriously Rajiv Gandhi took this responsibility. In particular, I still recall, as if it were yesterday, my lengthy discussion with Rajiv when I paid a short visit to New Delhi the following January to participate in a programme of events to mark the 75th anniversary of the ANC which was organized by the Congress Youth League. I also experienced the warmth of his humanity and the quality of his friendship. Once, when I broke my arm and suffered complications with my diabetes, a huge bouquet of flowers arrived – from Rajiv. I will never know how it was that thousands of miles away he learnt of my illness but I do know that such acts of friendship made the pain of my grief that much harder to bear when, tragically, he too, like his mother, was the victim of hatred and bigotry and never lived to see democracy triumph in South Africa. But it was a source of great joy for me to be with his widow, Sonia Gandhi, in Pretoria last May to witness the inauguration of President Mandela as South Africa's first democratically elected Head of State. The decolonialisation process which began with India's Independence in 1947, was closed on that historic day. Now we are in a new era in Southern Africa, where hope has to be turned into reality through a programme of reconstruction and equitable development throughout the region.

The Award I have been honoured to receive today is the Indira Gandhi Award for Peace, Development and Disarmament – objectives which have always united the peoples of

India and South Africa. Now for the first time the Government of these two countries have the opportunities to work together to promote these objectives. President Mandela in his Rajiv Gandhi Golden Jubilee Memorial Lecture two days ago set out a vision of a new relationship which will span the Indian Ocean bringing with it the prospect of the Indian Ocean becoming a zone of peace. I was particularly encouraged by the commitment to promote economic co-operation amongst all the countries which share this great ocean. Through trade, commerce and investment new initiatives can be taken to address root causes of under-development, thus bringing about a real improvement in the quality of life for all. This will also require a high priority to be given both to conventional disarmament as well as the outlawing of all nuclear and other weapons of mass destruction. This is in the Bandung spirit of Afro-Asian solidarity. But co-operation in the Indian Ocean should also be in the context of a new pattern of South–South relations which the South Commission under the leadership of Mwalimu Julius Nyerere has done so much to promote. One of the greatest challenges for the future of our planet is the confrontation between the hunger of the south and the affluence of the north. And I have no doubt that the future lies with the south. Whilst the north is gripped with a rising tide of racism and xenophobia, moral leadership is coming increasingly from the south – and there is no greater example of this than that now set by President Mandela. I believe that there can be no better tribute to Indira Gandhi than for the objectives of peace, development and disarmament to become a reality throughout the south, and especially the rim countries of the Indian Ocean, as a consequence of this week's historic visit by President Mandela to India. With these words I am honoured to accept the Indira Gandhi Award for Peace, Development and Disarmament.[14]

Before the Award ceremony President Mandela had delivered a lecture and, noticing Huddleston in the audience, spent the last five minutes in a brief encomium on his life-long friend: 'He lived among people who suffered the atrocity of apartheid, loved them as his own family, wiped their tears and encouraged them to carry on their noble fight. So close a bond did it become that when he was called away to other duties he continued for the next four decades to work, pressing the world to take action on the plight of the South African people.'

The failure of his final attempt to return to South Africa for good cast a long shadow over the rest of 1995. He returned to Mirfield from Johannesburg on 19 September after two distressing months and from then until his death two-and-a-half years later he was looked after by the young Mirfield brethren, Fr Nicolas Stebbing in particular. Huddleston was now much too ill to engage in the busy social round that had dominated his life for so long and made only brief visits to London – once to stay with the Ramptons, then to see friends while staying at the St James's Court Hotel. On 12 June 1996 he breakfasted at Buckingham Palace with Nelson Mandela. This was to be the last time the two men met. In December of the following year he was gazetted KCMG in the New Year honours' list and on 27 January 1998 he was present at the unveiling of his and Oliver Tambo's busts at South Africa House. His last public engagement was his investiture as a KCMG at Buckingham Palace on 24 March. Less than a month later, on the morning of 20 April 1998, Trevor Huddleston died.

Fr Nicolas Stebbing has written a moving account of Huddleston's last years:[15]

I first met Trevor properly when he came back here early in 1994 to stay for some weeks after falling and breaking his kneecap at St James's, Piccadilly. He stayed with us for several weeks then until he was well enough to go to South Africa for the inauguration of President Mandela and the new South African government. In October of that year he fell again and broke his hip. He came and stayed with us and it was then that really serious nursing began, as did my peculiar role of his *aide-de-camp* in all kinds of unusual situations. The first of these was the Mandela book launch at South Africa House. Then came the Indira Gandhi Peace Prize for which we had to go to New Delhi – an extraordinary journey –

Above: Huddleston and Fr Raymond Raynes CR (right) at the farewell concert for Huddleston, 1955.

Right: Huddleston arrives back in the UK after his tour of America, 1956.

The consecration as Bishop of Masasi, Dar es Salaam, 1960.

Huddleston with Julius Nyerere, President of Tanzania, 1964.

On the doorstep of 400 Commercial Road, E1, 1970.

Stepney, 1972.

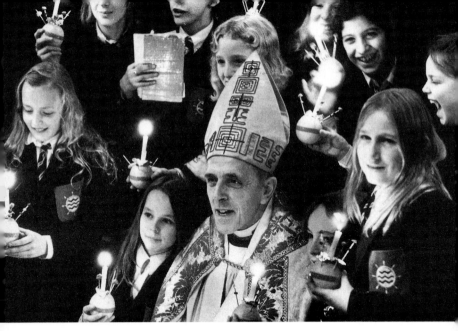

At a 'Christingle' service at St Clement's, Eastcheap, 1972.

Pastoral work, Stepney 1973.

Mauritius, 1980. Huddleston with Gilles (left), whom he adopted, and his friend Yasim.

Huddleston, Abdul Minty (left) and Desmond Tutu at the Hyde Park Rally, July 1988.

AAM protest vigil outside South Africa House, 1988.

Campaigning at the age of seventy-six. AAM protest rally, London 1989.

Above: Returning to South Africa in June 1991, for the first time in thirty-five years, to be greeted by Nelson Mandela (centre) and Alfred Nzo (right).

Left: Huddleston listens to the speeches after opening the ANC's first national congress on South African soil in thirty years, on 2 July 1991.

3 days in Delhi, one in Bombay, then on to South Africa where I spent one night before returning here. Trevor thought he was staying for good, at the Priory [St Peter's Priory, Southdale, Johannesburg], but after three months it became clear that this would not work and he came back here. After three months here he returned to Johannesburg, 'for good' but found life in a white old people's home intolerable. So he came back here. For about a year he kept talking about going back to South Africa but when we met Nelson Mandela in June 1996 he accepted Mandela's request that he stay in this country to work in every way he could to gain support in England for the new situation in South Africa. That was not quite the end of it. After a few months he tried again to persuade us to arrange for him to go out but we wouldn't. And in the end he accepted that his health simply would not allow it, that he would be too much of a burden on his friends out there. Accepting that was one of the hardest things he ever had to do, but it brought a certain amount of peace.

During that time, when he was continually going on about returning to South Africa, one could often see that he was caught in an impossible bind. He had not lived in South Africa for forty years. His health made it impossible for him to live anywhere but in an old people's home. He had an idea that he could rent a house in Soweto and have a nurse to look after him. Given his physical and mental state, and his immobility, this would very soon have ended in tears. Sometimes he knew this. Other times he refused to face up to it. Yet you could see that he was partly driven by guilt. His South African friends and admirers wanted him back. He himself was not at all sure he wanted to go back or could face the political hassles of the new South Africa. Very revealingly, as we drove away from Buckingham Palace after he had met Mandela and Mandela had asked him to stay in England, he said to me 'Well, that's a great relief. No-one can say now that I am chickening out of going back'. And, at the same time, he had his English friends whom he loved. One of the nicest things about looking after Trevor has been meeting his friends: they are all, without exception, delightful people.

Working with Trevor has been an amazing experience for me. Having him here has been very difficult for the Community and for him. I think it has been important for the wheel to turn full circle and for him to finish his religious life here where he began it more than fifty years ago. I don't think we should underestimate the enormous cost this has been to him. I do not understand all of this but I can guess. There is a long history of difficult relationships between Trevor and CR. I suspect (on the basis of what Sister Agatha Mary SPB once told me) that during Trevor's time in South Africa he was not much supported by his brethren who, however good they were as pastors, were politically and socially pretty conservative. Sister Agatha said it wasn't until she read Alan Wilkinson's history of CR that she realised how a (comparatively) socialist person like Trevor could have found himself in such a conservative community. Then, of course, leaving South Africa was immensely painful for Trevor. That obedience must have both broken him and made him what he is, for good and ill. He was of course a pretty disastrous novice guardian and those who were novices under him still resent the little amount of time he gave them since he was so taken up with apartheid matters. Trevor was, of course, a single agenda person. All was then and there. There has always been much tension between the kind of public stance he had expected the Community to take up and what the Community has felt able to do. All CR bishops find it difficult to return to the Community. Trevor was no exception. He was away for thirty-four years and had only spent four years of his Community life at Mirfield. The last three years really have been a kind of second novitiate for him. No wonder there have been tensions.

It was not all tension. Some of it has been amazing joy. Trevor had the most astonishing ability to engage one's feelings. When he was down, I was utterly down. When he was angry, I was devastated. A moment later (when I had just wondered how I could ever bear to set eyes on him again) he could be so utterly lovely, gracious, grateful, playful, enchanting that I would do absolutely anything for him. There was at such times a real pathos in him – an anxiety to be accepted, to be forgiven.

He was very brave. He was in increasing and continuous pain – from arthritis, from diabetic neuropathy, from the effects of immobility. From time to time this got on top of him and he raged against God for torturing him on and on like that. At the same time he was fighting with depression. I think he was a depressive but came from the generation that regarded depression as a weakness or a sin. So he said often: 'Of course I am not a depressive. It is just the insulin that makes me feel depressed.' He constantly rose above that and was the charming, delightful, energetic person that everyone knew him to be.

When Trevor went to South Africa House in January 1998 to be present at the unveiling of his bust he was in very good form, and gave a splendid speech. I think this concealed from most of his friends just how weak he was getting physically and mentally. Over the next few weeks we wondered whether he would make it to the palace to receive his KCMG. Up to the last moment we were prepared for him to decide he couldn't make it: or for us to decide he couldn't go. In fact his very strong will got him through. But although he was growing weaker, and sometimes more dotty, and was finding it increasingly difficult to maintain a conversation – at table for instance – that wasn't entirely on his terms, he also became sweeter, more interested in others, less obsessed with himself. He came to realise just how self-centred he had been and steadily began to make a real effort to change that. It was touching to see how much he put into the evening visits he had from students. Of course he always loved the young but he always put every last bit of energy into entertaining them and always told me afterwards how wonderful they had been.

Against all expectations the KCMG ceremony went very well and he coped well with the dinner. When I returned on Maundy Thursday I was amazed at how sweet, patient and light-hearted he seemed to have become. He seemed entirely free from self-pity. I wondered then if this was the change that often precedes the death of some of our more difficult characters. It was also true that we had at last persuaded him to take the proper painkillers and this was giving him a good night's sleep and (since they were morphine-based) probably contributed to his more euphoric state. On Holy Saturday he asked, with quite surprising diffidence, whether the Prior could find time to hear his confession. The Prior said afterwards that it was an amazingly grace-filled experience. Trevor told me then that the confession had been the most important single thing in his life.

On Easter Monday, after tea, he fell, trying to get to the basin to wash his cup. I found him on the floor in intense pain, which he did not bear silently. Connie called an ambulance. Trevor swore at everyone and everything and ripped off his dog collar to show he was not putting up any longer with a God who could treat him like this. The ambulance men thought he had broken ribs and shoulder. In fact, it turned out he had simply bruised them. However he was finding it impossible to stand and he himself said he would rather stay in hospital than be a burden to us. I took him to his ward but it became clear that this would not be a success. By 8.15 the next morning he had discharged himself and was on his way back. Connie and I thought this was a bad mistake, but, of course, it turned out he was right. Briefly I wondered if we should get him into a good local nursing home. Actually they had no room, but I know now he wouldn't have gone. He couldn't bear to be among strangers and even if they had been able to give him instant attention he would still not have been satisfied.

Nights were the worst. The painkillers seemed to have some effect but not enough. Fortunately, from the nursing angle, I was able to call in a college student, Lee Bennett, who is a splendid nurse and gave me the back-up I needed at night. It took time even for him to gain Trevor's confidence. Putting him to bed was horrendous. The first night I sat up with Trevor quite a lot and Lee could only come and help me move him (and reassure me there was nothing more we could do). The second night Trevor called two or three times and Lee had to call me. The third night I had a completely uninter-rupted night and Lee dealt with everything. In the morning Trevor insisted that Lee should tell me (in front of him) what he had told Trevor, that Trevor had been extremely good and was coping with the pain as well as it was possible to cope. There was a real sense of 'Mummy must know that I've been good'. In fact, it was a major concern during the last few days that he was doing things right, and he was much reassured when we told him he was being wonderful and doing very well, because he was so unsure of himself. On the Saturday night at about midnight Lee called me. Trevor had harangued him for not giving him enough painkillers and told him he had no right to be a priest (he had told him the previous night he already was a wonderful priest). He then harangued me and told me I had no right to be infirmarian since I didn't know how to stop the pain. I think he would have liked to call the Superior then and have me sacked. Then he sent us packing. We tried to call a doctor to do something about the pain, but we couldn't find one, which was just as well since Trevor evidently went off to sleep about 1 a.m. and slept through to 6 when he was sick, but went back to sleep and slept till lunchtime.

Why did he suffer such pain? Cracked ribs are notoriously painful. Probably the fall shook up his arthritis and inflamed his diabetic neuropathy making parts of his skin terribly over-sensitive to even the slightest touch. But I wonder if some of it was his struggle to let go, to learn how to die. On the last day he sat up through the afternoon, but couldn't eat at all, and drank just water. About suppertime I thought he was developing a death rattle, though he was intermittently conscious and we had some rational conversation. I asked if he wanted to be anointed and he did, so the Superior came and did that. I think that made an enormous difference. When James and I put him to bed there were no squeals or groans. He settled immediately into a comfortable position. I think he still had the pain but in some way it simply no longer bothered him. He had stopped fighting it. As the night went by he began slipping into semi-consciousness. Occasionally during the night he seemed to have conversations with angels or

God, hovering over his bed, mainly pleading with them to take him. Curiously in those few days, though he had kept saying he wanted to die, he had stopped railing at God for not letting him. He just kept pleading to be allowed to go. At 1.30 a.m. his breathing became more laboured. I called James and the Superior. We sat with him, and said the final prayers, but he didn't go. Morning came and I wondered whether to move him, to clean up the bed, but decided not to do much. He was beyond eating or drinking now, and the sleep had become much deeper. I think there was no communication at all after about 6 am. At 10.30 am, while Aidan was sitting with him, I popped in to see him and noticed that his colour had completely changed, his breathing almost gone. Aidan said that it had just happened. At that point I heard Jill Thompson arrive so I whipped her in and we just had time to say the Litany of the Dying and the final prayers before his breathing stopped altogether, so peacefully that it was some minutes before I could be sure it had really happened.

I learnt two things about Trevor during the last year. One was that he had a wonderful appreciation of poetry and music, and read widely and deeply, trying to keep it up to the very end, though in the end he was not capable of understanding or completing the many books he bought from Hatchard's (whose sales assistants he persecuted in an appalling fashion if they couldn't find the book or if the post delayed the book for more than a day.) Secondly, though it sounds a cliché, Trevor was a man of real prayer. Almost to the last day he said his Offices absolutely faithfully. Every morning he interceded for friends in a manner that left him exhausted. And those who gave him Communion always found him very collected, and many said how gratifying an experience this was. This was at a time when he was frequently cursing God to the skies for the appalling manner in which he ran the world – if he existed at all, which Trevor kept saying that ninety-eight per cent of him no longer believed.

His secretary, Jill Thompson, spoke the truth when she told a newspaper that he died of old age.

Demanding though he was he would surely have been gratified at the press response, the obituaries, the eulogies. In the *Financial Times* Joe Rogaly, whose name has recurred in these pages, wrote memorably of Huddleston as 'a man of God, a monk, a socialist possessed of deep faith in Christ and a consistent uplifter of the spirit. He held unwaveringly to his perception of humanity as an expression of the divine. He skilfully manipulated the great and the good in the interests of the wretched . . . He died with the flame of his great crusade, the betterment of the human condition for the love of Christ, held high.'[16]

The President of South Africa, Nelson Mandela, said he 'was a pillar of wisdom, humility and sacrifice to the legions of freedom fighters in the darkest moments of the struggle . . . Father Huddleston embraced the downtrodden.' Archbishop Tutu said he 'made sure that apartheid got onto the world agenda and stayed there. If you could say that anybody single-handedly made apartheid a world issue, then that person was Trevor Huddleston'. The British Prime Minister, Tony Blair said: 'Trevor Huddleston was a remarkable and a wonderful man. He will be remembered most for the role he played in the fight against apartheid in South Africa, a fight that would not have been won without the kind of courage and commitment . . . Huddleston showed.'

Ten years earlier, much the same was written of Huddleston in his *Festschrift*, by Sir Shridath S. Ramphal and Abdul Minty. In that book Julius Nyerere, then President of Tanzania but now in retirement, said: 'Bishop Huddleston has been . . . a fighter in the struggle for the triumph of human equality and dignity in Africa . . . he enriches the lives of those with whom he works.'[17] On 27 April 1998 Dr Nyerere wrote in the *Guardian*: 'Huddleston never faltered in his commitment to the anti-apartheid struggle; but while serving as Bishop of Masasi in the 1960s he served the people of that somewhat isolated diocese without reservation, clearly seeing the two tasks as one – the development of human dignity in Africa.'

It is easy to discount the *nihil nisi bonum* conventions of the editors of the world's obituary pages but difficult to discern any hypocrisy or overstatement in what was written about Huddleston's life, work and personality, in 1988 and in 1998. Life: work: personality: the three are inextricably tied. Often when moral theory is being discussed a distinction is made between what a person does and what he or she is. Sometimes it seems appropriate to define a person by what they do, perhaps because there may be little else, or little evidence of anything else (other than their observed or inferred activities) on which to base such a definition. But for others, a definition in terms of activity seems inadequate and such people – what they stand for, how people react to them, their place in history – must be seen as more than the sum of their actions. Where the match between identity and activity is total, you have a person of rare consistency and sanity. And where the actions over a long and active life are consistent with each other in the context of life-long vows ruling a changing lifestyle, changing work, changing events, a changing world scene, there you are likely to find a personality and achievement of true significance.

I have tried to use this distinction in defining and celebrating the life, activities and times of Trevor Huddleston and to show that the self is greater than its means of expression. An active and engaged public figure who has also taken the vows of chastity, poverty and obedience crucially points up this distinction. But the difference between his outer and inner lives is far from being paradoxical: the spiritual life fuelled the busy days of his life-long campaign for human dignity. Anyone who knew him or worked with him knows this.

If there is a discernible pattern in his career it seems to be a repeated creative response to a series of unconnected situations set up for him by other people. Perhaps this is what fulfilling a vow of obedience means. It was his vow of obedience that drove Huddleston into exile. It was given in 1941 at Mirfield and it was this alone that gave him the strength, when he needed it most, to part from what he loved. 'Nothing else could have torn me away from Africa at that moment.'[18] It was almost unbearable. 'What does it mean,' he goes on, 'this real agony of parting? Why does it cost so much?' He dreaded the darkness of the years that lay ahead but the vow of obedience carried him when otherwise he might have been totally adrift, and even though at times he must have felt it an insupportable burden. Just as it was in obedience to his Superior that he went to Sophiatown in 1943 and returned to Mirfield in 1956, he obeyed Raynes's successor, Fr Jonathan Graham, who brought about his next two moves: from Mirfield to London in 1958 and from London to Masasi in 1960. From there it was his ecclesiastical superior, Archbishop Ramsey, who made possible his eight years in Stepney and his immediate boss, Bishop Gerald Ellison of London, who directed him to Mauritius. In obedience, though sometimes loudly protesting, he went wherever he was sent.

This obedience led to many little deaths – exile, departure, grief, disappointment and a failure to see dead and buried his last enemy, apartheid. Despite the success of his writings, news stories and his own protests and jeremiads, public opinion against Pretoria's apartheid regime was only slightly stirred in the 1950s. Out of Christian Action in 1959 developed the Boycott Movement, the Anti-Apartheid Movement and the International Defence and Aid Fund. He presided at the start of all these movements but it took long years before Pretoria felt its policies under threat from world opinion. The social, economic and spiritual crimes he revealed were all happening a long way from the centres of world politics, and remained low on the international agenda.

It was from the wasteland of the townships that he said in 1992: 'We have forgotten the need to hate. We must hate what is evil. Apartheid is the most evil thing in the world.' His capacity for sustained hatred has been noted in earlier chapters as providing some of the energizing force of his lifestyle. Even at his deathbed he knew he had failed, for despite the sufferings of two generations of black South Africans apartheid was taking – and still is – an unconscionable time a-dying. He remained clearheaded about the identity of the last enemy – not death for that came as a friend from a God he had come to believe merciless – but apartheid, surviving all his efforts, his life, his lifework and the sufferings of his fellow South Africans in the armed struggle to end it. This self-knowledge, right up to the end, is a measure of his greatness, only achieved by someone whose identity, propensities and actions – what he wanted to do, what he could do, and what he did – combined into what and who he became. This surely is greatness and a guarantor of his secure position in the history of the twentieth century.

SOPHIATOWN REVISITED

Trevor Huddleston died on 20 April 1998. By then I had read the files, the references to him in the published literature, researched the origins of the Anti-Apartheid Movement and the history of the International Defence and Aid Fund from his files and the Rhodes House Library archives. I had drafted most of the chapters. Clearly, one vital element was missing, to be supplied (if I was lucky) by a visit to his hometown, Sophiatown. This unremarkable working-class suburb had been re-named Triomf after the 1955 removals and subsequent levelling of the township Huddleston knew and loved, and had been re-renamed Sophiatown early in 1998. I hoped to see his African friends, particularly those who served him at the altar in the 1940s and 1950s – Norman Montjane, Columbus Malebo and Fikile Bam. I hoped to see others recommended by Liz Carmichael and Anthony Sampson – Obed Musi, Joe Louw, Sally Motlana, Hugh Masekela, Jonas Gwangwa, 'Chinkie' Modega and other former players in the Huddleston Jazz Band. Archbishop Tutu said I should make a special point of seeing Michael Rantho, another 'Huddleston boy'. In Johannesburg a friend did sterling work on the mobile phone so that I had something like a programme of visits and interviews. The object of the visit was to flesh out Huddleston's often expressed devotion to Sophiatown and the love he gave and felt for so many of his neighbours and fellow workers there – young and old, male and female, Christian and Communist, atheist and Jew, and particularly to the 'creatures' for whom he created the guild of servers at the church of Christ the King.

A guild of altar boys in an Anglican church in a Johannesburg slum is an unlikely cradle for the revolution that fifty years later brought freedom to the country's black majority, but there is a nugget of truth in it when all rhetoric and hindsight have floated away.

In between visits I spent hours in the Johannesburg *Star*'s cuttings library where the files relating to Huddleston had been methodically archived. My most memorable meetings were with Judge Fikile Bam, Obed Musi, Columbus Malebo, Norman Montjane and Michael Rantho. I talked also to Walter Sisulu and Rica Hodson, visited the Hector Petersen monument commemorating the heroism of those murdered by the police in the Soweto uprisings between June 1976 and January 1977, twenty-two years earlier: quiet ceremonies marked the anniversary of the first terrible day when schoolchildren protested against being taught in Afrikaans. I celebrated and preached at the Sunday Eucharist held at the newly reclaimed Church of Christ the King in Sophiatown, toured Soweto with Columbus Malebo, visited Rosettenville, where the nuns of the Order of the Holy Paraclete still live opposite the former CR complex, which included St Peter's secondary school, the Priory and the theological college. I talked to the headmaster of the integrated private secondary school on the same site. I could have done none of this without my constant companion, driver and friend for those two weeks, Thulani Moyo, whom the staff of the Commonwealth Development Trust's Johannesburg office had found for me. It took him most of one Sunday to locate Obed Musi, who has no car or telephone, and bring him and his wife to my hotel at Rosebank where he gave a wonderful account of Huddleston in Sophiatown and wrote out Todd Matshikiza's poem in honour of him. I was not able to see at first-hand how he and several other million urban Africans actually lived.

Other friends visited Rosebank – Jim Bailey, the founder of *Drum* magazine; Esmé, widow of the poet, composer and jazz pianist Todd Matshikiza who wrote for *Drum* and composed the music for the musical, *King Kong*, a Sowetan *West Side Story*. She brought along her son John, daughter-in-law and two granddaughters, the youngest only three months old. I also met Horst Kleinschmidt whose work for IDAF was crucial in raising the credibility and transforming the performance of fund-raising and distribution to prisoners' families (cf Chapter Eight).

My talk with Michael Rantho was postponed several times because a student's threatened suicide demanded his immediate attention. He is a tall, slow-moving man suffering chronic back pain, the result of four severe car smashes in the last ten years, the most recent in 1994 when an elderly white gentleman smashed his car to smithereens with his BMW.

Michael Rantho was Huddleston's head server, a responsible and prestigious position in a society built around the liturgies of the Anglican church. He served at the monthly masses attended by all Sophiatown's many religious-affiliated organizations super-intended by Huddleston, and learnt Gregorian chant and Plain-song. He confirmed that the now standard 'Huddleston prayer' was indeed by Huddleston, proved by his changing the line 'guide our rulers' to 'guide our leaders'. He was one of four expelled from the teachers' training college for striking, but Huddleston said at the hearing, 'I'll look after Michael,' so he lived at the Priory, shared the Offices with the brethren and did the washing-up to earn his keep.

Rantho's father, a witch doctor, did not want him to leave home, so Huddleston and another CR father went round to collect him, manhandled his trunk onto the pickup, and when Rantho Sr tried to stop them Huddleston karate-chopped the father. '[Huddleston] was a strong man, and quite accustomed to township violence.' Michael Rantho was later befriended by Cyril Easthaugh (then Bishop of Peterborough, also very High Church). He visited Peterborough and met John Betjeman at the Cathedral. He specialized in social work in which he took a diploma. He knew Norman Montjane but he lived, worked and served mostly at Orlando, several miles away. He knew and loved Sally Motlana. There was a smallish swimming pool at the Priory where, in their early teens, they would all gather for diving parties for pennies in the pool. Widowed in 1985, he now lives with a nephew, who cooks for him. He still works for a private educational foundation-cum-social work company. He seemed to me to be a man of great potential who might easily have become a first-rate church musician or political activist or business tycoon but for the debilitating restrictions of apartheid.

The same could not be said of Fikile Bam whom I had met a few days earlier and who facilitated meetings with other former altar boys. His most painful memory of Huddleston was an occasion when several of them got drunk on communion wine and then failed to ring the angelus correctly. An infuriated Huddleston tore across the road from the priory, whipped them all with his belt and made them confess and apologize at the next servers' meeting. Judge Bam became an ANC youth league activist and was given ten years' hard labour on Robben Island for translating Che Guevara into Zulu. It was there that he met Nelson Mandela. One day (it happened to be Bam's birthday) the working party he was in heard the familiar strains of 'Happy Birthday' coming from a group nearby, in which the future President was the honorand. Sharing a birthday led to the two men studying the law together for further professional qualifications and a friendship, attested by Mandela in his autobiography, which remains close. Judge Bam observed that most South African law is based on English law, which only makes the distortions of apartheid more grotesque.

Also at work under the new government, Norman Montjane worked in the student support office at Witwatersrand University where I visited him on 22 June. In 1993 he travelled to London at the special invitation of Huddleston for his 80th birthday celebrations. Huddleston buried both Dr Montjane's mother and grandmother. 'Father Huddleston,' he told me, 'is not a white man, he's a Bantu'. Huddleston regularly travelled the few miles to Soweto, where Norman Montjane served for him every Friday at 7 a.m. They travelled together to the Jane Furze Hospital to see Montjane's brother, and to the Sisters of St Mary the Virgin (Huddleston was their confessor) and to Pretoria. He was present throughout Huddleston's return to South Africa in 1991, including Walter Sisulu's welcoming party of local ANC representatives, Montjane bringing Huddleston to the meeting without telling him what was in store. The rapturous welcome Huddleston received was one of the great moments of his return visit. Dr Montjane was one of the few Africans I met who had read *Naught for Your Comfort*, perhaps because it was dedicated to him. The others had their story to tell and followed the honourable oral tradition of their race, to which the writing of books adds little.

All those I managed to meet shared the experience of decades of apartheid impacting not only on them but their parents, relations, their spouses, children and grandchildren. They all knew what lack of freedom actually involved – poverty, diminishment, insultingly low educational standards, teaching given by order in an alien tongue, police harassment, the impossibility of getting a decent job. Many of their contemporaries had died, some murdered, some in accidents, some by avoidable disease. Many had been in prison – some for long periods – under terrible conditions now revealed by the country's new leaders. And they were a microcosm, the sparse and fragile survivors of fifty years of implacable oppression, cruelty, neglect, indifference and rejection inflicted by the white minority to maintain their lifestyle. It was this blasphemy – his own word – which drove Huddleston to despair and beyond. It was from his incarnational perception – that you cannot love an unseen god until you perceive Him in those you are sent to serve – that he concluded that the continual, unremitting assault on human dignity which was apartheid in action was an insult to God, and hence an unforgivable, unforgettable blasphemy.

APPENDICES

Trevor Huddleston left a mass of speeches, lectures, sermons and retreat addresses, many in his own handwriting, some in summary form but a substantial number written out in full. Some of these, which he himself might have drawn on had he lived to write another volume of autobiography, are included as appendices – those that in their time were key statements to key audiences, those which show how his mind was working, those that throw light on his relationships with close colleagues. Not all are by him, and those that are not are included as they contribute to the book's celebratory character, giving useful indications of how others saw him. But none of them, individually or collectively, can deliver the full magisterial force and directness of his impromptu orations – most of them concerning the evil of apartheid – attested to by many of his colleagues and friends in the 1980s and 1990s. He was a natural orator and he knew it, and made the most of his gift in the service of a cause he had made his own. These have never appeared in print, but some of their compelling power may be discerned in what follows.

Appendix One

Makhaliphile – 'Dauntless One'

*A chorale accompanied on the piano by the composer Todd
Matshikiza, conducted by Frank Dubasi and performed by the
choir of St Peter's, Rosettenville.*

   *Todd Matshikiza composed this chorale in Huddleston's
praise in 1953, after he had secured the funding for his long-
cherished project of an Olympic-size public swimming pool at
Orlando.*

Introduction

This work is humbly dedicated to Father Trevor Huddleston CR.
At all times when all else seems to fail, when darkness surrounds
us and there seems to be little else to do but weep ... weep for
the misery of our world and the lack of joyfulness in it ... at
these times, man finds eloquent self-expression in art. Yes, in art,
for, whatever else of man's own gifts man might himself destroy,
art he cannot destroy.

   And so it is that in our art of music, which must be Africa's
greatest gift, we sing the praises of them that are nearest and
dearest to us, and enshrine their endless toil and immortalise their
selflessness in our music, even in the face of those that wish to
destroy us.

Todd T. Matshikiza

I Chorus: Makhaliphile, please, please, pass this way,
                  Makhaliphile, please, please, pass this way,
                  Makhaliphile, please, please come and save us,
                  Your children hunger and thirst.

*Makhaliphile was a bold warrior of an unknown tribe, whose
leaders were lost or captured, who was adopted by this people.*

II Chorus: Well, tell us now Makhaliphile, you must be a
very strange creature man.
You could go to Florida, Riviera, India, Brazil
too –
But here you are in Africa.
Well, folks, let's eat him up, let's fry him up
No, he's not fat enough.

*This interlude is intended as a joke. A scherzo. It is a skit on
those people who say Africa is a backward, helpless savage. No
good can ever come of him. Nobody should waste their time on
him. Didn't they devour missionaries in the early days? It is also
full of remorse. When Father Huddleston tried to intervene for
the Basuto families who were being persecuted by the so-called
'Russian' gang during the Newclare riots, the 'Russian' gang
threatened to kill him. The 'enemies' of the African said: 'There
you are. You can't help the brutes. Leave them to finish each
other off.' But Father Huddleston is not discouraged.*

III Tenor solo: Sea water cannot be found at Orlando, therefore
there is no sea where we can bathe. There are
no means whereby we can bring the sea to
Orlando, so that we might bathe. What shall be
done?
     Well, if we can't bring the sea to Orlando,
we can do something to have a place where we
might bathe. But confound it! Makhaliphile has
already found a swimming bath for us. Gentleman, this will not do. We must try to help
ourselves and do these things for ourselves.

IV Chorus: Well spoke . . . well spoke . . . well spoke!

V Chorus: He gives our children food to eat,
He gives our destitute poor food to eat

Finale: The whole Nation thanks you, Father Trevor
Huddleston.
We give you the name of Makhaliphile.

Extract from a report by Fr Jonathan Graham CR on the Community of the Resurrection's work in South Africa, 1 June 1955.

'I am told there are two things I must see in Africa: the Northern Rhodesian copper belt and Huddleston': this was Archbishop Fisher's greeting to Trevor in May 1955 at Penhalonga. 'Ah, so you are one of Father Huddleston's congregation,' said an Irish Sister of Mercy to me on the boat coming home, 'he's a darling creature to be sure.' 'I can't bear to think of Father Huddleston leaving this country,' said an African solicitor and burst into tears. 'Well, I disagree with him and his principles,' said the Johannesburg businessman, 'but everyone who meets Trevor Huddleston loves him.'

Before the details fade from my mind I want to try and sketch some kind of portrait of Trevor in the setting where he has achieved a unique position in the course of twelve years' ministry. He landed in South Africa in 1943, was for six years in charge of Sophiatown and then moved to Rosettenville to be Provincial from 1949 to the present moment. In Sophiatown he lived and learnt in the heart of an African township and with immense thoroughness set himself to know, love and serve the underprivileged and the sinner. Not just to love and serve, but to *know* deeply and in detail, the life of the African. Though one may first be struck by his affection for Africans and go on to marvel at his unsparing work of service to them, it is not long before one meets evidence of a profound and detailed, if lightly worn, knowledge which lies behind them both.

Trevor is a striking figure, tall, well-proportioned, iron grey cropped hair and a singularly open and uncomplicated face; in repose, perhaps, a little forbidding, but how rarely in repose! Buoyantly he strides through the complex maze, swift and purposeful, yet never too preoccupied to greet and smile and laugh, never too impatient to listen to the most tedious of his brethren, never indifferent, always clear and outspoken and firm in any conversation of controversy.

One rapidly reaches the conclusion that he is heart-whole and single-minded and uncomplicated to a degree which is the envy and despair of lesser men. There are no reservations, no pettiness, no querulousness; everything about him is fresh and wholesome and in perspective and integrated; the whole man is there at every one's disposal always, whether the claimant for his attention is a dirty schoolboy or an archbishop, an eccentric or a bore.

'I've never seen him go to bed or get up,' said one of our brethren: and somewhere there lies the secret of his dedicated life. In the early morning he is kneeling before the Blessed Sacrament for an hour before he says Mass; after that the unceasing stream of visitors, telephone calls, letters, decisions, speaking in public and counsel in private, carries on throughout the day, day-in, day-out, week-in, week-out, without remission. And the power and efficacy of even the most trivial of his words or actions is the power of Charity, renewed daily at the Altar. And this is his entirely natural element from childhood onwards; and this is the air he breathes; one feels he would stifle in any other.

From the Altar comes his public life; he must bear witness to Charity, he must weigh up policy and oppression and injustice against Charity, he must deal with friends and opponents alike in charity; it is the Law of life and a Law is a Law; not as for so many of us, a vaguely conceived principle to which we revert in our better moments. It is this which makes it possible, as Charity works through a naturally friendly and affectionate disposition, for Trevor to oppose a politician strongly on a public platform and lunch amicably with him afterwards. It is this which makes it possible for him to lead and for others to follow; it is this which gives him a due sense of proportion about his 'indispensability' and endows him with a humility which faces squarely in the reliance of others on himself and enables him to make use of the less gifted and more half-hearted for the work of God.

In his more domestic work as Prior and Provincial it is this supernatural virtue which spreads itself and begets charity in the life of the Community; 'gifts of leadership' are there in plenty in his endowment, but they are never displayed, just naturally incorporated in the whole character.

It would be easy to be misled by newspaper reports into imagining that Trevor is a socio-political agitator who is driven by righteous indignation into pronouncing constantly on matters which are debatable and anyhow are on the fringe of his ministry. Trevor is 'news', and his opinion now is constantly sought by the press, on every conceivable subject, from vivisection to republicanism. What is really remarkable is the restraint he shows in refusing to comment on subjects where he feels no principle is at stake and in resisting the temptation to vanity; and the succinctness and clarity with which he states his opinion on matters on which he feels it right to speak. The immense difficulty of keeping a level head, of refusing to be drawn, of choosing the exactly right word, over a period of years, in which the pressures of injustice and oppressive legislation have grown rapidly greater, can only be guessed at: and to do all these things in the middle of a very exacting pastoral ministry is a very different thing from weighing one's speech in the seclusion of a study.

It is as a Pastor that he excels; a pastor to the boys of the Rosettenville school who crowd his office and make their confessions to him and come to him with their problems: several times a week he teaches in school; during the absence of a headmaster, he quietly assumed the whole of that work for several months; he never tires of schemes for expanding the lives and interests of these children; finding art teachers, violin tutors, inaugurating and fitting out a jazz band, even bringing the performers and their instruments into the church for a blessing! A pastor to the old parishioners at Sophiatown, to boys who have left the school, to their families, to hundreds who have fallen by the wayside, to innumerable of the oppressed and the proscribed, finding them jobs, fighting their battles, visiting them in illness and burying their dead.

And all this spills over into active and constructive philanthropy; he possesses the imagination to see great needs, the skill to reckon how they may be met, the charm and conviction to enlist the support of talent and money, and detachment sufficient to let others carry on what he has started, and an unpossessiveness which is content to see himself forgotten, if once the object for which he has worked is being attained.

One of the most imaginative works of this sort is the magnificent swimming baths at Orlando; one of the most extensive is the African Children's Feeding Scheme which is no mere piece of 'slumming' (though it has fed 5,000 children a day for ten years in the locations) but a school of study in malnutrition, its causes and its cure. Here he has enrolled a large number of people to help who have no Christian faith, including a high proportion of Jews.

Pastor, too, to the women religious: every fortnight going the rounds of seven houses, hearing confessions, giving spiritual instruction, advising and deciding upon their works, schools black and white, moral welfare, orphanages. And if an address on our Rule given at Chapter is any guide, his spiritual counsel is fresh, profound and unstrained. Pastor, too, to his brethren; setting and maintaining an example of obedience and charity, patient with foibles and consistently affectionate and ready to prick bubbles with an active sense of humour. It is he who makes a point of welcoming new arrivals, seeing brethren off on furlough, visiting the sick, deciding endless questions of major and very minor importance.

Pastor, also, to the educated, the puzzled, the overstrained who find their way to St Benedict's: planning and superintending retreats and shoe parties and knee-deep in an unceasing correspondence. And day by day there is a stream of visitors who find their way to him from all over Europe and America, because he is Huddleston: some in curiosity, others in sympathy, many in need of help and advice.

It is precisely because he is a pastor who gives his life for the sheep, that he has found himself forced into making a public stand for principle and into seeking the widest possible world-publicity for the expression of Christian principle. I heard him once addressing a meeting of university students, by invitation, on the subject of Bantu education. A lecture theatre was packed, undergraduates sitting on the floor and by the steps; a little oratorical trickery and he could have led them to Capetown: instead, with a superb restraint he gave them a factual, deliberate statement, carefully weighed and documented, on Christian principles in education and the effect of the government's policy upon Africans. Most of the succeeding questions were sympathetic in character; one young man tried a *ballon d'essai*: 'Isn't it true, sir, that mission-schools have been the chief influence in teaching the natives to despise the whites?' Trevor: 'Well, well, well!' Nothing could have been more effective.

He has been forced by his vocation into becoming a prophet; and prophets are rarely popular. He is bound to arouse the criticism and enmity of those who ought to be expected to understand and sympathise. This leads to isolation and – oh so easily! – to the temptation of self-pity: but of this there is scarcely any trace. But a prophet would be less than human if, with the sensitiveness which must be part of his character and the weariness which his vocation involves, he did not sometimes cry out in the bitterness of his soul.

The criticism and enmity of enemies is a great strain to the public figure. To carry on for years at a time, dogged by the CID, finding at every turn evidence of police interest and interference, and exposing oneself to the very real danger of imprisonment or deportation, is no joke! And to maintain Charity and truth towards enemies is a searching discipline, for which, it seems to me, Trevor emerges triumphant and quietly confident.

A young African, an old boy of St Peter's School, aged twenty-five, was teaching in a local school when the Bantu Education Act came into force; on principle he resigned, throwing away his training, his pension, his career; and found a job as a hand in a firm making packing cases, with no future, no hope, nothing but a life of submission to the false policy of apartheid. One day Trevor burst into my room and said: 'I've found a job for David, a job with a future.' The light of selfless triumph in his eyes was the reflection of the real heart of the man, a pastor giving his life for the sheep.

South Africa is fear; everyone is afraid of someone else; classes afraid of classes; white afraid of white; white afraid of black; black afraid of white. There is only one thing that can cast out fear: perfect Charity. There are very few people in Africa without fear. Trevor is one; for there is no fear in love.

APPENDIX THREE

*'Isitwalandwe' Citation – awarded to Trevor Huddleston
at the Congress of the People, Kliptown, Johannesburg,
25 June 1955.*

In recognition of his many years of honourable and selfless service
in the cause of human dignity and liberty, and as a mark of the
esteem and affection in which he is held by countless good men
and women, African, Indian, Coloured and White, who seek to
build a better life in our fair country founded upon Democracy
and Equality –

 the African National Congress
 the South African Indian Congress
 the South African Coloured Peoples' Organisation
 the South African Congress of Democrats

confer upon TREVOR HUDDLESTON CR the title

'ISITWALANDWE'

– the highest honour which the people can award.

Fr Huddleston's name is beloved by people of all creeds and
colour in this land because he has stood up without fear to
challenge the evil forces of hatred, injustice and prejudice which
are rampant in the country. He has refused to compromise with
wrong, whether in the field of education or in that of freedom of
speech.

On the occasion of the convention of the Congress of the
People in Johannesburg on 25 and 26 June in the year 1955.

*An extract from the transcript of a conversation between
Fr Andrew Blair CR and Joe Rogaly, at the Community of
the Resurrection, Mirfield, 4 January 1967.*

I think that the truest thing to say about my relations with Bishop Huddleston is that I have impinged upon him at certain rather critical moments in his life . . . far more than to say that I have worked closely with him for any length of time or influenced him in any way.

We first met at Bournemouth in 1933 when we were placed in the same billet on an Evangelistic campaign. He was then an undergraduate at Christ Church and I was a novice here. The background of this was the decision of the present Rector of Birmingham, Bryan Green, who was then head of the Oxford pastorate (a kind of Evangelical counterpart to Pusey House), to broaden the basis of the students' evangelistic campaigns which he customarily conducted at holiday resorts in the Long Vacations by inviting some Anglo-Catholics or High Church clergy and undergraduates to take part. Please excuse these party tags, but it is difficult to explain without them. He invited CR to send a couple of representatives and the then Superior (the late Fr Keble Talbot) sent Fr Harold Ellis, who was then one of our younger professed brethren, and myself. I saw a good deal of Trevor in the lodgings we shared and was greatly impressed by his goodness and evident strength of character: there seemed a latent potentiality there which ought to be nourished. At that time Trevor was not clear about his vocation to Holy Orders: I did my best to help him get his mind clear about this, but I honestly don't think I tried to push him. I felt, however, that he was a man to be kept in touch with: so I introduced him to Fr Ellis (who was then supposed to be CR's no 1 expert with young men) and he really took over from there. So my chief claim to fame would seem to be that I am the first Mirfield man Trevor met!

Fr Ellis was asked to take over the chaplaincy of a little group of men in Oxford called the Fellowship of the Transfiguration of which Trevor was one. He used to visit Oxford about once a term and occasionally I deputised for him. Members of the group, including Trevor, visited Mirfield from time to time for retreats, etc. During this time Trevor's sense of vocation to Holy Orders and also to membership of CR grew and developed: but Fr Ellis could tell you much more about this than I can.

Trevor asked Fr Ellis's advice about the choice of a Title for his Ordination and Fr Ellis consulted me. I happened to know that Canon Ross of St Mark's Swindon, whose curate I had been from 1924 to 1932, was looking for a man, so I suggested that Trevor might enquire into this. St Mark's was a big parish with four churches and a team of clergy who were a very happy band of brothers, and I felt that this was the kind of place where Trevor would be taught his trade as a priest competently and in a happy environment. Just at the time he went to Swindon I was sent to the Far East so I saw nothing of his work or life there at first-hand. But for many years I have kept in touch with my old friends there, and I know what affection and confidence Trevor inspired in them, both clergy and laity. The links between St Mark's and Mirfield were strong: besides myself there was one ex-member of Canon Ross's staff (Fr Justin Pierce) in CR: there were two Old Students from the college here working on the staff there: and for a long period there were always one or two ordinands from the parish in training either at the College or at our Hostel at Leeds. So my second claim to fame is that I forged the link between Trevor and Swindon. Hindsight is difficult: but I think it is right to say that the experience of the brotherly family life of the staff there did a good deal to bring out my own sense of a calling to Community life and I hoped it would do the same for Trevor.

When Trevor came into residence at Mirfield I was living at our Leeds house, so I did not see a lot of him during that period. But I would say that my third claim to fame was that I was indirectly responsible for his first going to South Africa. When Fr Raynes was elected Superior he had been in South Africa since

1933 – ten years – with only a very brief leave in the summer
of 1938 and a whole generation had come into CR during that
time whom he hardly knew. He wrote to me before he returned
to England asking me to come out and take over his work in
Sophiatown: he didn't really know me well, though he had known
me a little at Oxford and in my Swindon days. What he didn't
know was that I had some domestic problems of my own which
would make it very difficult for me to go off to a foreign land in
the middle of the war. This was represented to him and he made
a temporary appointment until he could come home and go into
things. Once home he was soon clear that I could not go and
asked me whether I thought that Trevor (whom he had only just
got to know) would do instead. I said that this had been in my
mind to propose if he asked me for a suggestion: Trevor was ten
years or so younger than me, much more malleable and lively,
and if his family circumstances were alright I thought he would
do excellently well . . . and so it turned out. He had made an
enormous impression on everyone here: and in fact when he went
to South Africa he was able to do all sorts of things which I
couldn't have begun to touch. It really was the hand of God that
made it difficult for me to go to Johannesburg in 1943 and open
the gate for Trevor.

About his return to England I won't say anything here, as I
gather you mean to take that up later on. But I can tell you
something of the circumstances of his election to Masasi, which
is perhaps my fourth major impact on Trevor's career. When
Trevor was working in London and at the height of his fame, our
then Superior, Fr Graham (now dead), said to me that he thought
Trevor could not go on as he was or it would kill him with the
demands on him as a speaker and radio and television star on
both sides of the Atlantic in addition to the day to day round of
his life in CR as Prior to our London house. 'We ought to get
him back to Africa for that is where his heart is: and if people in
this country after Sharpeville,' – the massacre was then recent
news – 'don't know what apartheid means they never will.' It
seemed clear that he would not be allowed to re-enter the Union
(though he was not, as was widely believed at the time, expelled

by the Union government) and the question was where could he go? Fr Graham mentioned that the See of Masasi was vacant and observed that if black men trusted any white man now, which he thought open to doubt, Trevor would be that white man. 'But,' he said, 'I can hardly write and suggest him to Masasi.' As it happened I was in touch with the Vicar-General, Archdeacon Lamburn on other matters, and knew about the vacancy already: so with Fr Graham's consent I wrote to him saying that perhaps they had thought that Fr Huddleston had turned him down on the grounds that CR wd. likely refuse leave for him to go out. It wasn't for me to urge them to invite him, and if he was invited the Community Chapter would have to give him permission before he could accept. I had no authority to commit the Chapter in advance: all that I could say was that they should not assume at this stage that if permission were asked it would be refused. This set things moving very quickly, and I dropped out of the business: the rest of it was conducted between Fr Graham, Trevor, the Masasi authorities and the then Archbishop of Canterbury (Dr Fisher).

So you see I'm not much good for a character study of Trevor: I only come into the picture as a kind of fortuitous eminence grise who has just happened to impact on him at rather critical moments in his life. It's just that things have worked out that way without my conscious volition, and I'm very happy to have been so used.

A sermon on the consecration of Desmond Tutu as Bishop of Lesotho in Johannesburg. St Paul's Cathedral, London, 11 July 1976.

No man is an island, entire of itself; every man is a piece of the continent, a part of the main; if a clod be washed away by the sea, Europe is the less, as well as if a promontory were, as well as if a manor thy friends or of thine own were: any man's death diminishes me, because I am involved in Mankind; and therefore never send to know for whom the bell tolls; it tolls for Thee . . .

from the *Devotions* of John Donne

1) If I begin by reminding you of those events which have hit the headlines in the past month – all of them violent, all of them tragic, all of them taking place on the continent of Africa – it is *not* because I think you are unaware or unconcerned: nor is it because I want to depress you or make you feel gloomy or despairing about our world . . . It is because I believe John Donne was right in perceiving that 'No man is an island . . . I am involved in Mankind.' And that the Christian faith demands a recognition of that truth as no other of the great religions of the world can possibly do. For Christianity alone asserts the identification of God with man: states without qualification that *God* is 'involved in Mankind': that he has 'emptied Himself and become of no reputation' in order to encompass that unbelievable and most mysterious proof of his love for the world – the giving of his only Son to share our life: to come where man is: to take flesh, be born, live, suffer, die and rise again *as Man*.

2) And the basic events are these: first, the trial, conviction and execution of men fighting as mercenaries in Angola; secondly, the outbreak of violence in Soweto, Johannesburg and elsewhere in

South Africa, and the deaths of over 170 people – some of them young schoolchildren; thirdly, the hijack and the rescue in Entebbe, Uganda – again involving armed force, violence and death.

So that, whether we like it or not, our television screens and our daily press have shown once again the continent and country of Africa as places of upheaval and terror and disorder.

3) Yet, as I speak these words, an event is taking place in the Cathedral Church of St Mary, Johannesburg which, I suspect, will have no impact on the television screens at all, and may only find a mention in the Church newspapers: not in the dailies.

The event is the consecration of a bishop to the diocese of Lesotho. He is the first black African to hold that office – his diocese being coterminous with the whole country and nation of Lesotho (Basutoland). His name is Desmond Tutu, who made history a year ago by becoming the first black African Dean of Johannesburg.

And the reason why I am speaking to you about him in this pulpit this morning is three-fold:

First – because I would ask your prayer for him as he is consecrated a bishop in the Church of God.

Second – because I have known him since childhood.

Thirdly – because had I been able to get a visa from the South African Government, I would have been preaching, not in this cathedral but in St Mary's Cathedral, Johannesburg.

So that, although this sermon cannot be the same as that which I would have preached there, it can at least perhaps say something about the significance of *that* event in contrast with, and standing over against, those other events which have made such an impact upon us over the past few weeks – the Angolan war and its mercenaries and massacres: Soweto and its eruption of anger and bloodshed: Entebbe and the hijack rescue operation with its accompaniment of violence and recrimination and unpredictable future consequences.

'No man is an island, entire of itself . . . any man's death diminishes me, because I am involved in Mankind.'

Much death there has been – in Angola, in South Africa, in Uganda. Much diminishment, therefore, in terms of our shared humanity, our age-long search for peace, our honour and dignity as sons of man made in the image and likeness of God.

Yet, just because 'any man's death diminishes me' so too, a man's life and its quality taken into God's plan and purpose – consecrated for use in His service and for His glory – can do the opposite: can enlarge and enrich and ennoble.

So – as Christians – we believe. For we are 'members one of another' and just as – 'if one member suffer . . . all suffer . . .' – so, 'if one member is honoured, all rejoice together.'

Desmond Tutu, as a child, had all the disadvantages of being born and bred an African in white South Africa. In addition, he spent two years in hospital with TB just at the time when – with great effort – he had managed to get into secondary school. In spite of that bad start he managed to gain entry to a South African university, to King's College, London – and to gain a BD and an MTh. He has used all of this academic excellence for *Christianity*. Writing a few months ago to his white fellow-Christians on South Africa on the text 'A new commandment I give unto you, that you love one another as I have loved you', he said: 'We speak too glibly of reconciliation and love and forgiveness in this country because we think they are easy things to accomplish. We forget that it cost God the death of His son to bring about reconciliation between Him and us . . . There was violence, confrontation and hatred – the dark terrible things summed up in the Cross on Good Friday before the light of the resurrection and the victory of Easter Day could be.'

It cannot be otherwise in our situation. Can you imagine the emotion of a black parent when he sees his children growing hate-filled and embittered because of the kind of lot that has been carved out for them by the omnipotent white man? When he sees them becoming more dehumanised and he utterly emasculated, unable to do anything about it all? *God* – are you serious that we must love those who have done this to us?'

Just before the outbreak in Soweto, as Dean of Johannesburg

and with his home in Soweto itself, he wrote an impassioned plea to the Prime Minister of his country, Mr Vorster.

'I have a growing, nightmarish fear,' he said, 'that unless something drastic is done very soon then bloodshed and violence are going to happen in South Africa almost inevitably . . . a people made desperate by despair, injustice and oppression will use desperate means.'

The Prime Minister's response was to tell him that his motives were political and propagandist.

And when the violence broke out and Soweto was in flames he prayed: 'O God please, please help us. O please make the white people hear us before it is too late.'

In Alan Paton's great novel, *Cry, the Beloved Country* – there is a moment when the young, black priest is speaking to his white colleagues about the future of their country and he says to them 'I have one great fear in my heart. That when *they* are turned to loving, *we* shall be turned to hating . . .'

Today – thirty years later – Desmond Tutu, proclaiming the love of God is echoing the same cry, the same warning, the same urgent plea. And, in an hour or two he will be a bishop in the Church of God. A bishop, surely, for whom all of us in the Anglican Communion can give thanks. A bishop who brings with him into our fellowship, a voice we so desperately need to hear – the voice of *Christian* Africa which even violence and terror and war have not silenced.

5) Those of us who have had the privilege of working in Africa as I have done, for twenty years: who know the people of Africa as *people*: who have seen at firsthand their patience in the face of adversity, their fortitude in times of poverty, their quiet dignity when confronted with the shrill, violent voice of racial prejudice – above all, perhaps, their deep wells of joy and gaiety, whatever the pain and sorrow of life – we know that the image of Africa as a continent of violence and turmoil is a total distortion of truth: as much a distortion as it would be to present *every* British city and *every* British country road as if it were Belfast or Armagh and nothing else.

6) 'No man is an island, entire of itself . . .'

And no nation, today, can be the sole repository of our patriotism and of our loyalty. For we belong to another as citizens of one earth, we are interdependent, we must 'love one another or die'.

And today, as never before, the Church of God must proclaim the love of God not by words and words and words, but by its very life. It must show itself to be what in truth it is: the Body of Christ – the hands, the feet, the eyes, the voice of Christ, filled with His spirit.

It is for this reason that the consecration of a bishop – whoever and wherever he may be – is of such moment to us all. It is the proclamation, in Christian terms, of what the world – torn by violence and strife and terror – most needs to hear: 'Ubi episcopus ibi ecclesia'.

'Fear not, little flock, it is your Father's good pleasure to give you the Kingdom.'

APPENDIX SIX

*A sermon delivered at Pentonville Prison
on Christmas Day 1976.*

Yet he did not think to snatch at equality with God, but made himself nothing, assuming the nature of a *slave* . . . bearing the human likeness revealed in human shape He humbled Himself.

Philippians 2.6.7.

1) Carols and carol-singing. Specially composed for Christmas. Always associated with the joys and pleasures of Christmas. The words and the tunes together

God rest ye merry gentlemen . . .

Hark the herald angels sing . . .

O Come, all ye faithful . . ., etc.

But what was the *original* carol? And what was it all about?

A fragment of a hymn (carol) used in the earlier Christian communities . . . used in a letter that St Paul wrote from *prison* probably in Rome, awaiting trial. Perhaps therefore the first carol ever written. And it is a carol (like all other carols) about the meaning of that birth at Bethlehem.

[Looking at Jesus in the manger] He did not think to snatch at equality with *God*, but 'made Himself nothing, assuming the nature of a slave, bearing the human likeness.'

So the first Christmas carol is about Jesus choosing to come into the world *not* (as He might have done) with all the glory, the splendour, the majesty of *God*. But with the nothingness of a slave.

Reminder of this last month: the celebrations in Masasi. 100 years ago – how did Christmas act as a reminder that the God we worship is a God who comes to *share* in the world's pain. Slavery: the clearest picture of it all through history – taking different forms: eg slavery itself – having nothing. The slavery of sickness, of poverty, of hunger. Today, of life under governments which deny all freedom. So – Bethlehem and Calvary, the beginning and the end of His human life in poverty. *But* 'God raised Him to the heights and bestowed on Him the name above all names, that at the name of Jesus, every knee shall bow.'

*A lecture given as part of a conference on Christian outreach
to the world of unbelief, 1977.*

I am going to begin my lecture with two moments, far apart in
time and place but both illustrative, I hope, of what I wish to
speak about. And if this was a sermon and not a lecture, I know
exactly what verse I would choose for my text. St Matthew, 6:33
and I'm sure you all know what that verse is. In fact it is: 'Seek
ye first the kingdom of God and his righteousness and all these
things shall be added unto you.'

Two months ago I revisited my old diocese in Tanzania to
take part in the celebrations of the centenary, not of the diocese,
but of the first proclamation of the Gospel in that part of Africa.
We gathered, a great crowd of African Christians, and a few
dozen English ex-missionaries of different vintages around the
actual spot from which the Gospel was preached and where the
first small church was built. And as I listened to the young
African priest from central Tanganyika speaking to us against
that background of rugged rocky outcrops, in front of him a fully
equipped modern hospital, to the side of him the present beautiful
church building, behind him the large primary school, and around
him people of all ages, born and bred in the Christian Church, I
tried to picture the moment, one hundred years ago when it all
began. And in fact it began a few years after David Livingstone
had made his great appeal to the universities to send men out to
Africa with one simple objective, to destroy slavery and to preach
freedom. It began, in fact, with a handful of slaves, just set free
from their slavery to the Arabs, from the island of Zanzibar, and
making their way up from the coast of Tanganyika to their homes
in Nyasaland (now Malawi) – homes some of them had never
seen, for they were born in slavery. They had travelled through
countries stricken with drought and famine. At last they had
arrived, hungry, thirsty and very weary, at a little place called

Masasi. And they asked their missionary leader Edward Steer,
later Bishop in that part of Africa, if they could stay because they
could go no further. Here was water, here was land for cultiva-
tion, here were friendly tribal chiefs. It seemed to be, to them, a
bit of heaven. And Steer agreed, and so they stayed. And from
that small group of freed slaves grew the Church of God. Not, of
course, a unique event in the long Christian centuries and certainly not unique to Africa. But in the context of the Christian
life quite a memorable event, nonetheless, because, remember,
they were slaves. That is to say they had nothing of their own,
no possessions, no relationships (for slaves are not free to marry),
no homes, not even a name. They were in very truth 'the things
that are not', the embodiment of a poverty so complete that it
could not be nearer to nothingness, save for one common entity:
they were human, they were men.

That is the first picture: and now another one. London, on a
foggy November morning in 1914. It was the day when a young
priest named H.R.L. Sheppard was to be inducted to the living of
St Martin-in-the-Fields. There were eleven people in the church.
And in his sermon he told them of his vision for the parish to
which he had just been appointed, and I want to quote his actual
words. In those bleak surroundings, in that almost empty place,
he said, 'I saw the great church standing in the greatest square in
the greatest city of the world, and I stood on the West steps and
I saw what the church would be to the life of the people. There
passed me into its warm inside, hundreds and hundreds of all
sorts of people, going up to the Temple of their Lord with
all their difficulties, trials and sorrow. I saw it full of people
dropping in at all hours of the day and night. It was never dark.
It was lighted all night and often tired bits of humanity swept in.
And I said to them as they passed, 'where are you going?' And
they said only one thing, 'this is our home. This is where we are
going to learn of the love of Jesus Christ. This is the altar of our
Lord where all our peace lies. This is St Martin's.' They spoke
two words to me only. One was the word 'home' and the other
was 'love'. And I left that wonderful church then and looked on
the thousands that streamed by and I recognized that into them

were going all the great flood of those who loved their Lord. They were mixing with the crowd and telling them 'we know the Lord and love him.' And then he asked his small, surprised congregation, 'will you give a hand? Will you give a hand and try, even if we fail, to build up this church in the greatest city in the world?'

When Dick Sheppard died, twenty-three years later, 100,000 people filed past his coffin in that same church of St Martin-in-the-Fields. And most of them were the 'tired bits of humanity' of his vision. And yet in between the vision and its consummation, a life of desperate struggle against sickness, of the championing of many lost causes, of bitter domestic sorrow, of a lonely and solitary death. Looking outwards, the weak things of the world confound the things that are mighty.

Note both the contrast and the similarity in these two historic moments point, I believe, to a fundamental theological truth about the nature of Christianity itself, of faith and life in the Christian community. It is this truth that I shall seek to develop tonight. But before I begin to do so, may I emphasize, quite truthfully, the fact that I am fully aware of my own limitations. The three speakers who are to follow me can, each one, claim mastery of his subject: dogmatic theology, history, spirituality. I know only too well that in speaking of mission, (for that is really what 'facing outwards' means to the Christian), as I understand it, I am bound to be drawing on my own experience, such as it is – and all the peculiarities of that experience, in different parts of the Anglican Communion and in different countries of the African continent. I am well aware (at least I hope I am) that I am not speaking only to Anglicans. I suspect I may be speaking to some at least who know Africa better than I do. But this is the only experience I had. And by expressing my knowledge of its partiality, I am simply trying to convey to you that 'looking outwards' is essentially and necessarily 'looking outwards' from oneself. As Michael Ramsey never ceases to remind us, the glory of God is seen in both Cross and Resurrection. It is one glory. The understanding of facing outwards in the Christian context is what he calls 'open-ness'. Always the portrait of Jesus in the

Gospels and epistles is the portrait of one who Himself is facing
outwards, pointing men away from and beyond himself to the
Father and to the Kingdom. He is always exhorting Man, not to
a Jesus-cult, a Jesus-worship, but to seek first the Kingdom of
God and His righteousness. The Son can do nothing by Himself.
If Jesus calls men to follow, if He says to them 'come to me and I
will refresh you' it is never with the object of drawing them to an
acknowledgement of His sovereignty. Indeed when He recognizes
that at a certain moment they wish to take Him and make Him a
king by force, He removed Himself from them, and departed into
another place. 'You call me a king. It is *you* who call me a king.
My kingdom is not of this world.'

Secondly, the authentic portrait of Jesus shows Him as concerned not with saving souls – however you define the word souls
– but with reaching out to the whole person – to his emotions,
his affections, his imagination, but also to his intellect and to his
will.

And thirdly Jesus is shown supremely as the man for others in
the sense that His Gospel is concerned always with people where
they are. I often feel that the most important phrase in the
parable of the Good Samaritan is the simple 'when he came
where he was he went to him and bound up his wounds' – when
he came where he was. Like the Samaritan, Jesus reaches out to
people in their infinite diversity of relationships, of conditions of
need, and Himself relates to them there. Old and young. Rich
and poor. Men, women, children, sick, whole and even dead. He
touches them – or like the woman with the issue of blood they
touch Him – from within the context of their own social environment, and His words and actions are directed to them there, and
not to some purely personal individual soul-saving exercise which
would assume their isolation from the world.

Now I have found it necessary to begin thus theologically
because I have suffered quite a lot, I must confess, from the
assumption that people make that because one is politically
involved, somehow or other, one is diverting attention from the
truth of the Gospel. Nothing, I would suggest, can be further
from the truth of the Gospel than the failure to recognize that the

mission of Jesus, and therefore the mission of his Church – the 'facing outwards' of the Incarnate Lord, and the 'facing outwards' of His body, the Church, is supremely, fundamentally and always God-centred.

What I want to say about facing outwards is bound to be subjective and personal. There is no other way in which I can say anything of value about Christianity, the Church and its mission to the world than from within my own experience, however limited, however partial, however prejudicial. But as it happens I have been given the opportunity and the privilege in three widely differing areas of responsibility – first as a priest, then for the past sixteen years and more as a bishop in the Anglican Communion – of 'facing outwards' upon what I regard as three of the greatest challenges confronting the Christian Church in our day and generation. That is my good fortune. I have been confronted precisely with these three things which are basic to 'where life is' in our world today. They are the issues of race and colour conflict; of the hungry world; and of the secular city. Twelve and a half years in Johannesburg, South Africa at the time when Soweto – or what existed of it then – (about half the present vast urban conglomeration) – was my parish. When I saw on the TV screen in June last year the first pictures of the riots in Soweto, I recognized the church in which I preached my first sermon in South Africa. And then, after that, eight years in Tanzania – a country which President Julius Nyerere said does not even belong to the Third World. In the latest parlance it belongs to the 'Fourth World'. And he added, 'Poverty is a very urgent matter to us. Along with the freedom struggle it is at the core of all our national activity.' And now for the past nine years, in the East End of London in Stepney, a jurisdiction embracing the London Boroughs of Tower Hamlets, Hackney and Islington – old inner city areas caught up in redevelopment so vast and so radical that the concept of community, and indeed community itself, are overwhelmingly threatened. Now I want to look at these three issues with you tonight, however briefly and sketchily, from within the context of the Christian life. What does each represent by way of challenge to us as Christians, whatever our church allegiance, wherever we happen to live, however our particular Christian and local community makes its demands upon us? And primarily to have a perspective upon all of them, we need to make our own the truth that is, in fact, bound to determine our attitude whether we like it or not: we have only one earth. And however obvious and banal such a statement may appear to be, it has to be affirmed emphatically, precisely because man is acting as if he did not believe it to be true. And it is the Western nations, owing their civilisation to Christianity, who seem to me to be the chief offenders. Is not the world our world? Is it not worth our love? And as Christians we have to add: is it not worth also God's world? If this is true, then race and colour conflict, that which inescapably divides man from man for no other reason than the totally irrational one of pigmentation, presents a massive challenge to human survival: massive because it is a world issue, however localised it may appear to be. It is so because we live in a world of mass communication. The politician who in an election speech, let us say in Birmingham or Wolverhampton, uses the presence of black immigrants as an electioneering gambit, is heard not only in Birmingham and Wolverhampton, not only in Britain, but in remote African villages as he speaks. And he is heard not electioneering, not attacking the immigrant communities, but assaulting the dignity of all black men. The phrase 'Black Consciousness', more effectively even than the phrase 'Black Power', is descriptive of a mood which is of immense significance because it expresses a depth of meaning as well as its extent and spread. If South Africa is the focus of race conflict, as it is, and Soweto, like Sharpeville, has become a symbolic word, it is because Soweto epitomises a basic evil – that of racism – the deliberate killing of schoolchildren, many of them not even in their teens, for protesting, peacefully, against a perversion of education, and everything that underlies that perversion. And this being done in the name of a political or ideological philosophy of race and at a moment when, a few hundred miles to the north in Rhodesia and Namibia, a state of war already exists between black and white. Where even in our world of violence and terror, where even here can we discover a more potent example of the violence and terror used by a government, not by a terrorist group, but by a government claiming to uphold Christian standards and Christian values. A government, moreover, with which – in terms of investment – our country contains strong links. Racism in one form or another has found or finds expression in most countries including our own. But nowhere else in the world is racism built into the constitution, the political, economic, social, even ecclesiastical institutions of the nation as it is in the Republic of South Africa. It is for this reason that the Christian Church and the Christian individual who looks out upon our world, God's world, today is bound to take issue, not only with the South African philosophy of apartheid, but with those in authority in our own land who by economic or political or diplomatic support sustain it. But we are in a weak and indefensible position to do this if in fact we are not prepared to meet the challenge of racism wherever it exists in our own land. If in fact as Bishop Eric Treacey, the former Bishop of Wakefield, who certainly knows his facts, said in the *Church Times* last week, 'thank God Parliament takes the problem of race more seriously than the Church of England'. He was referring to the new Race Relations Act. And he continued, 'The Synod wittered on about the closed shop, about the appointments of bishops, and side-stepped what is in all probability the most urgent and explosive social and moral problem of our day.' Twenty years ago in the book I wrote then, which I truly have never re-read since I wrote it until the last week – in its last chapter I said this: 'In opposing the policies of the government of South Africa I am not prepared to concede that any momentary good thing, which might conceivably be learnt from them is good. Nor am I prepared to concede that the motives which inspire such policies have any qualities of goodness about them. For both the acts and the motives are inspired by a desire which is fundamentally evil.'

I was extremely fortunate in being allowed to return after a brief spell in Britain, to another African country in 1960. Tanganyika, as it was then called, Tanzania as it is today. And I was even more fortunate to be elected Bishop of Masasi, whose origins I have already described. Fortunate, for not only is

Tanzania one of the twenty-five poorest countries on earth and therefore wholly typical of the Third, Fourth, or hungry world; but much more fortunate in being there during the transition from colonial to black African sovereignty and the emergence ten years ago at a place called Arusha of a political philosophy of unique value not only to Africa but to the world. The poverty of a developing country, is, of course, not the poverty of a slum. There is no assault on human dignity in a poverty which is shared and against which the nation is determined to fight until it overcomes. But nevertheless it is a real poverty. In that part of Tanzania which I know best and which I revisited only a month or so ago, even in a good year, even assuming there in no drought or flood, the children never get more than one meal a day and meat is a luxury. This is the poverty of two-thirds of our world. There is no time, of course, in an address of this kind, to enlarge in detail on how Tanzania is attempting to face the problem of development. I shall content myself with two quotations from President Nyerere in the Arusha Declaration: 'we make a mistake to use money . . . independence means self-reliance' and 'development is brought about by people, not money'. I was especially privileged, indeed called, to work in one of the poorest regions of a very poor country, to see for myself the working out of a development programme at the grass roots, to do what I could to urge our Christian community to recognize behind such policies their own Christian commitment to familyhood as the family of God; and to self-reliance as those made in the image and likeness of God, whose human dignity must depend upon and express the changeless and eternal dignity conveyed to them by the Incarnation of the Son of God. Their poverty becomes the expression of wealth because He for our sakes became poor, that we through His poverty might be rich.

And now for eight-and-a-half years the East End of London, a contrast so great with Masasi and Tanzania that at first I felt I could never even begin to understand the challenge. I'm not sure that I do now. Where priorities had been simple – the conquest of poverty, ignorance and disease – now they were infinitely complex, the very word poverty having a totally different meaning, yet its reality even more challenging because deprivation in affluence, which is our condition, is psychologically the most destructive poverty of all. And it is multiple deprivation about which I'm speaking. Multiple deprivation in our own affluent world and in our own affluent country. In the borough in which I live one child in four is in the courts before the age of seventeen. One in twenty-nine is placed in care because of family breakdown. We have the highest truancy rate, the highest illegitimacy rate, far the highest unemployment rate in any inner-city area. And each one of these factors affecting adversely the newcomer – the immigrant – who is made the scapegoat for social ills which existed long before he arrived on the scene, and totally unconnected with his presence in the neighbourhood. But above all else, and producing a basic challenge to the Christian church, there is the breakdown of what had been in those years, when poverty was material poverty on a massive scale, the most warm-hearted, caring community in any great city, and I would guess in the Western world. Redevelopment, the replacement of the old streets with high-rise flats, the wholesale removal of neighbourhood populations, the creation of barriers in the form of highways for articulated lorries between the old neighbourhoods, the elimination of play space for children, the inbalance of population caused by housing shortage which drives the young out and leaves the old in loneliness behind. The secularization of the city is caused by the breakdown of community more than by any other single factor, for it is community that allows man to transcend himself, to find the other, and having found him, to love him.

And for the Christian, community is something God-given. It is the one essential condition for mission, for evangelism, for meaning and purpose in this world, at least that is how I read the history of the Church in its golden years. 'They had all things in common.' Those little handfuls of insignificant men and women flung across the face of the great pagan persecuting empire, what had they to offer? How did they face outwards upon a world so terrifying in its alienation from the message which they knew themselves commanded to proclaim? They had no access to the corridors of power, they had no status, they had no buildings, they had three hundred years of secret meetings for prayer and eucharist under the threat of death. And yet they turned the world upside down. How? By being Community, but community so on fire with supernatural love that those outside had to come in. That is what, as a Christian, I understand by the mission of facing outwards. The effectiveness of the church's mission does not depend upon attitudes: but it does depend of priorities. 'You are the salt of the earth' is a mistranslation. 'You are salt *to* the world'. And the purpose of the salt is to preserve. You don't make a meal of salt. The Church, however unlikely an instrument it appears to be, is set in the world for only one purpose – to save it. And it cannot do so if its concern is for its own preservation, for its own buildings, for its own rituals, for its own functions; then it is fit only to be cast out and trodden underfoot. It must be the sign and symbol of the Gospel, by its presence, facing outwards, upon God's world in all its splendid variety and challenge and exciting possibilities. Facing outwards, for there is its mission and purpose. Facing outwards for although it is dark out there, and often a fearsome place, we are called to that and nothing else. We are called to be salt to the world. And maybe, if we are faithful in responding to that vocation, maybe one day we shall hear the greater compliment, 'You are the light of the world'.

Speech to the United Nations General Assembly as President of the Anti-Apartheid Movement, 5 November 1982.

It is difficult to find words adequate to such an occasion as this. I am conscious only of the fact that, however hard I try to do so, I shall fail in both my expression of gratitude and in measuring up to the significance of this moment.

I am also deeply conscious of the fact that an award such as this is not made, and should not be made, to an individual like myself for what must of necessity be such a limited contribution to such a vast challenge – nothing less than the elimination of racism in our world.

I can only say that I thank God for giving me the opportunity over the past forty years to have been actively, personally and wholeheartedly committed to this cause. It is a cause that is not only worthy of a total commitment of one's human energies, but deserves nothing less.

But it is too easy to speak in abstractions; I would like rather to speak for a few moments from my heart. For me, at least, the battle against the monstrous evil of apartheid in South Africa, began not as a battle of conflicting ideas within the whole field of international relations (though certainly it is necessary *always* to see apartheid as a massive threat to world peace and an assault on human rights). But it began for me in the streets of Sophiatown and Orlando in 1943 when, as a Christian priest and pastor, I was confronted with a system so evil that it attacked the very meaning of human life; the very purpose for which, as I believe, man is created. Apartheid, in its application to ordinary daily life in black Johannesburg, was the daily assertion and proclamation to the African people, not only of their permanent role as serfs and cyphers, but to those who, by reason of the colour of their skins, must aspire to being nothing else.

Apartheid said (and says) to African *children*: 'your education is an education for servitude.'

Apartheid says to African *workers*: 'we need your labour, black man. We must have your labour, black men, to give *white* South Africa the power and energy it needs to keep you for ever where you are.'

Apartheid says to African *families*: 'so long as you are here in our white city (eighty-seven per cent of the land area of South Africa) you can have no security, no permanence, no peace. For you have no citizenship – and you will never have it.'

'Keep over there.'

But these Africans were and are my friends – some, like Bishop Desmond Tutu, schoolchildren when I first knew them, some, like Nelson Mandela, Walter Sisulu, Oliver Tambo, my contemporaries. In those great days leading up to the Freedom Charter and the Kliptown Congress that approved it, *we* knew what we were doing. Or at least we knew what we were *trying* to do. We were appealing to the world community to recognize that apartheid was not – as many at that time liked to believe – a matter of South African political practice, a matter of purely local and internal concern – but an issue of worldwide significance. As much a challenge to the future of mankind as the Nazi ideology that had brought about the Second World War and as potentially dangerous.

So, in expressing my thanks to the United Nations Assembly, to the special Committee Against Apartheid, and to the Centre Against Apartheid which has done so much in the past twenty years to make the nations of the world aware of this challenge, I am speaking on behalf not only of myself but of all those with whom I have had the privilege and the honour to be associated over the years. The Award and all that has been said here today must give us renewed strength with a last and final battle for human rights and human dignity.

The most compelling reason for my gratitude for this gold award and for the opportunity of addressing the General Assembly has been summed up for me by the late Barbara Ward in *Only One Earth*. 'Our links of blood and history, our sense of shared culture and achievement, our tradition, our faith are all precious and enrich the world . . . But we have lacked a wide rationale of unity. Our prophets have sought it. Our poets have dreamed of it. But it is only in our own day that astronomers, physicists, geologists, chemists, biologists, anthropologists, ethnologists and archaeologists have all combined in a single witness to tell us that, in every alphabet of our being we do indeed belong to a single system . . . depending for its survival on the balance and the health of the total system . . . Governments have already paid lipservice to such a view of the world by setting up the whole variety of United Nations agencies whose duty it is to elaborate worldwide strategies. But the idea of authority and energy and resources to support their policies seem strange, visionary and Utopian at present, simply because world institutions are not backed by any sense of planetary community and commitment. Today in human society, we can perhaps hope to survive in all our prized diversity, providing we can achieve an ultimate loyalty to our single, beautiful and vulnerable Planet Earth.'

It is the total contradiction of such a vision and such a goal that I find most deeply offensive as a Christian in the concept of institutionalized racism known as 'apartheid'. I believe that one of the strongest motives which ought to compel this Assembly to exert its greatest efforts to defeat apartheid is the appalling waste of human resources which is its inescapable consequence. And this waste is recognizable at every level and cannot be contained within South Africa itself. Our world, bewildered and torn apart as it is by conflicting ideologies, nationalisms and – alas – religion, cannot afford *any* waste at *any* level. We need effective leadership – yet the government of South Africa exiles, restricts, imprisons and even kills those who are its leaders.

We need the enrichment which comes from multi-cultural, multi-lingual, multi-Faith societies – such as that which I have the privilege to live and work in – Mauritius and the islands of the Indian Ocean.

It should be intolerable to the world that men like Mandela and Sisulu: men like Beyers Naudé and women like Helen Joseph should be forcibly prevented from communicating their thoughts and ideas to mankind.

This waste of life, of human ability and talent, of idealism and wholeness, is an affront to the rest of mankind.

As a Christian leader I bow my head in shame at the failure of the Christian church to witness effectively against what – if the faith we profess means anything at all – is a blasphemy. The blasphemy of throwing in the face of God as if it were a useless thing, the crown of his creation: Man 'made in His image and likeness'.

Four years ago, in this very place, the President of the UN said: 'I believe that we shall have realized one of the ideals of the people gathered together in the United Nations when there is no need for the General Assembly to hold a meeting like this dedicated to the observance of the International Anti-Apartheid Year. That will mean that a political regime that runs counter to all the political and cultural ideals underlying the UN Charter has been swept away.' He was followed by the then Secretary-General who reminded the Assembly that: 'Apartheid is not only amoral and inhuman, but also a grave danger to the international peace and security,' and he continued: 'There is no single issue on which the Members of this Organization are more united than the one before us. We therefore speak today with one voice in expressing our determination to do everything in our power to help ensure the establishment in South Africa of a just society in which all people of all races will enjoy their inalienable rights. We must succeed in the interests of peace in Africa and, indeed, in the entire world.' And he was followed in turn by the then Prime Minister of Jamaica who posed the question: 'How does a world that produced Lincoln, Marx, Lenin, Mao and Franklin Roosevelt *still* stand impotent before this vicious edifice of shame and degradation?' Apartheid has been denounced in the rhetoric of every significant political leader of the twentieth century. It has been the subject of the furthest reaches of political indignation. It has been officially designated a crime against humanity. How, then, does this great Assembly of Nations find itself today virtually mocked by South Africa's unyielding position with respect to its racial policies? What of this latest impudent rejection of the specific will of the United Nations in Namibia?

All this – and much more – was said here *four years ago*. And only two weeks ago, in Johannesburg, a former US Secretary of Defence and President of the World Bank, Robert S. Macnamara, said: 'The greatest tragedies of history have occurred not so much because of what was finally done but what had earlier been left foolishly undone. And if what is left of the 1980s does not witness real movement towards sharing of political power, South Africa may, *and I believe will* become a great threat to the peace of the world in the 1990s as the Middle East is today.'

I make no apology for quoting these speakers at some length for the burden of what I have to say is that *the time for rhetoric is past*. This place has heard great speakers, great orators, great statesmen, proclaiming the great truths and witnessing to great causes in the interests of world peace.

It would not only be an impertinence but a folly for me to try and emulate them. My only concern is that this moment, in this Assembly, should be remembered not as a moment of oratory – however passionate – but as a moment of *decision*: a moment of *action*: a moment of *truth*.

But we are entitled to ask – as Mr Michael Manly asked in 1978 – how is it that the Republic of South Africa can still stand defiant of world opinion? How is it that, over the past four years, South Africa has been immensely aggressive both in its internal repression of its own citizens and in its external assaults on neighbouring States in Africa and in the Indian Ocean? And what can be done by this organization of United Nations to *compel* a change of direction where persuasion, diplomacy and the mobilization of world opinion have so conspicuously failed?

I believe at least that we can make a start by refusing to accept the word of *any* representative of *any* nation who begins what he has to say by affirming 'Of course my country is totally opposed to the iniquity of apartheid . . .' It is the certain prelude to the assertion that sanctions will not work.

One of the chief reasons why we are still so urgently in need of an effective, all-out sanctions policy against South Africa is that the West – and particularly the United Kingdom, the United States and France – the powers with the use of the veto in our Security Council – has so perfectly mastered the art of doubletalk: Great Britain, my own country, has led the world in such hypocrisy. For years it has declared its abhorrence of apartheid: for years it has used its veto to prevent any effective action against it. 'Sanctions do not work' – yet when it is a matter of a war in the South Atlantic, the first act of the British government is to call upon its allies . . . sometimes very reluctant allies . . . the US, the European Economic Community, the Commonwealth, to impose immediate and comprehensive sanctions against Argentina.

'Sanctions do not work' – so we will spend years in negotiating with the South African government over its illegal occupation of Namibia: knowing full well that South Africa will use every possible and impossible excuse to escape from the negotiating table. 'Sanctions do not work' – so we will accept the constant, openly defiant consequences of the South African policy of 'destabilization': the massive air and ground attacks against Angola and the occupation of its Southern provinces: incursions into Mozambique, Zimbabwe and Botswana: the attempted coup d'état in the Seychelles. And all the violence and terror that accompany these assaults – with appalling loss of life in defenceless villages and yet another tide of refugees pouring across the frontiers and into hungry lands. 'Sanctions do not work' – and so we are prepared to read of mass removals of people in their own land to dumping grounds and Bantustans where there is no future and no hope. We are prepared to accept imprisonment without trial; the police interrogation with torture; the deaths in police custody of men like Steve Biko and Neil Aggett; the murder by letter bomb of Ruth First, the most recent victim of such total villainy.

'Sanctions do not work' – because those who have the *power* to use them have not the *will* to use them. Because the lure of investment in South Africa is and always has been infinitely more attractive than the desire for justice and Human Rights. 'Sanctions do not work' they will say, because their effectiveness will punish the African more immediately and disastrously than those who rule them. It is better therefore, to insist on standards of employment and invest in those companies which enforce them. But do not disinvest: that gives you no language at all! *It is a strange argument.* Like the keeper of a brothel calling for support so that he does not have to turn his employees out onto the streets!

At a recent conference in London I said: 'We are in the last phase of the conflict between those who believe in human dignity and the rights of man and those who support and sustain a racist ideology which totally denies these things. A choice *against* an effective sanctions policy is a choice *for* apartheid and can be nothing else. If the West cares about peace in our world, it must act *now* to root out the cancer of racism represented in its most extreme form by 'apartheid' and such action *is* within our competence.

If we choose rightly, and if we choose *now*, we can be certain that we shall be contributing to a future for our world in which justice and peace will be infinitely more secure.

But we cannot avoid the choice. And we dare not delay in making it.

The Assize Sermon at The University Church of St Mary the Virgin, Oxford, 14 July 1983.

Anyone invited to preach from this pulpit on this day should be both pitied and forgiven. It's totally impossible to pretend to be anything but utterly inadequate to an occasion like this. After all, 150th anniversaries in fact occur only once – whatever is being commemorated and whoever is being remembered.

But as we well know, those of us here in this church, this day for the Church of England and for the whole worldwide Anglican Communion, marked an event, in John Henry Newman's view, which was the beginning of what has become to be called the Catholic Revival, with all its unforeseeable consequences. And the character of the preacher standing in this pulpit, addressing the judges of the Assize, did even more to shape and fashion the church to meet the challenges of his day. It was precisely because John Keble was so completely the opposite of what has become to be called a trendy clergyman that he created the trend, a trend powerful enough to alter the whole direction of church life in England. A trend moreover which gave to the Church in this land for the first time since the Reformation the sense of its own identity separate from the State and, in fact, led the Church into confrontation with the State at many levels of the nation's life, not least in matters concerning the ordering of its worship, the expression of its doctrine and above all the thrust of its mission to the wide world.

Those somnolent judges gathered in this lovely church on a summer's day 150 years ago, might conceivably – because even judges can be good Christians – have read Mr Keble's popular volume of poems, *The Christian Year* and they might have approved most of the sentiment expressed there. We need not bid for a cloistered cell / Our neighbours and our work farewell / Nor strive to wind ourselves too high / The sinful man beneath

the sky / The trivial round, the common task / Would furnish all
we ought to ask / Room to deny ourselves a road / To bring us
daily nearer God. I think His Majesty's judges wouldn't have felt
such sentiment any great threat to their position as the guardians
of law and order. After all, Victorian values had not yet emerged
within their society (the sermon was preached 4 years before
Queen Victoria ascended the throne).

And yet, the more intelligent of them, or perhaps those who'd
managed to keep awake through that long discourse, must at
least have recognized that this was a sermon addressed to a
specific issue, and that for once it was not piety but politics that
lay at the heart of the message. Its theme was not as might
perhaps have been expected for an Assize sermon, the relevance
of the divine law to the breakdown of social morality – the steady
increase in numbers of those who deserved to be hanged, for
instance – but the relevance of the church itself to the user patent
of its authority by the State. National apostasy was the cry. When
I was given that as a title for this sermon I wondered how many
people in England would even know the meaning of the word
apostasy. But, still, there it was – national apostasy, in the sense
of confrontation between church and State over suppression of
the Irish bishoprics: it was that which gave its meaning to this
particular sermon of 150 years ago. But it cannot be so understood today, as indeed the immediate and wide publicity given to
recent debate in the General Synod, on the overwhelming issue of
nuclear weapons and the restoration of capital punishment has
made clear. It looks almost more like consensus today than
confrontation. I think it may not be too far-fetched to suggest
that John Keble himself reflecting on what he had said in the
vicarage at Southrop, the following day, had no idea whatsoever
of the potential explosive power of his quiet and scholarly
sermon. Nor could he with his innate modesty, have envisaged a
way of communicating what he'd said, beyond the walls of this
university church, and into the homes and the hearts and the
minds of churchmen throughout the length and breadth of England. 'Tracts for the Times', quite a trendy way of describing a
method of communication in those days, before the excitements

of TVam etc, and that was only to be a beginning. But it was strong enough to give birth to a movement whose name is remembered and without which none of us, I suppose, would be here this afternoon. Wherein you'll forgive me if I dwell no longer on Mr Keble, on his Assize sermon and the early history of the Oxford Movement. You certainly wouldn't be here if you didn't already know, not from reading history but from experience at a deep level of the heart and of the mind, the impact of that movement, the reality of the catholic faith as held by the Church of England and its renewal 150 years ago.

I've begun my sermon in this way in order to avoid the accusation of an appalling presumption, of a kind of arrogance, which in my view, would be unforgiveable. This sermon is not and could never be comparable with its original, in form or in content or in impact. It couldn't be thus, any more than the political, the social, the economic climate of England today can be compared with that of the 1830s; any more than the role of the Church itself today could be so compared and defined; any more than the turbulence of the world in which we now live has even the smallest similarity to the world of Trafalgar and Water-loo. This sermon could not be comparable to that of John Keble's sermon for another and even more obvious reason, I am not a John Keble: he was by any standards an outstanding and brilliant scholar, an academic of this university, taking a double-first-class degree before he was eighteen. I am no scholar, and I'm certainly no academic. He was pre-eminently a great priest and pastor who lived out his life in country vicarages, who loved the trivial round, the common task in small villages. My life, for good or ill, both as priest and bishop, has taken me to a Ministry about as different from his as could possibly be imagined. He was a saint; I need say no more to point the contrast. Indeed, perhaps the only thing we have in common is our love for the Anglican church, our belief in its catholicity, our sharing in its prayer and worship, and above all else, our understanding of its vocation as the Body of Christ, the instrument of the Holy Spirit of God, the witness of His sovereignty over His world. The message I care to get across to you today, is that if the Church of England is not free to be the Church then certainly it is better that it should die. I would claim, however, that in spite of inroads made on the establishment over the past fifty years or so, it is in fact true that the establishment of the Church of England still prevents the attainment of that freedom and is a hindrance to it, as I well know, in its relationship with the rest of Christendom – and particularly with the worldwide Anglican Communion – of which today let us remember, the Church of England in its two provinces, is only a small and numerically insignificant part. Here we are strangers and pilgrims with no continuing city, as Fr Stanton of blessed memory, once remarked: 'who has ever heard of established strangers and endowed pilgrims?'

Clearly, in trying to proclaim his message I have to draw on my own experience because it is all I have. If that appears egotistical I can't help it, if it appears limited, well, so it is; or partial or overlaid by failure; well, it is all those things. But I think perhaps I was invited to perform this almost impossible task precisely because at least my experience has been one of contrast. One couldn't have a greater contrast than that between those provinces of the Anglican Communion in which over half a century I have been called to minister. Sophiatown in the Province of South Africa: those teeming streets and those marvellous Christians. Tanzania, one of the poorest countries in the Third World. Stepney, in the Province of Canterbury, the point of arrival for so many hundreds and hundreds of thousands of immigrant strangers, who have contributed so greatly to the wealth of our country, and who in doing so have been caused deep pain by those to whom they came in their poverty. And finally, the Indian Ocean and those fascinating and enthralling islands of Mauritius and Madagascar and the Seychelles. Beautiful, diverse, holding out hope for a multi-cultural, multi-faith, multi-lingual church. No doubt by divine inadvertence, as the Bishop Hensley Henson once said of a fellow bishop. I also have been a Bishop in two of those Provinces, and Archbishop of one. But I have also served in the Church of England, as by law established, for almost half my ministry – ten years as a Bishop. So today I'm speaking or trying to communicate with the Church in this land, to which I've only just returned after five exciting and challenging years. Five years, which in our country, I think you'll agree, have been years of massive change at many levels – years also which have presented, and still present, to the Church, an equally massive challenge. A challenge, which if we meet it, could lead us into the way of life, but which, if we evade it, will inescapably lead us into the way of death.

What is the nature of this challenge? I believe it centres around certain quite clear and easily identifiable issues. And those I've chosen are those which seem to me to be the inescapable challenges of our day. As, perhaps – and I know I've been described in these terms – a trendy clergyman in the tradition of John Keble; as a Christian Socialist in the tradition of Charles Gore, the founder of my own Community; and as a Christian humanist in the tradition of Anglicans like Fr Keble Talbot of my Community, who preached on this occasion fifty years ago. Like Fr Basil Jellicoe, that great priest who understood the inner city and the slums that he was the pioneer in clearing in the name of God. And Bishop Frank Weston, the symbol and sign of those of my generation, of the vigour and intellectual and spiritual thrust of the Oxford Movement in its Anglo-Catholic days of the 1920s. Now I don't make any excuses for my choice of issues, but of course you are free to choose others if you will. It seems to me that the central challenge to the Church, and the central challenge to the world outside the church, is unmistakably the challenge of authority: its meaning, its exercise and its limits. But along with this, and indeed part of its true meaning, is the challenge of scientific and technological discovery, and the pace of change in moral and ethical terms brought about by this. And then linked with both of these and inescapably part of them, the unification of mankind, our universal inter-dependence, which to me is at the very heart of the meaning of the word 'catholic'. If the Church of England is unwilling or unable to face these challenges, it seems to me it has already forfeited its claim to be called catholic. And I sense, for I have tried at least to keep in touch with events while I've been living so far away, that there is within our Church in this land, a deep reluctance on the part of many,

who claim the name of Catholic to avoid or evade precisely those
challenges by claiming a spirituality and a doctrinal integrity
opposed to anything so uncomfortable as the turbulence they
create. It would be only too easy, in fact, to talk about authority
in its theological or ecclesiastical sense alone. And I don't doubt I
would find many echoes in John Keble's sermon, and in John
Henry Newman's writings, because they were men of their age.
An ecclesiastically or theologically dominated age. Indeed, in the
whole catena of Oxford Movement literature it is only too easy
to find the subject of authority both divisive and central. But
that's a temptation I'm going to resist. What I'm talking about is
something much simpler, and more easily recognizable. It is the
total breakdown of the old accepted concept of authority. That
concept expressed by such phrases as 'The Bible says this, therefore . . .' or 'The Pope says this, therefore . . .' or 'The Church
says this, therefore . . .'

Man today is no longer ready to accept this kind of statement,
not because if he's a Christian he questions the validity of the
Bible, Pope or Church, but because he requires deeply, at the
centre of his being, an authority which makes sense to him where
he is, not within the four walls of the Church. A self-authenticating authority, not an imposed authority, however strong its
credentials. And I dare to prophesy – and I'm old enough to do
so without being found out if I'm wrong [laughter] – but I dare
to prophesy, because the beginnings of this are already evident,
at least to me, that the authority of Marxism itself is subject to
the same human desire and longing, and will not be able to
survive in any form unless somehow it measures up to this self-
same challenge. The Oxford Movement, the Tractarians individually, and gradually, over many decades, the leaders of the
Church of England, both clerical and lay, by breaking out as best
they could of establishment fetters, had a vast influence in this
matter of authority, showing amongst other things, that Catholic
tradition in theology was concerned with the truth of God's
Word and with rational argument for that truth; that the authority of Holy Scripture itself did not rest on a simple acceptance of
literal inspiration unbalanced by tradition; that the authority of

the Church did not rest upon its relationship with the State, in England or anywhere else, and in consequence of this, it liberated the Church to speak with authority on the great social issues of its day. For example, as long ago as 1844, W.G. Ward in his *The Ideal of a Christian Church*, could write, 'a pure church would, with eager and urgent zeal, have pleaded, clamoured, threatened on the workers' behalf. The Church ought to be the poor man's court of justice, and her ordinary condition one of opposition to those in worldly status.' Scientific and technological change has thrown up immensely challenging moral and ethical issues which simply cannot be met by a purely authoritarian response, whether that response be to a Church or to the majority religion in non-Christian lands, or to some ideological embodiment or institution. Time forbids to give more than some simple illustrations. But we only have to cast our minds over the headlines in our daily press or our television screens to recognize them and to shrink, because of our perplexity of mind, from knowing the answers. Genetic engineering, the manipulations of human intelligences, the assault on natural resources, the power to stop life starting, or to prolong it beyond its natural term, and so into the brave new world of space exploration, computer sciences, and the like. Challenges which each in their own way throw up immense complexity – there is no easy answer, and it would be the height of folly and an expression of arrogance for the Church, particularly for the Church of England alone, through its leaders, or its Synods or its Commissions, to imagine it could pronounce with authority, with self-authenticating authority, on any of these issues if it attempts to do so alone. Indeed, it is losing or has lost its authority precisely by making this attempt in the past. It is talking to itself, it is answering questions that would not have been asked, and therefore it is sealing itself off from humanity. What is needed, as I believe, and thank God there are many signs that this is emerging within the Church, is some kind of moral or ethical body in which all the expertise now available can be brought together, Christian or non-Christian alike, and which can provide not the answers but the information upon which the answers can be based. Surely this is one meaning of the word

Catholic – universal – to use the created and creative intellect of mankind for good. And it leads on to the last challenge on my list.

I'm going to tell you a story of a small village in my old diocese of Masasi, Tanzania, because I've never discovered a better way of illustrating what I want to say. It was my first visit, as Bishop, and the people, as always in Africa, had prepared a great welcome beginning with a Eucharist leading on to a feast and dancing until the sun began to sink and the villagers began to drift home before it was dark, because it was inconvenient to be picked up by a leopard on the way. I was left sitting outside a small hut under the stars and children gathered round my feet. I switched on my little transistor radio, and the first voice I heard was the voice of a Russian astronaut somewhere in space, and the children at my feet said in Swahili, 'Who is that? Where is he? What's he saying?' I wonder how many of you could have answered those questions in Swahili, or even in English? But I had to do my best, and the only thing I could think of to say was . . . 'It's a man.' Not a very profound remark you may think. But in fact I believe it was the most profound remark I ever made. It was man out there in space. It happened to be a Russian man but only because Americans and Russians have the money to get there, but it was man. Looking down at the small globe and saying: 'That's where I belong.' Not Africa, not China, not Russia, not Europe but Planet Earth. 'That's where I belong. That's home.'

In the great challenges facing mankind, all those that I've mentioned, the threat of nuclear war, the ideological conflict between East and West, above all and transcending all in its immediate urgency, the widening gulf between North and South, the affluent and the hungry world, what is our response to be? Are we, as the Church of England, to be for ever ambivalent and indecisive about such issues as the first use of nuclear weapons? Are we to be for ever diplomatic about the way to compel the South African government to give freedom and human rights and human dignity to its own citizens? Are we in our diplomacy to condemn what we call terrorism but to condone the spreading institutionalized violence of the state in Africa, in Central America and elsewhere? In just over two weeks from now, another 150th anniversary will be commemorated. The death of William Wilberforce. I think it's somehow providential, as that great Evangelical of the Clapham sect might have said, that these two events, John Keble's sermon on national apostasy and William Wilberforce's death, should so nearly have co-incided. On Friday 26 July 1833, the Bill for the Abolition of Slavery passed its second reading in the House of Commons. And three days later the man who had initiated and carried through what was arguably the greatest humanitarian reform in human history was dead. I wonder of the many millions who pass his epitaph in Westminster Abbey how many ever trouble to read it? It says: 'He was amongst the foremost of those who fixed the character of their times, because to high and various talents he added the abiding eloquence of a Christian life, that in the progress he was called to endure great obloquy, and great opposition.' It couldn't have been otherwise, unquestionably the battle for the abolition of slavery was seen in its own time as a specifically English concern, a conflict of interests within the country itself, not to be taken notice of by those who did not happen to live in this sceptred isle. A conflict not so much between Church and State, as between widely differing views of the role of the Church held by Christians themselves. In this respect it was in no way dissimilar to the issues raised from this pulpit by John Keble in his sermon on National Apostasy. Both Wilberforce and Keble, perhaps without recognizing it to be the case, were proclaiming Christianity to be universal – to be Catholic – concerned not with the religion of the Church of England but with man where he is. For this very reason I have to confess a weariness with Christian ecumenism and its laboured procedures. Please don't misunderstand me. I long for the visible unity of the church. I do not doubt for one moment the integrity of those who believe in that visible unity within the Roman Catholic or the Orthodox or the Protestant churches; I do not doubt the integrity of those who believe that to be the first priority. But I do greatly doubt the validity of their arguments. If we are truly catholic, then universality, the proclamation of our belief that this is God's world, God's universe, is surely a prior concern to that which would make institutional Christianity our chief objective. What is needed desperately is a context in which to set the ecumenical movement, the kind of context, indeed, which is proclaimed to us by the unwearying journeys of His Holiness the Pope to so many different parts of the world, carrying to each one a message of human dignity and human interdependence. But if we are to move forward, then we cannot neglect or ignore the need for interfaith ecumenism. The recognition that dialogue between Hindu and Christian, Muslim and Christian, Buddhist and Christian, must have priority if indeed the Christian Church is to be able to proclaim the Gospel. How can you proclaim God's truth if you are not prepared to listen? How can you proclaim to others the meaning of the Christian faith if you have no conception of the meaning of their own? I believe this to be a matter of the deepest urgency, and I believe that the Church of England is very late in the day in coming to recognize it; and I confess to my shame that it is only within the last five years, within the experience of Mauritius, where the Christian church is a minority church, where the Hindu religion is the majority faith, where all the great religions of the world can meet together with respect and reverence, where it is possible, on a certain day each year, for Muslims, Hindus and Christians to visit the Shrine of one of the great Roman Catholic missionaries, and to pray together. I have taken part in a mass where 150,000 were present, and where all the great religions were allowed to pray within the context of the mass in their own tongue. Barbara Ward, that great Christian prophet, wrote over ten years ago, 'we have lacked a wider rationale of unity, our prophets have sought it, our poets have dreamed of it, but it is only in our own day that astronomers, anthropologists, physicists, theologists, chemists, biologists and ethnologists have all combined in a single witness of advanced science to tell us that in every alphabet of our being we do indeed belong to a single system, powered by a single energy, manifesting a fundamental unity under all its variations. Depending on its survival on the balance and the health of the total system. If this vision of unity', she concludes, 'can become part of the common insights of all the inhabitants of Planet Earth, then we may find that beyond all our inscrutable pluralism we can achieve just enough unity of purpose to build a human world.'

Is this not a precious home for us earthlings? Is it not worth our love? It is against this background that I deeply deplore the National Apostasy of our day, in Europe, in this lovely Country of ours. A Church, which even to the smallest degree is inspired by a national regional jingoistic patriotism, is a church which may have a message to suburban England, but can have no Gospel whatever. [*Applause*]

That's very encouraging! And as I come near to the end of my active life and to the knowledge that such aims and such endeavours as mine will soon cease to be my concern, I would like to hope against hope that the Church of England might turn from its preoccupation with its own structures, its own liturgical and doctrinal quarrels, even its own identity, and discover anew, a theology of creation. This is the only challenge open to those who today would claim to be the heirs of the Oxford Movement, because it is a challenge to our catholicism, and it is posed for us by the simple fact that today we do belong to a Worldwide Church. The freshness and the joy of moving into those provinces of the Anglican Communion where I've worked and to compare them, as one has to so often, with the stultification and the preoccupation over detail which cannot by any circumstances, by any feat of imagination, be regarded as crucial to the proclaiming of the Christian religion. This is something which in my own heart dominates everything else, and I'd like to end not with any words of mine but with the words that Fr Keble Talbot of my Community used to end his sermon from this pulpit fifty years ago. He said, 'Broken indeed is the witness of the Church to the divine society, by the sin of its disunion and the worldliness of its members. That in faith and will we are to cleave to it, prizing it, prizing in our own Church not first what is peculiar to England, nor what binds it to the state or to a social system which is passing away, that were to defraud the nation of what it most needs.'

*An address at the Requiem Mass of Oliver Reginald Tambo
at St Mary's Cathedral, Johannesburg, 30 April 1993.*

The light shines in the darkness and the darkness has not
overcome it.

John 1. 3

To stand in this pulpit in this lovely Cathedral of St Mary's is,
for me, an awesome experience. The memories it evokes go back
half a century. It is thirty-seven years since I preached my farewell
sermon in this place and fifty since I first met the subject of this
Requiem Mass, Oliver Reginald Tambo. So it is not only that I
am overawed by events: it is my sense of responsibility for the
words I speak to you all. How can I ever do justice to the memory
of one who changed the course of my life? How can I even begin
to express what his friendship has meant to me since we first met
in St Peter's, Rosettenville, when he was only twenty-six and I a
totally immature and inexperienced thirty, sent by CR to Sophiatown and Orlando. And, in any case, how can anyone spell out
the meaning of friendship itself? But I must try and I ask your
forgiveness now for all inadequacies: 'The light shines in the
darkness.'

In a letter Oliver wrote to me five months ago in reply to one
of mine written as President of the Anti-Apartheid Movement
concerning the difficulty and dangers of a breakdown in communication at the critical time, he wrote this: 'I wish to address
myself to the concluding words in your letter, namely: "I know
that I can write to you as I know that you will fully understand
my motives for doing so".' (And he continued) 'I modestly wish
to stress that nothing is more precious to me than our unbroken
friendship over fifty years. Your kind words can never be
improved upon. Their wholesomeness is an embodiment of the
truth as *we* know it . . . Your concerns, Father, are also mine . . .

I cannot say how much we value your consistent support and clarity of mind about our political situation. It will remain a shining force of example long after we have gone. The immortality of it all will be emblazoned on the grave of apartheid . . .'

Perhaps that quotation could be regarded as a form of boasting. If so, I do not apologize for there are certain things we have a right to boast of and a lifelong friendship is one! Indeed one of the great English saints of the Middle Ages, a mystic and a scholar, St Aelred of Rievaulx, dared to say: 'God *is* friendship.' A contemporary theologian writes: 'If someone were to say to me, "But as a priest, isn't God more important to you than any of your friends?" I'd have to say that God is above all and through all and in all, and it's in and through my friends that I think I have learnt and still do learn, most about God and receive most from Him. With every true friendship we build more firmly the foundations on which the peace of the whole world rests.' And that is exactly as I believe myself about my friendship with Oliver. What I am saying is that Oliver not only gave me this gift but also enabled me to recognize the fundamental truth about the consequences – political, economic, social, cultural and theological – of South Africa's ideological philosophy. Apartheid.

I did not learn the meaning of apartheid by academic study. I learnt it in the streets and homes and schools of Sophiatown and Orlando. I learnt it from the people whose parish priest I was and for whom, under God, I had pastoral responsibility. I learnt it from the young and the old, from the family struggling to live when all the force of institutionalized racism was mobilized against them. When every effort was made to destroy and destroy and destroy their human dignity. I was there, in Sophiatown when the Minister of Native Affairs, in introducing the Bantu Education Act in Parliament, said: 'We are telling the native he is being educated for certain forms of labour: there are green pastures in which he has *no right* to graze.'

And there, at St Peter's, was Oliver, an outstanding educationalist and teacher, wholly committed to providing young and intelligent Africans with a future in which their gifts and talents could be used for their *own* country. Of course I was in

South Africa as a member of the Community of the Resurrection which had worked in Johannesburg since *before* the beginning of this century, whose chief work was in education and specifically in teacher-training, who had established the first Anglican college for the training of men for priesthood. Oliver was so completely at one with the Community's ideals and practice that he felt a strong vocation to priesthood himself and – in 1955 – asked me to recommend him to Archbishop Geoffrey Clayton for ordination. But, as you all know, in the following years came the Treason Trial and the long years leading to Sharpeville – the banning of the ANC and the decision of Albert Luthuli to send Oliver out of the country to hold together the ANC in exile.

It is difficult, even for myself, to recollect the major events of the liberation struggle in which we were involved. But I do remember the moment when Oliver received his banning order and his movements were restricted, deciding that I had to appeal to the *outside* world and particularly to the *Church* in my own country about its total failure to act against the Western Areas Removal Scheme and, of course, the Bantu Education Act. 'The Church sleeps on', I wrote to the *Observer* newspaper. 'It sleeps on while 60,000 people are moved from their homes in the interests of a fantastic racial theory. It sleeps on while plans are being made and implemented; it sleeps on while a dictatorship is swiftly being created over all Native Affairs in the Union – so that speech and movement and association are no longer free. The Church sleeps on – though it occasionally talks in its sleeps – and expects (or does it?) the Government to listen?'

So long ago. Forty years. Was it really like that? Standing here in this Anglican cathedral today – recognizing so clearly how in the past ten years the voice of the churches has *been* the voice of liberation when every other voice was silent and the release of political prisoners was so loudly demanded by the Council of Churches that at last came the beginning of the end: the battle of Cuitri Carnavale and Namibian independence. It was Oliver in those long lonely years of exile, first in Tanzania, then in Zambia, who held the ANC together: was ready, after the Soweto uprising, to receive that great rush of exiles and – at last – to be recognized as the international statesman that he was.

During those years, as I well know, he depended on his wife Adelaide for keeping a home for the children and for himself to return to on his many journeys. Without her and her courage and determination he could not possibly have achieved what he did. And of course, he could not have survived successfully the first stroke and the painful process of rehabilitation that that involved.

Indeed those last three years were a triumph of faith and hope and love, and even deeper understanding of friendship too. Poetry is the only medium I can use to bring together and to end these words of mine . . . *Oliver*!

> O Captain! My captain!
> Our fearful trip is done.
> The ship has weathered every track,
> the prize we sought is won . . .
> The port is near . . .

Well – is the prize won? No doubt the coming few weeks will tell. But I am certain that this Eucharist, this thanksgiving for Oliver, is far more than a memorial. It is a *rededication – making hope a reality* for Southern Africa, not tomorrow, but today. The best memorial for him is free and fair elections for a truly democratic constituent assembly in the shortest time possible.

Let that great Christian political prisoner, John Bunyan, speak the last words: 'When the day that he must go hence was come, many accompanied him to the riverside into which as he went he said "Death where is thy sting?" And as he went down deeper he said "Grave where is thy victory." So he passed over, *and all the trumpets sounded for him on the other side.*'

The light shines in the darkness, and the darkness *has not overcome it.*

Tribute to the Most Reverend Sir Trevor Huddleston CR, KCMG by Archbishop Desmond Tutu.

St Mary's Cathedral, Johannesburg, 5 May 1998.

Job 6–8

God is boasting about His servant Job: 'Don't you think he is something; don't you think he is really the cat's whiskers?'

I think God would do similarly with His servant Father Trevor, die Jerrie – God would ask the heavenly court what was really a rhetorical question, 'Have you considered my servant Trevor?'

Some, no, most, would describe Father Trevor Huddleston as a man with a passion for justice. That is not for me the first quality I would identify as what characterised this remarkable man most. I would say he had a profound sense of the infinite value of each individual person. This filled him with a deep reverence for each such person. Some of you will know the story I have now told many times over. I was a boy of about eight or so, and was standing with my mother who was not very educated having done no more than a few years of primary school. She was a domestic worker, at this time of the story she was working for blind women at Ezenzeleni near Wilgespruit in Horison at the blind Institute for blacks started by the extraordinary Blaxalls. We were standing on the verandah of the women's hostel, when this white man in a flowing black cassock swept past and he did what was unthinkable in the South Africa of those days – he doffed his hat to my mother. I was bowled over that a white man should raise his hat for my mother, a black woman and one who was not even educated.

Politically and socially it was unthinkable but Trevor's theology made it natural and unavoidable. He believed fervently in the doctrine that all of us are created in the image of God. That made us each one not just important, but endowed us with infinite worth so that we deserved not just respect but veritable reverence, for each of us then was God's viceroy, God's representative. We were sanctuaries of the Holy Spirit. This is what fired him and gave him his extraordinary passion to fight against all injustice, racism and oppression. It was the imperatives of the Gospel, not political concern. It was a working out of his faith. And so it was for him natural to doff his hat to a black woman. It was natural to fight against the destruction of Sophiatown because God's children lived there, people of infinite worth who were not nonentities to be shunted about at the will of those with political power.

He laughed like an African with his whole being and exuded a warmth and love that drew people like a magnet. His office in Sophiatown at 74 Meyer Street would at one time be filled with street urchins he called his 'creatures' playing marbles on its floor or with some sitting on his lap and at the next would be the venue of a meeting with distinguished personages, business moguls. He had this extraordinary capacity to attract all sorts of people – I heard my first classical concert in Christ the King Church when Yehudi Menuhin played there, one of several eminent artists who came there. He touched many, many people in the world and they are the better for having fallen under the magnetism of this wonderful servant of God, people who have subsequently gone on, most of them, to distinguished careers.

Walter Makhulu, now Archbishop of Central Africa; Michael Rantho; Hugh Masekela, who got his first trumpet from Father Trevor, a gift from the great Louis Satchmo Armstrong – it would be a veritable who's who of South Africa. Sally Motlana was helped educationally by the Community of the Resurrection for whom her father cooked – I used to help him wash up for a delicious plate of supper. He hob-nobbed with Oliver Tambo and Madiba [Nelson Mandela] and was there when the Freedom Charter was endorsed in Kliptown. He saved leading lights of the ANC when they might have been mown down when the police surrounded the Odin Cinema where a mass meeting was being held.

He could electrify audiences with his brilliant oratory and his book *Naught for Your Comfort* turned many black university students into activists for justice and freedom. There is no question at all that he was an enormous thorn in the flesh of the authorities and his own church leaders were not entirely comfortable with him. So he was re-called to his mother house – and then was in turn Bishop of Masasi in Tanzania, forming a lifelong friendship with Mwalimu Julius Nyerere: Bishop of Stepney and Bishop of Mauritius and Archbishop of the Indian Ocean. His house in Commercial Road in Stepney was overrun by unkempt cockney urchins so reminiscent of 74 Meyer Street. Archbishop Trevor galvanised the conscience of the world and as President of the AAM ensured that apartheid got on to the world's agenda and remained there until its demise, and if we want to honour anyone for doing that single-handedly then that person would have to be Archbishop Trevor.

He had a marvellous rapport with young people. In 1988 he urged them in Britain to mark Nelson Mandela's seventieth birthday in a special way – they responded overwhelmingly. They walked from all corners of Britain and converged on Hyde Park Corner – 250,000 of them, and he said that should be Madiba's last birthday in prison. Not far wrong, for he was out in 1990.

What a spectacular vindication there has been for Archbishop Trevor – he used to say apartheid would die before he did. How wonderfully prophetic. He saw the death of apartheid and he voted as a South African in 1994, and attended the inauguration of his friend on 10 May 1994 as the first democratically elected President of the New South Africa.

God's sense of humour is tremendous. Trevor and others used to stand outside South Africa House in London protesting, and now, in what used to be the citadel of apartheid, as you enter you are met by this extraordinary spectacle – a bust of Oliver Tambo and a bust of Trevor Huddleston. What could be more eloquent, a more dramatic demonstration that apartheid is gone, that a new dispensation has come, and then, a few weeks before his death the splendid accolade, public acknowledgement by Britain of his part in the history of the United Kingdom and South Africa: the knighthood so richly deserved.

Who he was was formed by his faith. A man of deep spirituality and prayer, he depended so very much on his Community and their faithful and regular round of prayer and adoration. We pay a warm tribute to them as well in paying tribute to Archbishop Trevor for the contribution to South Africa and to our church.

The most fitting monument is a living monument: to uphold and value our new-won freedom. Not devalue it. Rout out corruption; end nepotism; increase efficiency; fight crime; end the culture of entitlement and élitism.

Ensure that the quality of life of ordinary people, God's special friends who meant so much for Archbishop Trevor, that quality of life is vastly improved; that freedom is better than repression.

NOTES

Preface

1 Trevor Huddleston, *Naught for Your Comfort*, London, Collins, 1956. All references in the text are to the Fontana paperback edition, first published 1957.
2 This point is further developed in Deborah Duncan Honoré (ed.), *Trevor Huddleston: Essays on his Life and Work*, Oxford, Oxford University Press, 1988, pp. 201–3.
3 Sermon on Huddleston's eightieth birthday, at St James's Church, Piccadilly, London, 15 June 1993. The text is held in the Huddleston archive, Rhodes House Library, Oxford.

ONE HIDDEN TIMES, 1913–1943

1 Trevor Huddleston, *The True and Living God*, London, Collins Fontana Books, 1964, p. 77.
2 Writing as 'Spierpoint' in *The Times Literary Supplement* of 5 March 1982, a short story entitled 'Charles Ryder's Schooldays'.
3 Taken from the transcripts of Huddleston's conversations with Joe Rogaly which took place in Masasi in December 1966. The transcripts are in the Huddleston archive, Rhodes House Library.
4 Ibid.
5 Ibid.
6 Quotes from Rogaly's files, with his kind permission.
7 See Appendix 4.
8 Letter to Rogaly, 19 January 1967.

TWO SOPHIATOWN, 1943–1953

1 Ndabaningi Sithole, *African Nationalism*, 2nd edn, London, Oxford
   University Press, 1968, pp. 47ff. T.W. Wallbank, *Contemporary Africa:
   Continent in Transition*, London and Princeton, Van Nostrand, 1964,
   pp. 51, 59.
2 T.W. Wallbank, *Contemporary Africa: Continent in transition*, 1964,
   p. 53.
3 Thomas Pakenham, *The Scramble for Africa: 1876–1912*, London:
   Weidenfeld and Nicolson, 1991, p. 673.
4 Ibid., p. 673.
5 Ibid., pp. 669–80.
6 Allister Sparks, *The Mind of South Africa*, London, Heinemann, 1990,
   p. 184.
7 The author is indebted to Anne Yates for this information.
8 Br Roger Castle, CR letter to Rogaly, 1966.
9 Nicholas Mosley, *The Life of Raymond Raynes*, London, The Faith
   Press, 1961, p. 88.
10 Ibid., p. 88.
11 Ibid., pp. 127–28.
12 Honoré (ed.), *Trevor Huddleston*, p. 2.
13 See also Chapter Nine for his own reflections on his love of children.
14 Rogaly.
15 Modisane, *Blame Me On History*, London, Thames and Hudson, 1963.
16 *Guide to the Religious Communities of the Anglican Communion*,
   London, Mowbray & Co, 1955, p. 6.
17 Huddleston, *Naught for Your Comfort*, p. 99.
18 Ibid., pp. 99–100.
19 Rogaly. In addition to the transcripts of his conversations with Rogaly,
   Huddleston's confirmation addresses and advice to those under his
   spiritual direction are now part of the Huddleston archives at Rhodes
   House Library. 'Never shorten because of spiritual dryness, never
   lengthen because of unaccustomed fervence (*sic*). Be quiet and content
   in the presence; no self-torture; offer the dryness as prayer. All growth
   in prayer depends on growth in simplicity.'
20 Rogaly.
21 Freda Troup, *In Face of Fear: Michael Scott's Challenge to South
   Africa*, London, Faber, 1950 pp. 132–3.
22 Huddleston, *Naught for Your Comfort*, pp. 43–44.
23 Anne Yates, biography of Michael Scott, forthcoming.
24 Alan Wilkinson, *The Community of the Resurrection: A Centenary
   History*, London, SCM Press, 1992, p. 217.

25 Anthony Sampson, *Drum: A Venture into the New Africa*, London, Collins, 1956.
26 Mosley, *The Life of Raymond Raynes*, London, The Faith Press, 1961, p. 114
27 Pippa Stein and Ruth Jacobson (eds.), *Sophiatown Speaks*, Johannesburg, Junction Avenue Press, 1986.
28 Rogaly.
29 *Star*, Johannesburg.
30 Rogaly.
31 Rogaly.
32 Wilkinson, *The Community of the Resurrection*, London, SCM Press, pp. 229–30.
33 *Star*, 18 May 1947.
34 *Rand Daily Mail*, 16 October, 1947. Huddleston, *Naught for Yor Comfort*, p. 63.
35 *Star*, 3 January 1948.
36 *Star*, 3 January 1948.
37 Huddleston, *Naught for Your Comfort*, p. 35. Johannesburg *Sunday Times*, 14 November 1948.
38 Huddleston, *Naught for Your Comfort*, pp. 36–37.
39 Huddleston to Baring, 16 December 1948. Earlier he had written 'things are going from bad to worse and the future looks very grim indeed for our people', (11 November 1947) and to Lady Baring on 21 June 1948: 'I am a poor hand at helping people in the spiritual life because, after five years here I feel absolutely sucked dry.'
40 *Star*, 24 December 1948.
41 *Star*, 10 January 1949.
42 Bishop Anthony Hunter to Eric James.
43 Rogaly.
44 Sir Ernest Oppenheimer was the founder of the Anglo American Corporation in 1917, which later gained control of De Beers and most of South Africa's gold-mining interests.
45 Sampson, *Drum*, 1983, p. 132.
46 Sampson, *Drum*, pp. 130–38
47 Huddleston, *Naught for Your Comfort*, pp. 111–2.
48 Huddleston, *Naught for Your Comfort*, pp. 105–7.
49 Trevor Huddleston, *Return to South Africa: The Ecstasy and the Agony*, London, Collins/Fount, 1991, p. 131.
50 Rogaly.
51 Rogaly.
52 Quoted in the *Star*, 13 May 1950.
53 Huddleston, *Naught for Your Comfort*, pp. 77, 79.
54 Huddleston, *Naught for Your Comfort*, pp. 80–88.

55 *Star*, 30 March, 1952. Huddleston, *Naught for Your Comfort*, p. 55.
56 Huddleston, *Naught for Your Comfort*, p. 4.
57 T. Karis and Gwendolen M. Carter (eds), *From Protest to Challenge: A Documentary History of African Politics in South Africa 1882–1954*: Vol. 3 'Challenge and Violence, 1953–64', Johannesburg, Hoover Institution Press, 1977, p. 5.
58 *Rand Daily Mail*, 16 February 1953.
59 Sampson, *Drum*, pp. 134–5.
60 Nelson Mandela, *Long Walk to Freedom*, London, Little, Brown, 1994, pp. 180–2. Writing 38 years later, but perhaps composed in his years on Robben Island when an early version of his autobiography was written and smuggled out of prison by Mac Maharaj, a fellow inmate and now South Africa's Minister of Transport.
61 This was Harry Bloom, a local human rights lawyer who later wrote the libretto of *King Kong* and published a chillingly authentic novel of Transvaal township life, *Episode*, London, Collins, 1957.
62 Huddleston, *Naught for Your Comfort*, p. 56.
63 Michael E. Worsnip, *Between the Two Fires: The Anglican Church and Apartheid 1948–57*, Pietermaritzberg, University of Natal Press, 1991, p. 98.
64 Mandela, *Long Walk to Freedom*, p. 181.
65 Don Mattera, *Memory is the Weapon*, Capetown, The Ravan Press, 1987, pp. 204–8.
66 Anthony Storr, review in *The Observer*, autumn 1997 of Anne Seba, *Mother Theresa: Beyond the Image*, London, Weidenfeld and Nicolson, 1997.
67 Huddleston, *Naught for Your Comfort*, p. 188. Italics in original.
68 Nicholas Mosley, *Efforts at Truth*, London, Secker and Warburg, 1994, p. 137.
69 Peter F. Alexander, *Alan Paton: a biography*, Oxford, Oxford University Press, 1994, p. 169.
70 Huddleston, *Return to South Africa*, p. 25.
71 Huddleston, *Naught for Your Comfort*, pp. 97–103.
72 Huddleston, *Return to South Africa*, p. 71.
73 Related to the author, June 1998.
74 Sampson, *Drum*, p. 130.
75 Sampson, *Drum*, p. 132.
76 Sampson, *Drum*. pp. 132–33.

THREE AFTER SOPHIATOWN: CRISIS YEARS, 1954–1956

1 *Star*, 8 February 1955.
2 Karis & Carter (eds.), *From Protest to Challenge*: vol. 3, pp. 10, 83.
3 From Huddleston's Address to the 50th Anniversary Year dinner of Kent School Connecticut given at the Waldorf Hotel, New York, on 10 March 1956.
4 Huddleson, *Naught for Your Comfort*, p. 133. See also Wilkinson, *The Community of the Resurrection*, p. 305.
5 Huddleston. *Naught for Your* Comfort, pp. 134–5. Robert Resha was the chairman of the Transvaal Youth Section of the ANC.
6 Alexander, *Alan Paton*, p. 301.
7 Patron to Wilkinson, 29 July 1983.
8 Karis & Carter (eds.), *From Protest to Challenge*, vol. 3, pp. 184–7.
9 See Appendix 3. Police shorthand note-takers were unable to record speeches in vernacular languages or those drowned out by train noises offstage. (Karis.)
10 Karis & Carter (eds.), *From Protest to Challenge*, vol. 3, p. 235.
11 Alexander, *Alan Paton*, p. 169.
12 Clayton to the Bishop of Ely, 3 December 1954.
13 Clayton to the Bishop of Ely, 3 December 1954.
14 Huddleston to Raynes, 8 December 1954.
15 Raynes to Clayton, 13 December 1954.
16 Wilkinson, *The Community of the Resurrection*, p. 309. See also Appendix 2.
17 Jonathan Graham, handwritten report to Raynes composed on the voyage back, June 1955. See Appendix 2.
18 Related to the author by Dorothy and Deane Yates, June 1998.
19 *Star*, 31 October 1955.
20 3 November, reprinted in the *Star*, 4 November 1955.
21 *Rand Daily Mail*, 1 December 1955.
22 Jonathan Graham, private diary entry.
23 Reprinted in the *Rand Daily Mail*, 7 November 1955. See also the London *Sunday Times*, 13 November.
24 *Star*, 19 November, subheaded 'deserved to be drummed out or strung up from a lamppost'.
25 Mrs Dorothy Yates to Canon Eric James of 20 November 1994.
26 *Star*, 25 November. The correspondent was Ezekiel Mphahlele.
27 *Star*, 14 December.
28 Honoré (ed.), *Trevor Huddleston*, pp. 3–4.
29 A pictorial record of Huddleston's life, containing a transcription of his

spoken commentary from a film called 'Makhaliphile – the Dauntless One'. Published by Kliptown Books, London 1990.

30 Huddleston, *Naught for Your Comfort*, p. 24.
31 Huddleston to Molly Baring, 14 February 1956.
32 Huddleston to Molly Baring, 4 July 1956.
33 From a typed report in the Huddleston files evidently reacting to a second report on CR in South Africa by Jonathan Graham (cf the first report reproduced as Appendix 2). I have not been able to locate a copy of this second report but the essence of Graham's position is conveyed by private diary entries.
34 Sampson journal entry.
35 Related to the author in a conversation with the late Peter Wyld, April 1998.

FOUR   HOME AND AWAY, 1956–1960

1 Huddleston, *Naught for Your Comfort*, pp. 182–3.
2 Related to the author, June 1998.
3 Rogaly.
4 Rogaly.
5 Huddleston, *Naught for Your Comfort*, pp. 165–6.
6 I have attempted without success to re-read the reviews and report the sales and foreign rights sales: Collins's files are unavailable.
7 I supplied this information as a note in Mosley, *The Life of Raymond Raynes*, pp. 260–1.
8 Alexander Steward, *You are Wrong, Father Huddleston*, London, Bodley Head, 1956.
9 Huddleston to Molly Baring from Rosettenville, 11 February 1956.
10 Rogaly.
11 Rogaly.
12 Rogaly.
13 Mosley, *The Life of Raymond Raynes*, p. 270.
14 Private letter to Joe Rogaly, 1966.
15 Sampson: private journal, 1956.
16 This quotations, and all those from Huddleston to Mischa that follow, are taken from letters kindly shown me by Mischa Scorer.
17 Rogaly.
18 Private letters kindly supplied by Molly Baring (Lady Howick).
19 Ibid.
20 Lady Howick to Rogaly, 21 December 1966.
21 Huddleston, *Naught for Your Comfort*, pp. 172.
22 Fisher to Rogaly, 18 December 1966.

23 Lamburn to Canon Eric James, 27 December 1991.
24 Cf. Appendix 4, Blair to Rogaly, 4 January 1967.
25 Lady Howick to Rogaly, 21 December 1966.

FIVE   MASASI, 1960–1968

1 From the Lancing Lecture, delivered by Huddleston in Lancing College, 1963.
2 UMCA joined up with SPG in the early 1960s to become USPG. Evelyn Baring was UMCA's President and could thus exercise his influence in ecclesiastical as well as political affairs in the area.
3 Terence Ranger, 'Trevor Huddleston in Masasi, 1960–1968' in Honoré (ed.), *Trevor Huddleston*, pp. 35–52.
4 Letter to the author from Dr Bevis Cubey,19 May 1998.
5 Maurice King, *Primary Health Care*, Oxford, Clarendon Press, 1982.
6 Huddleston kept a log of most of his eight years at Masasi and I have drawn upon them extensively throughout the chapter. The originals are now in the Huddleston archive, Rhodes House Library.
7 Canon Lamburn to Canon Eric James, 27 December 1991.
8 Lamburn to James, same date.
9 *New Statesman*, 27 December 1968.
10 Rogaly.
11 Dr Eric Mascall to Huddleston, February 1962.
12 Sampson, private journal, June 1962.
13 Walter Oakeshott to Huddleston, 6 March 1963.
14 Miss Worth was our neighbour in Ladbroke Square. They met at our house.
15 Rogaly.
16 See David Holden's profile of Nyerere in the *Sunday Times*, 1 October, 1972.
17 In his later years, Fr Mark developed the symptoms of manic-depression, but despite the unhappiness this caused him and his friends inside and outside the Community, he continued his excellent studies in comparative liturgies and the music of J.S. Bach. He preached at the magnificent liturgy at St James's, Piccadilly, when he and Huddleston celebrated the fortieth anniversary of their profession in 1981.
18 This was never completed, but his typescripts of conversations with Huddleston are one of this book's most important and useful sources.
19 Huddleston's address to the clergy assembled at Mtandi on Thursday, 13 June 1968. Source: Huddleston archive, Rhodes House Library.
20 Honoré (ed.), *Trevor Huddleston*, pp. 35–52.
21 Letter to the author, 19 May 1998.

SIX STEPNEY, 1968–1978

1 *New Statesman*, 27 December 1968.
2 *Guardian*,14 June 1968.
3 This and many of the references to follow are taken from Huddleston's appointments diaries for the period, now in the Huddleston archive, Rhodes House Library.
4 Unpublished sermon, now held in the Huddleston archive, Rhodes House Library.
5 Quoted from a roneoed copy of his speech he sent to Huddleston.
6 *Observer*, 15 June 1969.
7 He did not keep logbooks of his Stepney years so the evidence here is inferential.
8 *The Times*, 8 October 1970.
9 Ibid.
10 *Church Times*, 9 October 1970, front page story, reporting a talk to the Anglo-Israeli Friendship Society (Enfield district) on 5 October.
11 *The Times*, 21 May 1970.
12 Letter to the author, 16 February 1996.
13 See Peter F. Anson, *Abbot Extraordinary: The Life of Aelred of Caldey*, London, The Faith Press, 1959.
14 Peter Hain, *Sing the Beloved Country – The Struggle for the New South Africa*, London, Pluto Press, 1996.
15 Private information.
16 Unpublished sermon, Huddleston archive, Rhodes House Library.
17 Unpublished sermon, Huddleston archive, Rhodes House Library.
18 Letter to the author from Peter Mandelson, June 1998.
19 Tambo to Huddleston, 19 September 1973.
20 Nyerere to Huddleston, 27 August 1970.
21 *Scarborough Mercury*, 20 October 1973.
22 Interview with Bruce Kent, 4 August 1997
23 Lewin to Huddleston, 29 November 1973.
24 Letter, 10 April 1974, Huddleston archive, Rhodes House Library.
25 *Guardian*, 12 April 1974.
26 *Sun*, 22 April 1974.
27 John D. Brewer, *After Soweto: An Unfinished Journey*, Oxford, Clarendon Press, 1986, p. 407.
28 Ibid., p. 408.
29 Ibid., p. 415.
30 *The Times*, 7 December 1985. This, with hindsight, seems an accurate description of how apartheid managed to stay alive and well right through to the 1990s.

31 Brewer, *After Soweto*, p. 409.
32 An earlier Pentonville Christmas address is given in Appendix 6.
33 Pearce to Huddleston, November 1977.
34 E.A. James, *Indian Ocean Odyssey*, London, Christian Action, 1994, p. 7

SEVEN   MAURITIUS, 1978–1983

1 Paton to Alan Wilkinson, 29 July 1983. Paton believed Huddleston was never the same after he left South Africa. 'The love of his life was Sophiatown. No other love ever replaced it.'
2 An annotated appointments diary for this period survives which I have quoted from extensively. The other main source is Huddleston's regular three-monthly newsletter, produced for and distributed to friends and colleagues all over the world, which continued all though his time in Mauritius. Both are in the Huddleston Archive, Rhodes House Library.
3 'There was wonderful rapport between this little gnome-like Malagasy Papa Simon and Trevor despite the language barriers. He was the ultimate *animateur*.' The Revd Hall Speers in a letter to Canon Eric James, 27 July 1994.
4 George Briggs had been a friend of Huddleston's for twenty years, an African missionary for thirty-six years and was Archdeacon in Masasi during the period that Huddleston was bishop. In 1981 he had recently stepped down as Bishop of the Seychelles. He now lives in retirement in Surrey.
5 No. 2 Newsletter – December 1978.
6 Ibid.
7 Honoré (ed), *Trevor Huddleston*, pp. 103–114.
8 No. 4 Newsletter – June 1979.
9 Quoted in the letter from Revd Hall Speers to Canon Eric James, 27 July 1994.
10 No.5 Newsletter – September 1979.
11 No. 7 Newsletter – June 1980.
12 Ibid.
13 Paton to Gonville ffrench-Beytagh, 1 December 1981: quoted in Alexander, *Alan Paton*, p. 417.
14 No. 9 Newsletter – June 1980.
15 No. 11 Newsletter – August 1981.
16 No. 12 Newsletter – November 1981.
17 No. 13 Newsletter – June 1982.
18 Archbishop Peter Carnley to the author, 1 September 1998.
19 No. 15 Newsletter – November 1982.

20 See Appendix 8.
21 No. 16 Newsletter.
22 Honoré (ed.), *Trevor Huddleston*, p. 106.
23 Ibid., p. 110.
24 Trevor Huddleston, *I Believe: Reflections on the Apostles' Creed*, London, Collins/Fount, 1986.

EIGHT LOSS AND GAIN, 1983–1991

1 The former Bishop of Johannesburg, expelled from South Africa after condemning the Sharpeville massacre in 1960.
2 See Appendix 8.
3 See Christabel Gurney, *A Great Cause: the Origins of AAM*, Oxford, Rhodes House, 1998.
4 The Denniston family were all there, some in pushchairs and the smallest not quite born.
5 South African responsibility for the bomb outrage was freely acknowledged during the hearings of the Truth and Reconciliation Commission, at which Craig Williamson and others confirmed what many had previously only suspected. In fact the leaders of the assassination attempt had been given medals by Pretoria. The explosives came over from South Africa by diplomatic bag.
6 Brewer, *After Soweto*, p. 411.
7 The sermon and a transcript of the questions and answers which followed (Alan Paton shared the platform with Huddleston) are in the Huddleston archive at Rhodes House Library.
8 The annual reports are all preserved in the archives of the Anti-Apartheid Movement, held at Rhodes House Library, and are quoted here with their permission and full co-operation. Established when the AAM dissolved in 1995, the archive is managed by the AAM Archives Committee in order to provide a unique and comprehensive research resource covering the whole apartheid era and the world-wide campaign against apartheid.
9 Manuscript and typed transcript in Huddleston archive, Rhodes House Library.
10 On 4 May of that year he found time to preach and conduct the marriage ceremony of my daughter Sue at Christ Church, Oxford and two months later to charter a long-haul taxi driver to take him and another close friend to my wife's funeral in the depths of Worcestershire on 3 July 1985.
11 Letter to Mrs Thatcher, 26 September 1985 in AAM archive.
12 Foreword to AAM's Annual Report, October 1985.

13 From the introduction to the IDAF Archive, 1991.
14 This is related from first hand experience. I was one such volunteer from 1984 until the winding down of IDAF in 1991.
15 Herbstein to Canon Eric James, 11 May 1995.
16 President Obasanjo was subsequently imprisoned by Nigeria's military leaders but released in June 1998.
17 *Mission to South Africa: The Commonwealth Report*, foreword by Shridath Ramphal, London, Penguin Books, 1986, p. 23.
18 Foreword to AAM's annual report, October, 1986.
19 AAM's annual report, September,1987.
20 Victoria Brittain, *Hidden Lives, Hidden Deaths: South Africa's Crippling of a Continent*, London, Faber, 1988, pp. 173–75.
21 Brittain, *Hidden Lives*, p. 177.
22 Frank Chikane's address to the Harare Conference, September 1987. Transcript in the Huddleston archive, Rhodes House Library.
23 Brittain, *Hidden Lives*, p. 179.
24 It is the subject of a chapter in Robin Denselow's book, *Music and Politics*.
25 Foreword to AAM's annual report, September 1988.
26 Huddleston, *Return to South Africa*, p. 55.
27 Fr Aelred Stubbs, *CR Quarterly* No. 382, June 1998, refers to a crisis that was threatening to undermine the Community which Huddleston averted while at Stepney by alerting the Archbishop of Canterbury, Michael Ramsey, to it. This crisis probably involved Hugh Bishop. See also Wilkinson, *op. cit.* p. 341.

NINE   NOW IS THE TIME, 1991–1998

1 *Southern African Review of Books*, Feb/March 1990, quoted by Huddleston in *Return to South Africa*, p. 8.
2 There are appointment diaries covering this period which carry occasional annotations. All are now lodged in the Huddleston archive.
3 Huddleston, *Return to South Africa*, p. 12.
4 Ibid., p. 14.
5 Ibid., p. 13.
6 Ibid., p. 24.
7 Dedicated to Oliver Tambo, Hilda Bernstein and Abdul Minty (HarperCollins/Fount 1991).
8 Exact figures are not available from HarperCollins but the advance paid was not earned in royalties.
9 *Fortresses of Fear*, the report of an Independent Board of Enquiry, 1991, p. 15.

10 Huddleston, *Return to South Africa*, p. 28.
11 Ibid., pp. 69–71.
12 From his eulogy of 30 April 1993 on the text: 'The light shines in the darkness and the darkness has not overcome it', reproduced in full as Appendix 10.
13 Cf. Canon Eric James's obituary of Huddleston in the *Guardian*, 21 April 1998.
14 The text of this address is in the Huddleston archive, Rhodes House Library.
15 Some portions of Fr Nicolas's memoir were reproduced in *CR*, the quarterly review of the Community of the Resurrection (John the Baptist 1998, No. 382) in an obituary by Fr Aelred Stubbs CR. I have Fr Nicolas's permission to reproduce a fuller version here.
16 *Financial Times*, 21 April 1998.
17 Honoré, *Trevor Huddleston*, p. 16.
18 Huddleston, *Naught for Your Comfort*, p. 14.

BIBLIOGRAPHY

Adair, Herbert, and Moadley, Kogila, *South Africa without Apartheid: Dismantling Racial Domination*, Berkeley, CA, UC Press, 1986

Alexander, Peter F., *Alan Paton: a biography*, Oxford, Oxford University Press, 1995

Amnesty International, *South Africa: State of Fear*, London, 1992

Anonymous, *Guide to the Religious Communities, of the Anglican Communion*, London, Mowbrays, 1955

Berman, John Kane, *Soweto: Black Revolt White Reaction*, Johannesburg, Ravan Press, 1978

Bernstein, Hilda, *The World That was Ours: The story of the Rivonia · Trials*, Cape Town, SAW, 1989

Benson, Mary, *South Africa: The Struggle for a Birthright*, London, Penguin, 1966

—*A Far Cry*, London, Penguin, 1989

Blaxall, Arthur, *Sentence Suspended*, London, Hodder and Stoughton, 1954

Bloom, Harry, *Episode*, London, Collins, 1956

du Boulay, Shirley, *Tutu; Voice of the Voiceless*, London, Hodder and Stoughton, 1988

Brewer, John D., *After Soweto: An Unfinished Journey*, Oxford, Clarendon Press, 1986

Brown, Shelagh (ed.), *Drawing Near to the City: Christians speak about dying*, London, SPCK/Triangle, 1984

Brittain, Victoria, *Hidden Lives, Hidden Deaths: South Africa's Crippling of a Continent*, London and Boston, Faber, 1988

Bunting, Brian, *The Rise of the South African Reich IDAF: 1986, 1964, 1969*, New York, Basic Books, 1989

Chapman, Michael (ed.), *The 'Drum' Decade: stories from the 1950s*, Pietermaritzburg, University of Natal Press, 1989

Collins, Diana, *Partners in Progress: Life with Canon Collins*, London, Gollancz, 1992

Davies, Rob, with O'Meara, Dan, and Dlamini, Sipho, *The Struggle for South Africa: a reference guide to movements, organisations and institutions*, vol.1, London, Zed Books, 1984

Dingake, Michael, *My Fight Against Apartheid*, Johannesburg, Kliptown Books, 1987

Driver, C.J., *Patrick Duncan: South African and Pan African*, London, Heinemann, 1980

First, Ruth, with Steele, Jonathan and Gurney, Christabel, *The South African Connection: Western Investment in Apartheid*, London, Temple Smith, 1972

Hagemann, Albrecht, *Nelson Mandela*, Hamburg, Rowohlt, 1995

Hain, Peter, *Don't Play with Apartheid*, London, George Allen and Unwin, 1971

— *Sing the Beloved Country – The Struggle for the New South Africa*, London, Pluto Press, 1996

Hastings, Adrian, *A History of African Christianity 1950–1975*, Cambridge, Cambridge University Press, 1979

Hellman E. and Lever, H., *Race Relations in South Africa, 1929–79*, Johannesburg, Macmillan South Africa, 1979

Hinchliff, Peter, *The Anglican Church in South Africa*, London, Darton, Longman and Todd, 1989

Honoré, Deborah Duncan (ed.), *Trevor Huddleston: Essays on His Life and Work*, Oxford, Oxford University Press, 1988

Hope, Marjorie and Young, James, *The South African Churches in a Revolutionary Situation*, Maryknoll, NY, Orbis Books, 1981

Huddleston, Trevor, *Naught for Your Comfort*, London, Collins, 1956

— *The True and Living God*, London, Fontana, 1964

— *God's World*, London, Collins/Fount, 1966

— *Three Views on Commitment*, Oxford, Oxfam, 1967

— *I Believe: Reflections on the Apostles' Creed*, London, Collins/Fount, 1986

— *Return to South Africa: The Ecstacy and the Agony*, London, Collins/Fount, 1991

Hurrell, Muriel, *A Decade of Bantu Education*, Johannesburg, South African Institute of Race Relations, 1964

James, Eric, *A Life of Bishop John A.T. Robinson*, London, Collins, 1987

— *Indian Ocean Odyssey*, London, Christian Action, 1994

Jarrett-Kerr, Martin C. R., *African Pulse*, London, The Faith Press, 1960

Joseph, Helen, *Side by Side: The Autobiography of Helen Joseph*, London, Zed Books, 1986

Karis, T., Carter, G. M. (eds.), *From Protest to Challenge: A Documentary History of African Politics in South Africa 1882–1964*, vol. 3, 'Challenge and Violence, 1953–64', Stanford, California, Hoover Institution Press, 1977

King, Maurice, *Primary Health Care*, Oxford, Clarendon Press, 1982
Krog, Antjie, *Country of My Skull*, London, Jonathan Cape, 1999
Lapping, Brian, *Apartheid: a History*, London, Grafton Books, 1986
Luthuli, Albert, *Let My People Go*, London, Collins, 1962
Mandela, Nelson, *The Struggle is My Life, Speeches and Writings Brought Together to Mark His 60th Birthday*, London, International Defence and Aid Fund, 1978
— *Long Walk to Freedom*, London, Little, Brown, 1995
Mattera, Don, *Memory is the Weapon*, Capetown, Ravan Press, 1987
— *Gone with the Twilight: A Story of Sophiatown*, London, Zed Books, 1987
Meer, Fatima, *Higher than Hope: the Authorized Biography of Nelson Mandela*, London, Hamish Hamilton, 1998
Meli, Francis, *A History of the ANC*, Baton Rouge, Indiana University Press, 1989
Mission to South Africa: The Commonwealth Report, London, Penguin Books, 1986
Modisane, Bloke, *Blame Me On History*, London, Thames and Hudson, 1963
Mosley, Nicholas, *The Life of Raymond Raynes*, London, The Faith Press, 1961
— *Efforts at Truth*, London, Secker and Warburg, 1994
— (ed.) *The Faith: Instructions on the Christian Faith by Raymond Raynes, CR*, London, The Faith Press, 1961
Neame, L.E., *The History of apartheid: The story of the colour war in South Africa*, London, Pall Mall Press, 1962
Owen, Roger, *I Wish he were Black: The Story of Trevor Huddleston*, London, Religious Education Press, 1978
Pakenham, Thomas, *The Scramble For Africa: 1876–1912*, London, Weidenfeld and Nicolson, 1991
Paton, Alan, *Cry, the Beloved Country: A story of comfort in desolation*, London, Jonathan Cape, 1948
— *Apartheid and the Archbishop: The Life and Times of Geoffrey Clayton*, London, Jonathan Cape, 1974
— *Towards the Mountain*, London, Penguin, 1986
— *Journey Continued*, Oxford, Oxford University Press, 1988
Peart-Binns, John S., *Ambrose Reeves*, London, Gollancz, 1973
Raynes, Raymond, *Darkness No Darkness*, London, The Faith Press, 1958
Reeves, Ambrose, *Yesterday and Tomorrow: A Challenge to Christians*, London, Gollancz, 1960
— *Shooting at Sharpeville*, London, Gollancz, 1962
— *South Africa: Yesterday and Tomorrow: The Challenge to Christians*, London, Gollancz, 1962

Russell, Diana E. H., *Lives of Courage: Women for a new South Africa*, New York, Basic Books, 1989

Sampson, Anthony, *The Treason Cage*, London, Heinemann, 1958

—*Drum; A Venture into the new Africa*, London, Collins, 1956 revised 1983 as *Drum: An African Adventure – And Afterwards*, London, Hodder and Stoughton

—*Black and Gold: Tycoons, Revolutionaries and Apartheid*, London, Hodder and Stoughton, 1987

Scott, Michael, *A Time to Speak: An Autobiography*, London, Faber, 1958

Sithole, Ndabaningi, *African Nationalism*, 2nd edn, Oxford, Oxford University Press, 1968

Smith, William Edgett, *Nyerere of Tanzania*, Harare, Zimbabwe Publishing House, 1981

Sparks, Allister, *The Mind of South Africa*, London, Heinemann, 1990

Stanton, Hannah, *Go Well, Stay Well*, London, Hodder and Stoughton, 1963

Steward, A., *You are Wrong, Father Huddleston*, London, Bodley Head, 1956

Stein, Pippa and Jacobson, Ruth (eds), *Sophiatown Speaks*, Johannesburg, Junction Avenue Press, 1986

Stubbs, Aelred C.R. (ed.), *Steve Biko*, London, Penguin, 1988

Thompson, Doris, *Priest and Pioneer: A Memoir of Fr. Osmund Victor*, London, Faith Press, 1958

Troup, Freda, *In Face of Fear: Michael Scott's Challenge to South Africa*, London, Faber, 1950

Tutu, Archbishop Desmond, *Crying in the Wilderness: The struggle for justice in South Africa*, London, Mowbray, 1982, 1986

Villa-Vicencio, Charles, *Trapped in apartheid: a socio-theological history of the English-speaking churches*, Capetown, David Philip/Orbis, 1988

Wallbank, T.W., *Contemporary Africa: Continent in transition*, London and Princeton, Van Nostrand, 1964

Walshe, Peter, *The Rise of African Nationalism in South Africa: The African National Congress*, London, C. Hurst and Co, 1970

Wilkinson, Alan, *The Community of the Resurrection: A Centenary History*, London, SCM Press, 1992

Worsnip, Michael E., *Between Two Fires: The Anglican Church and Apartheid, 1948–195*, Pietermaritzburg, University of Natal Press, 1991

INDEX

Resha, Robert 38, 50
Rhodesia UDI 95
Rifkind, Malcolm 172
Rivonia Trial 88
Roberts, Ted 122, 135
Robinson, Charlotte Dawson (Aunt Potsa)
    2, 5
Robinson, John 124
Rogaly, Joe xxi, 1, 98–100, 122, 226
Roosevelt, Eleanor 69
Rose-Innes, Jasmine 53
Rosettenville 7, 19–20, 212
Runcie, Robert, Archbishop of Canterbury
    145
Runnymede Trust 128

Sachs, Albie 91
St John Stevas, Norman 118, 122
St Mark's, Swindon 7, 227
St Michael's, Golders Green 2, 3
St Peter's, Rosettenville 20, 31, 47, 57,
    212, 265
    closure 48–9, 63
Sampson, Anthony x, 23, 30, 43, 65, 74,
    89–90, 122, 211
    Drum xx, 70
Sargent, Fr Miles 6
Sargent, Malcolm 3
schools see education
Scorer, Mischa 75–6, 122
Scott, Michael 21–3, 41, 63, 69, 89, 92,
    154
Searle, Christopher 128
Separate Representation of Voters Bill 36
Sepeku, John, Bishop of Dar es Salaam
    103
Seychelles 143
Sharpeville massacre 87, 111, 154–5
Sheppard, David 123–4, 127
Sheppard, Dick 238–9
Sidebotham, Fr George 7
Simon, Fr 139
Sisulu, Walter 24, 36, 46, 48, 169–70,
    182, 186–7, 193, 196, 212, 248
    AAM International Conference 192
    relations with Huddleston xix 40
    sentenced 88
    world travels 47
Slovo, Joe 53
Smith, Ian 95, 99
Smith-Cameron, Ivor 123
Smuts, Field-Marshall 5, 12, 15
Sophiatown 10–46, 211–15
    destroyed 52, 57

Odin Cinema meeting 37–9
removals 46–7, 49–50
South Africa 5
    apartheid policy 11, 32, 35–6, 40, 111
    arms to 119, 123, 155
    boycott 123–4, 154–5
    Centre for Black Advancement 133
    government tribute to Huddleston xx
    Ministry of Constitutional Development
        133
    Mission to South Africa 172–3
    national anthem 51
    Nationalist native policy 32, 35–6
    Pass Laws 32, 111
    race relations see apartheid
    Sharpeville massacre 87, 111, 154–5
    Soweto massacres 132, 155
    sports boycott 123–4, 154–5, 180–1
    Treason Trials 63, 87, 111, 154, 166
    Truth and Reconciliation Commission
        189
    Western Areas Removal Scheme 47–50
    white supremacy 40, 48, 159
South Africa Police
    CID 37
    special political branch 36
South African Bureau of State Security
    (BOSS) 156
Soweto massacres 132, 155; monument 212
sports boycott 123–4, 154–5, 180–1
squatters 23, 34, 41, 52
Stebbing, Fr Nicolas xxii, 196, 200–6
Steel, David 154–5
Steer, Edward 238
Steward, Alexander, You Are Wrong,
    Father Huddleston 70
Stopford, Dr Robert, Bishop of London
    112
Storr, Anthony 40
Stradling, Bishop Leslie 80, 90
Strijdom, Johannes 12
Stubbs, Fr Aelred 132
Suppression of Communism Act 32, 48
Suzman, Helen 172

Talbot, Father Alan 86, 89, 123
Talbot Father Keble 226
Tambo, Adelaide 127–8, 193, 268
Tambo, Oliver 44, 101, 114, 122, 128–9,
    185–6, 196, 200, 248, 270
    ANC activist 48, 52
    ANC President-in-Exile 176, 179
    assassination attempt 156
    death and requiem mass 188, 192